Telling Our Stories

Telling Our Stories
Omushkego Legends and Histories from Hudson Bay

Louis Bird

EDITED BY
Jennifer S. H. Brown, Paul W. DePasquale, and Mark F. Ruml

WITH CONTRIBUTIONS BY
Roland Bohr, Anne Lindsay, and Donna G. Sutherland

broadview press

LOUIS BIRD TRAVELLING UP THE WINISK RIVER,
ENTERING FOX NOSE RAPIDS, JUNE 1996
Photo by George Fulford.

LIBRARY AND ARCHIVES CANADA CATALOGUING IN PUBLICATION

Bird, Louis
 Telling our stories : Omushkego legends and histories from Hudson
Bay / Louis Bird ; edited by Jennifer S.H. Brown, Paul W. DePasquale,
Mark F. Ruml ; with contributions by Roland Bohr, Anne Lindsay, and
Donna G. Sutherland.

Includes bibliographical references and index.
ISBN 1-55111-580-8

 1. Cree Indians—Hudson Bay Region—Folklore. 2. Tales—Hudson Bay
Region. 3. Cree Indians—Hudson Bay Region—History. I. Brown,
Jennifer S. H., 1940– II. DePasquale, Paul W. (Paul Warren), 1965–
III. Ruml, Mark F. (Mark Francis), 1962– IV. Bohr, Roland V. Lindsay,
Anne VI. Sutherland, Donna G., 1961– VII. Title.

E99.C88B526 2005   398.2'09714'111   C2005-903370-3

BROADVIEW PRESS, LTD. is an independent, international publishing house, incorporated in 1985. Broadview believes in shared ownership, both with its employees and with the general public; since the year 2000 Broadview shares have traded publicly on the Toronto Venture Exchange under the symbol BDP.
 We welcome comments and suggestions regarding any aspect of our publications—please feel free to contact us at the addresses below or at broadview@broadviewpress.com/www.broadviewpress.com.

North America
Post Office Box 1243,
Peterborough, Ontario, Canada K9J 7H5

Post Office Box 1015,
3576 California Road,
Orchard Park, New York, USA 14127
TEL: (705) 743-8990; FAX: (705) 743-8353

customerservice@broadviewpress.com

UK, Ireland and continental Europe
Plymbridge Distributors Ltd.
Estover Road, Plymouth PL6 7PY, UK
TEL: 44 (0) 1752 202301;
FAX ORDER LINE: 44 (0) 1752 202333;
ORDERS: orders@nbnplymbridge.com
CUST. SERV.: cservs@nbnplymbridge.com

Australia and New Zealand
UNIREPS University of New South Wales
Sydney, NSW 2052 Australia
TEL: 61 2 96640999; FAX: 61 2 96645420
infopress@unsw.edu.au

Broadview Press gratefully acknowledges the support of the Ministry of Canadian Heritage through the Book Publishing Industry Development Program.

Cover & Interior by Liz Broes, Black Eye Design.

Copy-edited by Betsy Struthers.

Printed in Canada

10 9 8 7 6 5 4 3 2 1

contents

list of maps and illustrations

maps

illustrations

preface & acknowledgements

Louis Bird grew up hearing the legends and histories of his people from his parents and other relatives in and around the small Omushkego (Swampy Cree) community of Winisk, Ontario, near the mouth of the Winisk River on Hudson Bay. He was born in 1934, to a family that still hunted, fished, and traded for furs, following the older ways except for adopting the Roman Catholic faith that Oblate missionaries brought to the area in the previous century.

His life has spanned many changes. Four years before his birth, government treaty commissioners flew into Winisk to have its leading men, Louis's grandfather and great uncle among them, sign an adhesion to Treaty No. 9, ceding their ancestral lands; the implications of that event were not clear at the time and are now the subject of much critical concern, as Louis observes in Chapter 9. As a boy in the late 1930s and early 1940s, he spent four years in St. Anne's Residential School at Fort Albany, run by the Oblates of Mary Immaculate. As a young man, he experienced the powerful changes that affected Winisk in the mid-1950s when the Canadian federal government built Site 500, a Distant Early Warning radar station, across the river from his community. Suddenly the global Cold War was on the doorstep of the Omushkego people. The arrival of about 1000 workers brought new influences and pressures that had a drastic impact on language, among other things. Acquiring fluency in English, Louis became a manual labourer at the radar station and went on to work as a tractor operator, stevedore, line cutter, surveyor's assistant, and section man for Canadian National Railways across northern Ontario and Manitoba.

In the 1970s, having upgraded his schooling through continuing education programs, Louis took on a range of new occupations. As he notes in

13

Chapter 1, he began in this decade his systematic recording of the old stories; he also held jobs as a translator, interpreter, and economic development advisor. In 1972–73, he served his community as Chief of the Winisk First Nation, a job that, as he notes in Chapter 9, was fraught with political challenges and tensions.

The following two decades saw Louis direct his energies increasingly towards what has become his life's work. While acting as translator and advisor on many issues facing Omushkego communities, he also became a storyteller with a passion for preserving and sharing his people's stories and history. In 1985, he was a featured performer in Amsterdam, the Netherlands, in a workshop organized by the Writer's Union of Canada. In 1988, he made the first of numerous appearances as a featured storyteller at the annual Northern Storytelling Festival, Whitehorse, Yukon. Since then he has performed at storytelling festivals and by invitation in Toronto, Winnipeg, and elsewhere, as well as at a number of universities and conferences; in 1999, he won second prize at the International Storytelling Festival held in Louisville, Kentucky. Countless school and university students have enjoyed and learned from his visits to their classes.

Since 1998, Louis's work has received support from the Canada Council, the Social Sciences and Humanities Research Council of Canada, and the Ministry of Canadian Heritage. The latter two supplied generous funding for Louis to work with a number of colleagues and students at the University of Winnipeg to transcribe his tapes and research on the historical contexts of his stories to make them accessible. In 2003, a grant from the Canadian Culture On-Line program of Canadian Heritage facilitated the digitization of several hundred English and Cree-language audiotapes and the creation of a web site, <http://www.ourvoices.ca>, which presents about 80 of Louis Bird's English-language stories. Unfortunately, the grant's narrow time frame and the lack of personnel skilled in Cree syllabics greatly hampered progress on Cree transcription. But the English-language stories that it made available serve as the rich reservoir from which Louis Bird, and the editors and contributors, have drawn to create this book. Please visit the site to view the story transcripts and to hear them in Louis Bird's voice. A brief history of his community is presented at <http://www.ourvoices.ca/index/winisk>.

Creating the Chapters

The nine chapters of this book came together as Louis Bird worked closely with each of the contributors on a wide range of topics expressive of his and their varied interests and areas of knowledge. Chapters 1 and 9 were created last and serve as bookends to the work. In November 2003, thinking about the book at his home in Peawanuck, Ontario, Louis recorded an audiotape reflecting on his work, concerns, and life goals. First he talked about his people's past from ancient to recent times, their modes of life, their values and worldview as taught through and expressed in the stories, and their ways of coping with changes brought by the fur trade and missionization, creating the narrative that introduces the book as Chapter 1. Then he spoke of recent changes and pressures, current conditions, and his concerns for the future, generating a text that, as Chapter 9, provides a powerful conclusion. His comments on education, language loss, the effects of modern media, and economic and political issues remind readers that Louis Bird's work is about much more than storytelling; it is about the survival of a people and the maintaining of their cultural knowledge, strength, and dignity through the media that he knows and loves best—the Cree language and storytelling. Louis oscillates between hard-working optimism and moments of great discouragement. Asked for a title for Chapter 1, his first suggestion, only half ironic, was "The Last of the Omushkego Storytellers." He settled for one that lacks such finality, but his work and this book are important to him because that undercurrent of loss is never far from his thoughts.

The editorial process for Chapters 1 and 9, as for the others, involved transcription and then a series of reviews of the text for clarity and accuracy. On these two chapters, Louis and Jennifer Brown worked over the transcripts several times. He added and emended some points; he also trimmed repetitions and false starts. For these, as for all the chapters, he developed his own editorial sense about presenting his words, both Cree and English, in written and print form. He has worked over the texts to polish them lightly, but his oral English-Cree mode of expression remains intact. Readers of this book are urged to listen to his voice on the web site; then they will be able to hear him speaking in their minds, as they read his words on the printed page.

The sequence of stories in Chapters 2 through 8 follows the order that Louis has worked out for his storytelling as he has gained experience telling

Omushkego stories to a wide range of audiences. The Omushkegowak, like many other Aboriginal people, distinguish two major genres of stories, legends and those of more recent (historical) times, and Louis begins in Chapter 2 with some of the founding legends of Omushkego traditions, working with Paul DePasquale to place them in context and to present his people's ways of thinking about beginnings and "the world before we came."

In Chapters 3 and 4, Louis Bird and Mark Ruml delve deeply into themes and stories of what Louis in English calls "shamanism"—mi-te-wi-win spiritual powers, the dream quest through which such powers are received, and the shaking tent—the ceremony in which those powers find their strongest expression and applications, sometimes positive and useful, sometimes deadly. Chapter 4 focuses on "shamanic showdowns," stories that evoke a central theme surrounding mi-te-wak or those who practise those powers as they confront each other in epic duels.

Chapter 5 brings together a series of stories that move into the historical sphere, telling of early contacts with and responses to outsiders, both Aboriginal and European. Louis's stories foreshadow and recount episodes of contact in ways that contrast with the written accounts by some of the earliest Englishmen to sail into James Bay, as gathered by Jennifer Brown. Side by side, they illuminate different ways of seeing and telling, showing how European moments of contact were given meaning and assimilated into a vibrant, enduring Aboriginal oral tradition in Omushkego country.

In Chapter 6, Louis Bird and Anne Lindsay have worked over a story passed down in his family to tell it more fully than in earlier taped and published versions. Set during the fur-trade period at the mouth of the Ekwan River, it recounts a celebration that got terribly out of hand, a warning about the "blasphemous" actions that were occurring, and the dire consequence, a terrible epidemic. Outsiders inadvertently brought deadly new diseases; Omushkego people developed their own means to respond and cope, explaining them in the context of their own strong values about respect and proper behaviour.

Chapter 7 presents the rich results of many conversations between Louis Bird and Roland Bohr, a German historian, archer, and bowyer, who was the first to ask Louis about Omushkego bows and arrows and other traditional weapons of hunting and warfare, and to record his observations about the uses, advantages, and disadvantages of these weapons, as compared to the succession of firearms introduced from Europe. Louis's insights bring us fresh perspectives on a subject that, while much studied on the Plains, has received almost no attention in the Hudson Bay Lowlands.

Chapter 8, the last of the collaborative "story" chapters, came about because Donna Sutherland, herself of Cree and Scottish descent, asked Louis to tell stories about women as well as men. Louis responded with a powerful story about his great-grandmother, Grand Sophia, who as a Catholic convert had an almost disastrous conflict with a traditional mi-tew or shaman. The story evokes not only women's roles and situations, but also the stresses that arose as Omushkego people, both traditional and Christian, coped with the tensions between religions and value systems when Christianity arrived. It leads effectively into Louis's final chapter about recent and current generations and about his hopes and fears for the future. As the father of seven daughters who have given him 25 grandchildren, he ponders the future a great deal, as he holds firmly to the past through his ancestral legends and stories.

A Note on Terminology

The terms currently used in Canada to refer to the various First Nations, Métis, and Inuit peoples—terms like "Aboriginal," "First Nation(s)," "Native," "Indigenous," and "Indian"—are each used by Aboriginal peoples themselves; each has its proponents and detractors and is open to debate. Because there is no consensus on the question of terminology (nor do we believe that a consensus is a necessary or desirable goal), we have not imposed a standard terminology on this book. Louis Bird keeps to his own terms of choice, as do the other contributors, Native and non-Native, from diverse scholarly and cultural backgrounds. Wherever possible, Aboriginal-language equivalents preferred by the peoples themselves have been used, such as Anishinaabe and Omushkego. We believe that the terminology used throughout this book reflects the heterogeneity of Canadian Aboriginal peoples as well as the range of scholarly and non-scholarly debates taking place within Canada today. A useful discussion on terminology is Greg Young-Ing's "Talking Terminology: What's in a Word and What's Not" (2001).

Acknowledgements

First, the editors and contributors to this book wish to express their warmest thanks to Louis Bird for making this work possible and for his wonderful help, care, and patience in checking the transcripts, answering endless questions, and reviewing numerous chapter drafts. As well, our thanks to his parents and grandparents and all the other relatives and community people who shared these stories with him and to his wife Thelma Bird and family for putting up with his absences in Winnipeg. We also thank one another for many conversations and exchanges of ideas and information over the last three to five years and for mutual assistance and encouragement.

We are grateful to the Social Sciences and Humanities Research Council of Canada and to the Ministry of Canadian Heritage for major grants that, in 1999–2002 and 2003 respectively, supported the Omushkego Oral History Project. They made it possible to bring Louis to Winnipeg on numerous visits and to copy, transcribe, and conduct research on the stories. In particular, the Canadian Culture On-Line program of Canadian Heritage provided major funding for digitization and the creation of the web site, <http://www.ourvoices.ca>. Please see the web site for credits to other supporters whose donations of matching funds made that project possible and to other members of the team involved in creating the web site. Special thanks to George Fulford (Anthropology, University of Winnipeg), who put immense energy into successfully securing and organizing the work on the above grants, marshalling the resources that provided an essential base and bringing Louis and us together in fruitful collaboration.

At the University of Winnipeg we also extend warm thanks to Mark Leggott (University Librarian) and Mike Langedock (Executive Director, Technical Solutions Centre) and their staff people for many hours of technical assistance and advice. University discretionary grants to those of us on the faculty, and work-study grants in support of student assistants, provided much added support. The Centre for Rupert's Land Studies hosted the project and continues to serve as home for the Omushkego Oral History Project. Since summer 2004, the Canada Research Chair in Aboriginal Peoples in an Urban and Regional Context, held by Jennifer S.H. Brown and funded by the Canadian federal government, has afforded support for the photographic and map research for this book, as well as

for valued assistance from Dr. Susan Gray, CRC Research Associate working with Jennifer Brown.

The Hudson's Bay Company Archives at the Archives of Manitoba,
Winnipeg, and the Oblate Archives Deschâtelets in Ottawa provided much
helpful research assistance from their collections. Renée Fossett brought
her professional skills and experience to the compiling of the index, and
Wilson B. Brown formatted Louis Bird's hand-drawn diagram for Chapter
1, and assisted greatly with the scanning and selecting of photographs.
Finally, our thanks to Broadview Press for their enthusiasm and support
for this project; special thanks to Michael Harrison, Barbara Conolly,
Betsy Struthers, Judith Earnshaw, and Liz Broes.

Jennifer S.H. Brown, Paul W. DePasquale, and Mark F. Ruml, Editors

glossary of cree terms

Prepared by Paul W. DePasquale in collaboration with Louis Bird

The following Omushkego words and English-language equivalents as they appear in this book are faithful to the usage and spelling of Louis Bird. Louis spells the words in his language by extrapolating from how they are written in Cree syllabics; these words are sometimes but not always consistent with the double vowel spelling used in the system of roman orthography now often used for the Ojibwe language. For comparative information on the vocabularies, structures, and the various orthographies used for the Cree and Ojibwe languages, see the list of suggested resources at the end of the Glossary.

Words and Personal Names

A-MOE: "Bumblebee." A-moe was a respected, powerful old **mi-tew** who possessed a reputation for honesty and leadership abilities, although he was often challenged by other **mi-te-wak** to prove his abilities. A-moe traded at the Hudson's Bay Company posts of York Factory, Fort Severn, and Fort Albany. See Bird 0011, and Hamm and Bird 2000.

AN-WAY: The name of a powerful **mi-tew** and sought-after "expert exterminator of cannibals." Contacted by elders through either the **koo-saa-pa-chi-kan** ("shaking tent") or by runners or other communicators, An-way travelled some unknown distance (he may have been Plains Cree but Louis is not certain) to rid the community of the feared **wih-ti-go** or cannibalistic peoples who threatened to take over the area. For stories about An-way (also spelled Anwe) and other cannibal exterminators, see DePasquale and Bird, in press, 2005.

21

A-TA-NOO-KA-NAK: Stories about events that happened so long ago that the personages are beyond living memory and take on powerful, even mystical qualities. Louis translates this word as "legends." The noun is grammatically animate, in contrast to ti-pa-chi-moo-wi-nan (see below), which is inanimate. The plural suffixes of animate and inanimate nouns also differ, as shown in these plural forms.

CHA-KA-PESH: "Midget," as Louis describes him. A legendary man who was very small but possessed the shamanic powers of a mi-tew (see Chapter 5).

E-HEP: The giant spider of Chapter 2 who lowered the first humans to this world from the world above.

IT-TWA-SOO-WIN: Unlike a legend, which is rooted in some actual, physical experience, it-twa-soo-win is a created myth that has no corresponding physical reality. As Louis explains, "It's the idea of a world beyond physical. People would try to understand where the something came from. So they think that there is a spiritual world and that spiritual world connected to this world.... People used to say there is god for thunder and all that stuff. There's a certain god that is there and it's not material, it's not physical. But he is there, and sometimes these beings that are not physical, sometimes they disagree with each other. That's what the [Omushkego] people say, so that's what we call it-twa-soo-win, it's a noun. This is not physical, it's only in the mind" (Chapter 2, fn. 15).

I-YAS: A legendary personage who left his son alone on an island because he wrongly believed that the young man had had sexual relations with the younger of I-yas's two wives. According to the moral custom, the young man was supposed to have been put to death (Chapter 4, fn. 3).

KA-PA-KI-SOOT: "He-who-explodes" or "He-who-explodes-in-the-face." A friend of Louis's great grandmother, Grand Sophia, and her second husband, John Anishinaabe. This nickname or real name is explained in Chapter 8.

KII-SHE-SWA-FII: Grand Sophia, Louis's great-grandmother. Kii-she conveys the sense not only of Grand Sophia's age but also that she was "a great lady, very much admired by the people."

KI-KA-SII-PAS-SKWA-TA-PIE-YAN: "Squeaking tight" used in conjunction with -an-ni-ka-i-ti-ta-man: "is what you hear." Literally, "you're squeaking tight [between your legs] is what you hear." Or, "it must be your thigh bone that you hear." The title of the quotation story at the end of Chapter 1.

KISCHE-PA-STA-HO-WIN: "A great sin against nature." See Chapters 1 and 6 for examples of "blasphemous acts" with severe consequences.

KI-SHAY-YA-HOW: "Older person, respected person; oldest of the people."

KI-STI-KA-MIN: "Big water," sometimes used for Hudson Bay.

KI-WAY-TI-NI-SIEW: "North" or "north wind." According to Louis in Chapter 2, the elders speak of the strongest, most dangerous wind, the north wind, as a person with a powerful mind and will.

KO-KUM: "Your grandmother." See Chapter 8 for details about Louis's ko-kum, **Kii-she-swa-fii**, Grand Sophia.

KOO-SAA-PA-CHI-KAN: A structure used when practising **mi-te-wi-win**; "shaking tent."

KOO-CHI-KAN: "Feared one" or "feared shaman."

MA-KA-AA-IT-TWAY-KOO-PA-NEY: "Quotation story," defined in Chapter 1.

MI-SHE-MA-SQWA: "Giant bear."

MI-SHI-PIS-SHEW: "Big Cat" in Chapter 2. The mi-shi-pis-shew is a "giant cat" or cougar.

MI-SHE-SHEK-KAK: "Giant Skunk," the title character of Chapter 2.

MI-TE-WAK: Those who practise **mi-te-wi-win**.

MI-TEW: "He acts out." An individual who practises **mi-te-wi-win**. In Chapter 1, Louis defines a mi-tew as "the totally educated person."

MI-TE-WI-WIN: "Shamanism" as Louis describes it in English. The traditional spiritual beliefs and practices discussed in Chapter 3. In Chapter 8, Louis discusses the differences between mi-te-wi-win and Christianity: "It's not a very perfect [nice or kind] thing—mi-te-wi-win—it's not love thy neighbour—it's not turn the other cheek sort of thing—no. It's something like an eye for an eye."

MUSH-KOO-TEW: "Prairie."

NA-TA-WI-PA-WAA-MO-WIN: One of two types of dream quests; an intentional dream quest in which the dreamer dreams about something specific, such as a feared animal. Distinct from **shii-shii-kwa-ni-pa-wa-mo-win,** a non-specific dream quest.

NA-TO-WAY-WAK: A term used in Chapter 5 to refer to Iroquois attacking from the south.

NIIS-STAW: A brother-in-law by marriage, by blood. Niis-staw can also be used as an informal greeting. The term **neeth-tha-wes** is used in a similar way in the Oji-Cree and Ojibwe languages.

O-KI-MAW: "Boss or leader" or "the boss human." Louis explains the name of his maternal grandfather, David Okimaawininiiw or Okimaaw, in Chapter 6, fn. 12.

OMUSHKEGO-ASKI: Omushkego land, the area around the west coast of James Bay and southwest coast of Hudson Bay.

OMUSHKEGOWAK: The Cree First Nations on western Hudson Bay and James Bay; literally, "people of the swamp or muskeg." Sing. Omushkego. This name, sometimes spelled Mushkegowuk, appears so often in English contexts that hyphens are omitted here.

O-MUSH-KE-GO-WI. KIS-SKI-NO-HA-MA-KE-WII-NA: "Traditional Omushkego teachings."

O-PA-WA-CHI-KA-NAK: Dream quest creatures or spirit helpers.

PAA-STA-HO: "Sin against nature."

PA-SOO-WAY-YA-NA-SKEW-PA-NI-WIN: Noun, "echo in the cloud," used with **chi-pe-ta-soo-win** ("you hear your own voice"). This is the sound the people heard in the story of the Wailing Clouds; it was a "ghost experience, a prediction of doomsday" (Chapter 6). Describing the meaning of "The Wailing Clouds," Louis translates the Cree phrase as "night before sound echoed to predict the doomsday for those people" (Louis Bird to Anne Lindsay, 17 July 2003).

PAS-STA-HO-WIN: A blasphemous act, distinct from **pas-sta-moo-win,** a spoken blasphemy.

PE-MI-TI-SHWAY-HI-GAN: A bola (cord with two weights attached, to throw around the legs of caribou).

PE-MO-TE-SQUAN: "Sling."

PIM-MI-TISH-SOO-WAY-PA-HI-GAN: "Stickhook ball swing." See also **we-pa-chi-skway-ask-wa-hi-gan**.

PI-MOO-TA-HI-GO-SI-WIN: "To be able to project yourself where you want to be instantly." See Chapter 3.

QUA-YASK-PI-MAA-TI-WIN: "Moral or righteous living."

SHAA-POO-TA-WAN: Omushkego type of "long house" made by joining two teepees.

SHE-WEE-PHAN: "Sweet lunged." The brother of **A-moe**, She-wee-phan was dishonest and, according to Louis, possibly crazy or mentally retarded. He lived as a kind of outlaw, stealing and having his way with women. See Bird 0011 and Hamm and Bird 2000.

SHII-SHII-KWA-NI-PA-WA-MO-WIN: One of two types of dream quests; a non-specific dream quest in which the dreamer does not try to dream about any one particular thing. Distinct from **na-taw-i-pa-waa-mo-win** in which the dreamer dreams about something intentional, such as a feared animal.

SINK-I-PIS: A legendary diving bird who was dull and homely unlike his handsome brother the loon. See Chapter 2.

TAN-SHI: "How are you?"

TI-PA-CHI-MOO-WI-NAN: Unlike **a-ta-noo-ka-nak**, these stories are of recent historical events and involve people known to or remembered by the storyteller.

WA-PA-WA-MO-WIN: Mirror, literally, "seeing yourself"—your face comes back at you (Bird, 25 November 2003). The theme of a story about a man trading furs for the first mirror he had seen, and what happened next (Chapter 5).

WA-SHA-HAY-NI-GOOM: "Cut-away Nose." The name of a stranger, possibly English, who came to stay with a group of Omushkego people when they were hunting caribou (Chapter 5).

WAY-PAS-TEN: Something that sails without control.

WAY-WAY-NO-NA-NA-YE-WA: "The bulgey cheek" (an insulting nickname for Giant Skunk in Chapter 2), used with ki-mat-ta-e-pa-nuk, "they have seen a track." Literally, "They have seen the track of the bulgey cheek."

WE-MIS-SHOOSH: In Chapter 4, the name of the bug that a legendary mi-tew turned into as a result of the mistakes he had made. This bug is a caddis fly in the larval stage. A caddis fly, also known as a sedge fly, is an aquatic insect usually found in freshwater habitats but sometimes in brackish and tidal waters.

WE-MIS-TI-GO-SI-WAK: White men, lit., men with wooden boats.

WE-PA-CHI-SKWAY-ASK-WA-HI-GAN: A game using two balls tied together and drawn with a stick that has a bit of a hook. See pim-mi-tish-soo-way-pa-hi-gan and Chapter 6 for more details.

WIH-TI-GO OR WEE-THI-GO: "Other-than-human" or "not proper human." A cannibalistic person or spirit.

WIH-TI-GO-MA-HI-KA-NAK: "Other-than-wolf." Dangerous wolves with a crazy sickness.

WI-SA-KAY-CHAK: "Pain in the neck" or "pain in the spirit." Wi-sa-kay-chak is the Omushkego trickster/culture hero similar to Nanabush (Wenabozho, Nenabozho), Raven, Coyote, and Glooscap in other Aboriginal cultures. Wi-sa-kay-chak is a complex figure, sometimes human, sometimes animal or spirit. See Chapter 2, fn. 3 for more details.

Place Names

Despite European renamings of Omushkego lands and waterways, the people retain place names in their own language to identify the areas within their home territory. As the following list of present-day place names with their corresponding descriptions in the Omushkego language suggests, the Native terminology reflects the shape, location, and/or conditions of the land and the animals and creatures that were (and still are in many cases) found there. In this way, Omushkego place names have enabled the people to precisely describe and locate specific lands, rivers, and lakes as well as the animals needed for their sustenance.

AKIMISKI ISLAND; a-ka-mas-ki: "The land across." The largest island in James Bay.

ATTAWAPISKAT; at-ta-wa-pis-kat: This used to be called kat-ta-wa-pis-kak (kat-ta-wa = "gorge," pis-kak = "stone"), after the outcropping of rock in this area. Europeans apparently found it easier to pronounce the Cree name without the first syllable, and so called it "Attawapiskat."

ATTAWAPISKAT RIVER; at-ta-wa-pis-kat-zi-pi: "Gorge stone river."

BIG TROUT LAKE; ki-chi-na-me-kos-za-ka-hi-gan: "The lake that has the largest lake trout [na-me-kos]."

CAPE HENRIETTA MARIA; moo-sha-wow: "Barren, treeless," a term describing the headland as a whole. Louis explains that the phrase, ki-ni-ki-moo-sha-wow, used for the Cape in Chapter 5, refers specifically to the point of land sticking out into Hudson Bay and marking the entrance to James Bay. It was here, according to the old stories, that Omushkego people first heard the guns of European ships as they fired at each other.

CHARLTON ISLAND; cha-a-ton-mi-nis-stic: This island was originally called (and still is called by some speakers) a-ka-mas-ski-shish, "a small land across." After it was named by the English, Omushkego people referred to it as cha-a-ton [an Omushkego pronunciation of "Charlton"] + mi-nis-stic ["island"].

EKWAN RIVER; e-kwan-zi-pi: While Louis explains that e-kwan is "just a name; I don't know the meaning," he understands it to refer to "the river frequently used" or "the preferable way to go" between James Bay and Hudson Bay. In Chapter 6, Louis describes a camping ground at the mouth of this river as "the most famous place where the Omushkegos used to gather together in the spring, to have celebration, to welcome each other, to reunion with their friends and also to have a celebration," at least before the disastrous sickness described in Chapter 6. In Chapter 4, Louis explains further that the Ekwan River was frequently used to go to James Bay from the Winisk River and that it is famous for its estuary and goose hunting. The red-throated loon was and is another popular bird to hunt, but its population has decreased significantly due to oil spills in the region.

FORT SEVERN; wa-sha-hoe: "The bay within the bay." So-called because of the way the land is shaped near the mouth of the river.

GREAT SPIRIT LAKE; ki-chi-man-doo-wi-za-ka-hi-gan or man-doo-wi-za-ka-hi-gan: "Spirit lake."

HAYES RIVER; ki-chi-wa-ska-hi-ga-ni-wi-zi-pi: "Great house river," the "great house" being York Factory. The location had an original name, not known to Louis, to describe the misty or foggy conditions in the area.

HUDSON BAY LOWLAND; te-nii-sha-wow: "Low land."

IT-TA-HON-NA-NI-ZI-PI: "Way to go river," a small creek that runs parallel with the Ekwan River and gives access to it via a portage.

JAMES BAY LOWLAND; te-nii-sha-wow: "Low land," or shi-ka-shi-mow, a "gradually declining [or sloping] land."

KASHECHEWAN RIVER; ki-shi-chi-wa-ni-zi-pi: ki-shi = "fast, strong" + chi-wan = "water moving." The Hudson's Bay Company renamed the Kashechewan River the Albany. In Chapter 4, Kashechewan is defined as "main channel."

KAS-SKA-TA-MA-GAN: "Something to eat or catch," or "a place you can eat from." Located about fifty miles inland from the shores of Hudson Bay, between the HBC settlements of York Factory and Fort Severn. Louis describes Kas-ska-ta-ma-gan as the "name of an area so famous for food," a "natural store" where people still come for caribou, moose, brown bear, rabbits, brook trout, and white fish.

LAKE ST. ANNE; mi-noo-twa-ha-na-za-ka-hi-gan: mi-noo-twa = "saint" + ha-na = "Anna" + za-ka-hi-gan = "lake." Near Fort Albany where St. Anne's Residential School was located.

MOOSE FACTORY; moo-zoo-ni-mi-nis-tic: moo-zoo = "moose" + mi-nis-tic = "island." A location plentiful in moose. The English name, "Moose Factory," connoting the sense of a place that manufactures moose, is puzzling and funny to Louis.

MOOSONEE RIVER; moo-soo-ni-zi-pi: "Moose river."

NELSON RIVER; pa-wa-ni-na-kaw-zi-pi: "River of white water."

PEAWANUK; pi-wa-nauk: "Where the outcropping contains some flint," or simply "flint."

SAY-SAY-MAT-TA-WOW: Describes the area in Chapter 6 where the "rivers spread" or where there is a "junction at the mouth." The area is west of

James Bay and north of the easternmost portion of the Ekwan River. In Chapter 6, Say-say-mat-ta-wow is described as a leg of the route to **It-ta-hon-na-ni-zi-pi** or "way-to-go."

SEVERN RIVER; wa-sha-hoe-wi-zi-pi: "The bay within the bay river."

SHAMATTAWA; ki-she-ma-ta-wa: Louis defines it as "the Great Spirit Lake" in Chapter 8. A junction of the Hayes River.

ST. ANNE'S RESIDENTIAL SCHOOL; mi-no-twa-ha-na-kis-ski-noo-ha-ma-to-wi-ka-mik: "Saint Anne's school building," which Louis attended for four years.

WA-SHA-HOE: "The bay within the bay"; see Fort Severn above.

WINISK; wi-nask: "Weenusk" means "ground hog."

WINISK RIVER; wi-nas-sko-zi-pi: "Ground hog river."

WIN-NI-PEG: Dirty (salted) water; Cree term for Hudson Bay.

YORK FACTORY; ki-chi-was-ska-hi-gan: "Great house." So-called because the English fort was three stories tall.

Suggested Language Resources

The following works provide comparative vocabularies and glossaries, and information on various ways of spelling Cree and Ojibwe words in roman orthography, as well as presenting introductory materials that help in under-standing the structure and patterns of Cree and its related sister language, Ojibwe (Anishinaabemowin).

Ellis, C. Douglas, ed. 1995. *atalohkana nesta tipacimowina: Cree Legends and Narratives from the West Coast of James Bay*. Winnipeg, MB: Algonquian Text Society, University of Manitoba Press. The glossary runs to over 100 pages and relates to the same region as this book.

Faries, Richard. 1938. *A Dictionary of the Cree Language as Spoken by the Indians in the Provinces of Quebec, Ontario, Manitoba, Saskatchewan and Alberta*. Toronto, ON: General Synod of the Church of England in Canada. Richard Faries was an Anglican Archdeacon who, from 1899 to 1951, served as a missionary at York Factory and also at Churchill. His dictionary is very useful for Omushkego (Swampy Cree) terms. For a biographical sketch and details of Faries's numerous publications including Cree catechisms, primers, hymn books, and various literary works, see <http://thunderbaymuseum.com/personal4.htm#A29>.

Nichols, John D., and Earl Nyholm. 1995. *A Concise Dictionary of Minnesota Ojibwe*. Minneapolis: University of Minnesota Press. This work uses a roman orthography without accents that renders long vowels simply by doubling them, a system that appears to be gaining popularity.

Wolfart, H.C., and Freda Ahenakew. 1998. *The Student's Dictionary of Literary Plains Cree Based on Contemporary Texts*. Winnipeg: memoir 15, Algonquian and Iroquoian Linguistics, University of Manitoba. This work is of interest for comparisons of Plains and Swampy Cree, and to broaden perspectives on the Cree language.

For a useful annotated guide designed to encourage young people to speak their Native languages, including Cree and other Aboriginal languages spoken throughout Manitoba and Northern Ontario, see "The Way We Speak: An Annotated Bibliography of Aboriginal Language Resources in Manitoba," Manitoba Education and Training, 1998, available at <http://www.edu.gov.mb.ca/ks4/abedu/abdocs/annotated_bib.pdf>.

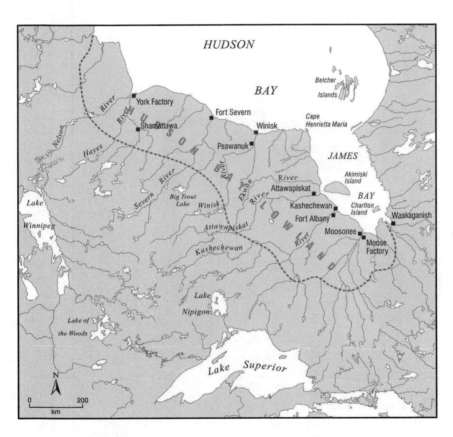

MAP 1: *The Western Hudson Bay and James Bay Lowlands. Adapted with permission from Lytwyn 2002: 2. Prepared by Weldon Hiebert.*

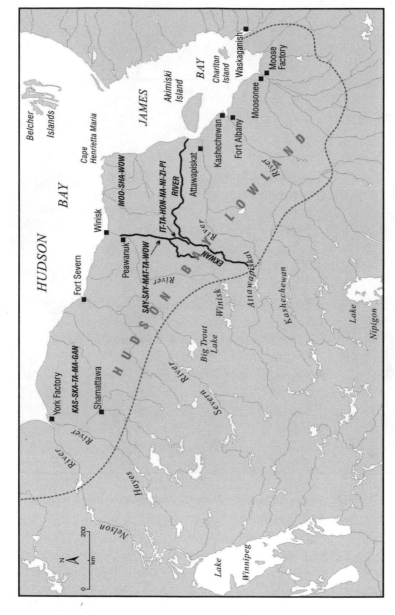

MAP 2: *The Hudson and James Bay Lowlands, showing places mentioned in this volume. Prepared by Weldon Hiebert in collaboration with Louis Bird and Paul DePasquale.*

1

An Omushkego Storyteller
and His Book

Hello, good day. This is Louis Bird, today is November 21, 2003, and this is Peawanuck, Ontario, where I live. This is my introduction to a book of stories that I have been working on for a long time.[1] A team of professors and some students at the University of Winnipeg helped me with the chapters. We sometimes call it "Louis Bird's book," but the stories are old and I did not make them up. I learned them mostly from my grandmother, Maggie Bird (Pennishish), her brother, David Sutherland, and my parents, Michel and Scholastique Bird, and then from many other people.

Here is the way I have tried to do it. The collections were there. I begin thinking about saving the stories in 1965, but my collecting did not actually begin in '65. It was only in 1975 that I actually begin to record the elders. In 1965, I listened to the elders, different elders, after my grandmother died that year. I begin to be aware that we were losing the elders that know the stories, and I begin to notice that recording the elders would be important. But at that time, I had no machine that could be used to record their voices, until very late in 1975. That is when I actually began recording them, from that time on, a little bit at a time.

After going through many periods of near giving-up in frustration, because of many things that I didn't have, I continued off and on to do the recording, to record some elders who at least allowed me to record them. At the same time, I recorded some stories on my own, of those people that spoke to me between 1965 and '75—recalling what they have said; and then I recorded in my own voice, so that I would not forget it, so that I would remember it. And I kept these recordings with me, as part of my col-

---

1 Louis Bird recorded the tapes for Chapters 1 and 9 on 21 November 2003, and Anne Lindsay transcribed them.

FIGURE 1: *My grandmother, Maggie Pennishish (Bird), making snowshoes in the 1950s. Her husband, John, and her brother, David Sutherland, were signers of the Treaty No. 9 Adhesion at Winisk in 1930 (see Figure 8). The treaty commissioners used Bird as our family surname, translating the Cree name, Pennishish. Photo by Father Gagnon, Winisk, Ontario. Credit: With the compliments of Archives Deschâtelets. Fonds Vita Rordam.*

lection. But I never yet thought to write those things down, I just wanted to record them. And it was only in 1975, when I began to recognize that these things should be recorded and be written down. I was not interested in legends only. I was interested in the cultural stories or the oral histories, which I call them, which took place before the European time, and also the stories that took place after the European contact. But I did not organize anything. I did not plot, like the writers do, because I am not a writer. I am only a collector of stories. I was not even trained to be a storyteller! I learned, along the way, to tell a story. My only interest was to record the stories that I have heard, that I remember, and whenever possible, to try to get an elder to sit down with me and tell me the story. I have learned a little bit how to communicate, so I began to apply a little bit of that.

Here is the way I have planned. The collection I have accumulated, I begin to think that I should place the legends in the first part, because in order to write these things down, they have to be divided. The first part is the legends, all five famous legends that we had from time immemorial. And also, the oral stories. Oral stories are different from legends; they are not made stories, they are actual stories that happened in the past. But the legends are created stories from the past—past experiences from our ancestors. That's what the legends are. And the legends are teaching material. They are like a book, different kind of books, different subjects, different events in the history, way back. That's what they were. So, visualize the movement of life in time, going from east to west, as an arrow, or as we usually visualize on television about jet stream in the weather report. I have tried to put the pattern of the stories, our history, in a diagram here, with arrows (Figure 2). So the beginning would be to place the legends where the First Nation people live on their own in this land and have lived for many centuries, that is, tribes by tribes, families by families. The way they live—they live on the land; they did not settle anywhere. They move on the land; that is the reason I say that. That is where the legends came from, at that time. And dividing the space and time, I call that period, "before contact." Not "Before Christ," but "before contact period."

So that's where I place the legends and also some oral stories and quotation stories.[2] They fit right there, because all these stories, they do not mention anything that is originally from a European. In all five major legends, and in the other old stories about An-way, cannibal beings, tribal skirmishes, etc., there is no mention about the steel, metal, or anything. It only happens after contact. During that period, before contact, our First Nation had their own lifestyle. So their way of teaching was different; they had developed the teaching system which requires learning at a very early age, by observation, by hearing, by feeling, by imagining.

The legends were used as historical events, to teach the upcoming generation. Quotations were remembered as cautions, or to make the new generation aware of life experience upon the land. They also have oral histories in time before contact. These oral stories are actual events of their ancestors. And all these stories were memorized by the young people, and as the people got older, they redefined and applied them as the educational

---

2 A good many of the stories in this book are quotation stories. Each one contains a quotation, a short phrase that expresses or condenses the whole story. For listeners who already know a story, it is a cue about what they will hear. A short example of a quotation story is at the end of this chapter.

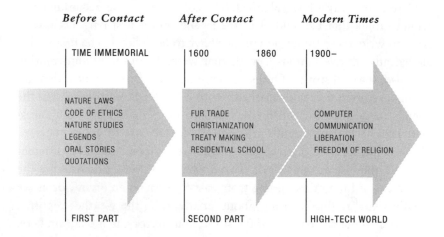

FIGURE 2: *From time immemorial to modern time.*

stories. They were equal to books. Those stories were used to educate the young people, to introduce the life experience to them, before they actually experience it. And some stories were designed to activate the mind and interest of the young people, the young persons of five years old, so they will be introduced to the things to come for them to encounter, so that they won't be so shocked when it happens. The stories were all kinds. Some were exciting stories, some were dramatic, some were fantasies, to create excitement in the children. And some were horror stories, some were scary stories, some were totally bad stories. But they were all useful, to train the youngster in the daytime, to absorb from the parents how they work, each day, morning to night. To learn the survival skills they are trained that way, by observation. They were told to observe the actions of the elders, and any adults that set to work in hunting, in fishing, and many other stuff, so they learned by watching, every day. They also learned by watching the men creating tools that were required in each season. The young girls watched their parents, their mother especially, and then they listen to their grandmother as she tells the story, as she recalls her life experience. And they watch their mother work with the skillful hands, as she creates things they need, as they listen to their grandmother.

Evenings were set aside time for the elders to tell the legends. They were created stories; they were often comical in nature. They were not necessarily true, but they were very useful. Quotation stories are true in life experience, human experience. But they are just as old as legends. And all these [stories] were used to introduce [knowledge] into the mind of the youngster. In the daytime, he watches both parents; mothers are watched by their daughters, father is watched by his son, probably hunting around short distance, fishing away from home. And the girls watched their mother do around-the-home hunting. The women hunt small game: squirrels, weasels, rabbits, and spruce partridges. They fish by hooks by the river, by the creek. In the wintertime, they fish on the ice, under the ice. They sit with their daughters to do that, show them how to hook the bait, and how to take the fish out, and how to clean them. The boys learn to walk very early with their father, to hunt whenever they can. Men knew how to hunt a rabbit also, and also the spruce partridge, and also other partridges, in a certain time of the year.

In winter, it's a hard time. This was before contact. There were no guns then; there were no steel axes. Wintertime was hard because the bow and arrow does not work well in cold weather, extreme cold weather. The axe they used was not as sturdy as steel, because it is only a bone axe or a stone axe. The stone axe does not cut well in ice-cold frozen sticks. The boys will watch their father looking for some kind of a tree, for tools, for snowshoe making; they learn exactly what kind of a tree they have to cut down, and where to look for it. They camp out with their father, and in the nighttime, they don't have to listen to legends, but they just have to watch the night sky, to study the stars' position, to study which star is what, also to watch the moon. Their father would tell them what these are. And also they absorb the weather, the coloration of the morning, and also in the evening and during the day. The father will point these things to the boy, and he will learn as he grows up.

In the meantime, if the boy is already walking around, he would be more than five years old. Listening to the legends at home, he would hear the stories about five characters that we have, and how those people possessed some mystical and magical powers. A young boy himself would ask, how does he get to do those things? Then the grandmother or the grandfather will explain; and when the father walks with the little young man with him, he will show the places where people begin to start what they call fasting or retreat, or dream quest places. They learn those things in their training, along with the survival skills, by great, careful observation of their father and their uncle or their grandfather. So this is how the young boys learn. But the girls learn the same way at home. Whatever the mother has to do in home, they learn that from their mother. And together, in the evening, the girls and the boys can sit quietly before bedtime, to listen to the elders tell the legends.

Getting back to the tool making. The creating of hunting tools is what I wanted to add a little bit about—snowshoe making. Also to look, in summer time, what is a tool? How do you create a canoe, how do you create your paddle, and where to find these woods, what kind, is what the young boy has to watch. And exactly how the man who creates the canoe makes it, where does he get the materials, how does he prepare it? How does he shape the canoe? All these, and the grandpa also will sit there and watch and teach.

Now, we come to the physical world; our physical training is limited, because our bodies can only stand so much hardship. Strength is not almighty power; it comes to exhaustion, at times. And there are things that are necessary to be done in order to survive. For example, hunting is not that easy. Sometimes, a man, to hunt the caribou, is not always successful to sneak up on the caribou, which is the easiest way you can get one. But in order to kill more than one, you must, as a man, have the strength and stamina and endurance to run after the caribou, and you must also know the terrain, the tundra, where the caribou will go, so you will know how to take a short cut. The boy has to know this. These are the things that a young boy has to know in the winter. In summer he will have to learn also the same thing, but it's much easier. Tool making—where do you find a tree to make a bow? And where do you find the stick to make an arrow? How do you make an arrow? All these have to be learned. And also the tools that can be used at home, like a wooden blade, a bowl, a spoon, all these have to be made—a paddle, as I say, for canoe, and other special tools that are required. The boy has to find these, and also the young girls have to absorb and see how it's done. They are not required to make them, but they would have to know.

Now, we have mentioned about the limitation of physical power and, in that, for the strenuous and continuous required strength for strenuous work, one has to have a will to do that. But the will is limited. That's where the spirituality comes in. That is where the young person has to go into the dream quest. Many things that he learns, that he absorbs, which he did not understand, was sometimes even afraid of, during his early years, he would have to go, once in awhile, to the dream quest. His father would take him there, show him where it is, if he is able to overcome his fear of being alone. So he has to go there to have a dream quest. It means to condition himself to dream and to visualize things that he feared and to be able to understand it, so he doesn't have to be afraid of it. And also to have a dream about animals, all kinds, that are fearful or dangerous to humans, so he can dream about them, so he will have a controlling system in his mind. All kinds of animals, he must [dream about]. Also, the weather, that is fearful sometimes; the thunder is scary, and he has to get over his fear about the thunder and lightning, and a danger of wind, that he will have to understand. He also has to learn the observation of the weather, so he can predict the kind of weather he will experience during his hunting.

So the spiritual development comes along as you are five years old, and it increases as your body grows up. And you bring along your spiritual development as you grow up, because you need it when you get to be an adult, to be able to will yourself beyond your physical strength; when you hunt, or when you have to defend your family by a threat of another person, you will have to have this. Also to have an ability to foresee the future, you may have to depend on these skills. So you, in doing so, make observation of everything; your father or your grandfather will tell you, there are creations. These things did not emerge themselves. These things, like stars and the moon and the sun and the earth, have been set by the power beyond physical being. And that's where the Great Spirit lives. That's where the Creator is mentioned, because this creation that we see— there has to be a Creator, there had to be a source of those things that we see. And living in the wilderness creates the beliefs out of the dream quest, also the vision, then [the boy can] apply them to life to understand more and to withstand the hardship of the environment.

So why all this training? Well, the physical, as I say, is limited, and this spiritual process adds to the total being of the individual to survive, at least in the northern area. And in the harsh environment, in northern North America, this can be achieved by living in the wilderness. You cannot achieve those things if you just sit home and do nothing. You will have to be involved in the harsh environment, and the environment causes you to develop a defence system in your body and in your mind. And if you increase this hardship by retreating, by fasting, by a denial of good food or gorging yourself with food—you have to avoid that—you have to give yourself less comfort so you can build yourself into a state of half a dream and half awake, so your dream vision can come very clear. When you achieve to do that, that's when you begin to seek the answers on the questions that you have—to seek any assistance with what you are afraid of in nature, whatever it is, even if it is a creature that you are afraid of.

So, this is a total education. As we know, natural human needs are something else that you have to study. What are the human needs? When you are born, you need to be cared for, because you're helpless, and when you receive care from your mother, you have love. Your father loves you. After that you need food. Of course, the parents will give you that. You need protection, because you cannot help yourself. Your parents are there, and that is a comfort, and that is what you received at the beginning when you were born. So, any human, what he needs is to receive love, kindness, and parents' love. Food, for the body to grow. And the spirituality—that is introduced in stories, legends, quotations, plus personal awareness. So when does it happen? As early as possible. To understand or to be introduced to the spiritual part of life, it's usually before the age of five. To listen, to absorb, to desire, and then to believe, then practise.

Respecting the environment is also very strong. The elders would teach you about land; how do you respect the land? Why do you have to respect the land? Total environment: land and whatever it contains, living or not living or moving. Everything is living, they say, but some may not move. Some things move, in water, underwater, and above. All the living things are supposed to be understood and respected. This is the part where the First Nation knew all those things, at the beginning, when there was no other nation around them.

Now we will go back briefly, to visualize the arrows moving towards your right. The first part, it's an open end, it only has a point in the direction where it goes. There is no closure at the left-hand side, because there is a famous word which Native people always use. They say, "Our ancestors, we have been here since time immemorial." That's why these arrows have no ends, in this vision. And they go on to point at the contact period. This is extra information. As far as the European know, and the different kinds of intellectuals that study the history, they have explained to us that life begin, long time ago. And then, people spread all over the world and somehow separated. The countries, I mean, the earth moved. Its continental movement is there. Well, let it be so. Maybe that's why the humans were found here, when the Europeans came to this country, which they didn't know existed. So we will leave that, but this is the idea.

When the Europeans saw these human beings, automatically they think they were less intelligent than them. But these people live here many years before that, five thousand, maybe ten thousand years. And they learned. The thing that we have to understand is that they adapted themselves into the land, at least as far as we can see, in a certain part of this country. And different tribes have different customs, experiences; they developed a variation of cultures, because of the geographical locations in which they lived as a tribe.

To thoroughly explain everything about the past before the European came is important: how and why these people did these things. How did the First Nations before contact accomplish something that seems so strange? For example, how did they do to have a process and spiritual practice they call "shaking tent?" There is a story that tells us the Omushkegowak truly were practising this shaking tent. There were those who did not; they were just pretending. But those who did the right thing, they usually require a very respectable location. They don't do this shaking tent right around the camp; they do it away from the camp so there can be quietness, and also they would do it at a certain period. They prepare it, the tools, the teepee structure; the materials that they use are truly made very nicely. It's a ritual; one has to go through with it. Once they get in the tent, they make it work.

The question is: how do they do this? We have mentioned about something called "dream quest." During that dream quest, someone will, in his dream, have it revealed that shaking tent will be his thing. It will be his achievement during his life. Not everyone is given to be a shaking tent user. Those people who want it, they can have it. But they have to go through a certain kind of a ritual during the dream quest. They'll have to go through severe tests and conditioning for them to acquire such a thing. So these are the things that are very important in the past, amongst the First Nations, Omushkegowak.

Why do they have to have this? It's for them to survive. As we said before, the human physical power is limited, but if you have an extra power in you—there is something we know that is called "mind over matter," I think it is called. It's when your physical being cannot accomplish anything, then you apply your mind to be able to do something that you cannot do, and it's possible. That is what I mean. That is why they condition themselves to have a dream during the dream quest, so they can know how to do this. So they can train their mind to take over what the physical power cannot do. That is why they have to do that dream quest.

We have mentioned about caribou hunting—sometimes it's very hard to do that. So the Omushkegowak have a system what they call: sneak up on the caribou the best you can. If it's early in the day, you could follow the caribou and take a short cut, catch up to them if you can, then shoot again with your arrow. And then, if you still have daylight left, you can still follow them and shoot them three times a day, even in the shortest day. That is almost impossible to do. Caribou can travel a long distance in one hour. They can travel at approximately thirty-five miles an hour, forty-five miles at their top speed. The only thing that stops them sometimes is the deep snow and the bush and the terrain, or because they have to stop and eat. That's the only time you can gain on them. If you push them all the time, they will not stop. There are some men who have a skill, to know exactly how to do, because they have studied the terrain and the landscape, what it looks like, where the caribou usually run—they can take a short cut and accomplish this impossible feat, to be able to shoot the caribou three times in the shortest day of the year. That's the highest achievement for the hunter. But he requires the will to do it. No ordinary man can do that.

So that's why these things have to be learned at the early age. That is why the person has to go into the dream quest so he can have it in his dream state of mind that he will be able to do these things. How is he going to do that? When the mind is trained to do things impossible, the body can too, at least for the time being. Our ancestors achieved this by living in the wilderness—harsh environment. And because it's harsh conditions where they live, they don't necessarily have to fast so much. Not much need to retreat or deny food or comfort, because they already live in the harshness of nature.

The human body needs these things, kindness, love, protection, and food and clothing. That's the most. Then spiritual need is introduced in the stories, also in legends and quotations, plus seasonal awareness. When can these things be possible? As soon as the person is able to understand the language. Five years of age is when you begin to listen to the stories, to absorb what you have dreamed, and then to believe what you acquire in your dream quest, then apply it in practice. You have to learn at the same time, when you have training, to study the land, the animals, birds, fish, insects, and weather, seasons, wind, and all the nature's forces. You have to include them in the dream quest. It has been said that everything that is fearsome in the human mind, in your own body, has to be questioned during the dream quest exercise. Whatever a young person fears, he has to question it during the dream quest. It is during that time that he will receive the answer and instruction how to overcome his fear, and what he should do.

There are many other things that have to be revealed during the dream quest. The things that you may require, that could be practised during your lifetime. Aside from the famous shaking tents amongst the Omushkegowak, there are other things that one should know or should try to acquire. For example, drum. One has to dream the drum and how to make it, every detail, to be a drummer. Drumming and singing, also how to heal with the drum. Song, or songs, reveal to you. What items should be used when one sings, if one needs a rattle—the skull of an otter, beaver, mink, or marten skull with round stones in it, a cymbal, something to make a noise. Something to make a sound, music that you can use. Probably a flute, the musical thing, with the air, and you use fingers to play with. Dancing—it is in the dream quest that one is told how to dance. To smoke, to do some smoking. All these things are supposed to be revealed during the dream quest. The use of sweet grass, which we had to get from other tribes. Most of all, how to use the shaking tent. How do you create it? What sticks to use, how many? And also, water vision. There is a way that the Omushkego people were able to do this; they just put water into the wooden pan, even the cloth or hide, to see the vision in it. If they are expecting some kind of attack by someone, they would put the cloth over their head, over this water pan, and see the vision in there; they could see what they want to see. That's because the water acts like eyes with binoculars; it extends your vision. These things were very famous amongst the Omushkegos.

Tools. Personal items, like medicine. What sort of a medicine should be used: it will be revealed to you on the dream quest. A medicine bag means a little bag that you put things in that you have dreamed. Probably animal bones, the teeth or claws of bear or lynx or wolf—things like that. Porcupine quills, that is a very powerful and dangerous thing to use against your enemies. Any other object that has been revealed to you during the dream quest. There are many things that happen during the dream quest that will help during your lifetime. That is why the dream quest must be. It's necessary before you could become what they call a mi-tew. A mi-tew is the totally educated person. It's almost like today: a person goes to a certain degree of education, goes to the high school, to the university or college if he wants to get specialized in something, goes on to many years in university, and then he has many degrees of different kinds. After that, he is capable to work in one of those jobs whenever he needs to, if he could apply it. It is the same thing with this mind development, a further education, beyond the physical education.

As I said, physical capability is not enough for this kind of harsh life, but a person needs to have the spiritual part. The mind is where the spirit lives. That's what the elders believe. They think that in the mind, that's where the spiritual life is located, and that the mind has about three levels of consciousness. One of those levels of consciousness is the one that has the power over matter, and that is why they go into the dream quest, to try to awaken it, so they can apply it whenever necessary.

It has been always cautioned that anyone who acquired such authenticity of this achievement was not to reveal it to anyone; otherwise he would lose it. Also, he was instructed by an elder never to abuse it; otherwise he would lose it. It would not protect him; it will fail to protect him, even to help him, so there's a restriction to it. These are the things that happen before contact; and in that period, because of this mind structure of a person, because most of the individuals who lived acquired these capabilities and knowledge, they are powerful. The other people respect them. No one can fool around with such individuals. One has to respect them, to listen to them. That is why the elders were most respected, because most of them had acquired such knowledge and power in themselves; they were fully capable of applying it when it's necessary. Therefore, they have acquired such a knowledge and power and capability that they were looked at as the leaders automatically and also expected to be the judges of matters, to enforce the righteousness when necessary, and to prosecute the wrongdoers when they are called for.

Most young people understand that, and they know it because they are told in the stories; these were implanted in their minds, to believe that. The more they believe, the more they behave well, and for that reason alone, because there was so much mi-tew in each individual elder, it was just like having a law inside your home, a policeman, the judge, the prosecutor, the intellectual who may be just on the side of the Creator himself. That's how these things were looked at in the past. Young people have not lived so long in this world; they didn't acquire all those things, because it takes years to acquire these things. It takes twenty years, at least.

But by some curse or some benefit, maybe, some young people can acquire it, especially those who have been born in a very rough condition, like an orphan, the boy who has no parents, who has not experienced love from his parents. Denied all the comfort and happiness in the early age, he automatically acquires this gift. All he has to do is—extreme unhappiness will bring it into his being. Extreme sad, mistreated, being abused, these things were accumulated in him, and when his mind can take it no more, he would just summon these things automatically. He has it. The abused orphan, the more mistreated, the more the power is created in him; that is what has been said in our culture. That is the reason our elders as judges, as instructors and teachers, have said to us, "Do not abuse the orphan, or the widow, do not abuse them," they said, "because they are protected by the Great Spirit."

All these things have been said, before the contact. There was no need to have a policeman, there was no need to have a jail or a judge; there was no need to have a prosecutor, or a prison, because everything was there, on the land; that's how these people lived. So the question is, were they savages? Were they uncivilized? Were they crazy? Maybe it is some form of craziness, but they have survived. Somehow, the Creator they call, or the Great Spirit, has allowed that to happen.

It has been said the orphan child will acquire these mystical powers, if need be; he doesn't have to go to the exercise of dream quest or anything. He doesn't have to go to retreat or fasting, he already has it. For his protection, the Creator gave the child this protection. This is revealed in the story of the orphan who defeated the powerful mi-tew (Chapter 3) and in the legend called Cha-ka-pesh, about an orphan who was mi-tew. That's what it does; the legend applies here in what I'm saying. If there is one lesson to the story about Cha-ka-pesh, it tells us exactly what happened.[3] And these legends existed thousands of years before European contact.

There is another subject that I want to include here. Our ancestors, mostly the elders who have accumulated the knowledge and experience and a great observation of nature, all the creation, they call it, the Creator had created, they have learned a lot of righteousness amongst them. As

---

3 There are several stories about Cha-ka-pesh, an orphan who lived with his older sister and was always causing her distress by testing his mi-tew powers; he traveled to the moon, snared the sun, and, in a story told in Chapter 5, he traveled through time and space to encounter the first foreign ship in Hudson Bay (Bird 0035; Bird 0114; Bird 0130).

today, they were all human; they were not all "holy people." But they knew. They had things out of these stories that we hear. Out of these things, the elders became encyclopedias. They also became churches, the righteous enforcers, the source of information for the proper life. So they have created some unwritten code of ethics which states in some legends not to kill human without any good reason, without a last effort to avoid it. That's what it says in the stories. The legends tell us that and also quotation stories. It tells us this story about not to kill, and also it tells the story about how to respect your elder, your parents, and what must not be done. Similarly as the Jewish Bible tells us God gave Ten Commandments.

These ideas existed amongst the First Nations before the European came, because the First Nation people did not kill for no reason. They kill sometimes to defend or to acquire something that they need, in their belief, for life. It's a just cause, whether they have to kill another human being for a reason. Which stories tell us about that? There are some old quotation stories about skirmishes that took place between the Omushkego and other tribes in James Bay Lowland, the tribes that came to attack the Omushkegos, without any reasoning that the Omushkego could understand. They just considered it savagery, useless massacre, or total insult— or is it God's will, or Creator's will? So, having to react to this tragic event, some stories tell us our Omushkego people sometimes retaliated and captured the aggressors and questioned them: "Why do you kill? Why do you do this so harshly?" Sometimes the attackers came from the land far to the south, and their spiritual belief and practices required them to become warriors, to go to far distant lands, and to kill people and bring some captives back for the sacrificial offering.[4] The stories are there, but we have not yet recorded many of them.

That's where this teaching came from that similarly says, "Thou shall not kill without any reason." And there are other codes of ethics that are extremely emphasized in legends—like where it's forbidden to a boy to sexually abuse a stepmother, let alone his mother. Because these things have happened long time ago, and they were written in the mind of every young person, these are not right. So they were condemning sins; when a person has been caught or been accused of doing such things, he was ostracized, that means totally abandoned from the tribe and not to be pitied, and that he should die, if it's necessary, in the wilderness, or he would starve to death. No one must help him, and that's how strong these

4 See Chapter 5, "The Omushkego Captive and the Na-to-way-wak."

things were. That means no man should abuse a mother sexually, and stepmother, or his own sister. These three were very strong. And it works in the opposite way too. The woman should not go after her own father on her initiative, and her stepbrother, and her own brother. These things were forbidden.

And the next one also—the young person; for example, if a woman marries an old person and has a son, she should not go after the son, when she finds herself dissatisfied from the older husband. It is really forbidden for her to do that. It has happened, in the past. There is a great story about this, the story of I-yas; it's a very lengthy story.[5] It emphasizes how forbidden this act is. It's a woman who did some bad things and causes much pain between father and son even though she failed to seduce her stepson, because the stepson understood the forbidden stuff; the custom was against that.

Then there is stealing. Again, the same custom applies, I mean the code of ethics that says you shouldn't steal anything that belongs to your fellow man—his possessions, to begin the list, like canoe, bow and arrow, his ax, and then, most important, his wife. You should never steal his wife unless there's a situation that a woman is actually running from her husband. You should not steal anything that belongs to an individual, a man or woman. The stealing was forbidden, because it was taking a possession from the man that belongs to him. His possession is his life. When you take it away from him, it is very close to killing him. When you take his wife away, you take his love away—the reason he lives. This is what they say, in our code of ethics.

Another thing that was emphasized was that each individual, either boy or girl, was told to respect animals, and that is also a very strong emphasis. Not to abuse animals by any means. There has been experienced a long time ago a man and woman sexually abusing the animal. That is ostracized sin. It's a blaspheming act. Blaspheming act means you could be killed for doing it. Like in the Jewish religion, a stoning sin. All these that I have said, to steal, to fornicate with your father's wife and his step-wife, or your sister, these were like a stoning sin, as in the Old Testament, the punishment was being killed with stones. For a woman to do the same thing was a stoning sin; and to abuse the animals of any kind, sexually abuse or use them, is also a stoning sin. These things have happened.

---

5 For the I-yas story, see Bird 0095.

Then there is also the law to respect the elders; it was very strong, not necessarily a stoning sin, but disrespect is a blaspheme act. It will catch up with you in consequence. Consequence can be very severe. Kische-pa-sta-ho-win, that's what they call it, a great sin. There are many other things: when you are harsh on the young people, when you severely punish them, you will also sin against nature. Two words, three words I have thrown in here. One is the blaspheme act, and the other one is ostracism—that means to be cast out, killed for doing something bad, and that's the Indian word, the ostracism. And also the blaspheme act, to be killed by it, and also I use the word stonings, just to make it more understandable what I mean. And then the respect of the animals is also defined. You do not kill an animal without using it all. You must use all the animal, all parts of it that you can eat or use in any way possible. And you should never overkill the animals that you cannot prepare or use, because it's a sin against nature. There is also on top of that, abusing, sexually abusing the animal. If you do something bad to the animal, you will get sick from it. That's another thing that is totally a most sinful thing.

Then there's the environment. Sin against environment means that you do something, damage to the land: setting a fire purposely, not putting a fire out, letting a forest fire start. Also leaving something behind that is dirty. Or, if you stay in one place, you shouldn't stay too long, and you should clean it before you leave, as best as you can, and let the nature clean it after. It is one of the reasons why our ancestors, our Omushkego people, follow the seasons in migration, because the nature takes care of the land. And you should respect it that way. You do not alter the land; you respect it the way it is, in all its environment. It's the most important code of ethics, I almost say law, but it is the law for the First Nation. It's called custom.

And of course, we hear so much about respecting the elders. We have heard that already. Why? Because they live long. They almost represent the Creator himself because they live long, those who live right. But those who led a sinful life or a bad life, they were less respected, but you still had to respect, regardless. And there is another rule that has said you must respect your parents, regardless. That means, if you know your parents are bad, you should never confront them or call them what they are. You should never do that. Otherwise the Creator will punish you. Because they are the servants for your health, for your life, for your wealth. For your life, mostly. They are servants for your wellbeing; the Creator has put them there. These are the teachings that were there a long time ago, but they were not written; they were stamped and written in the minds of each individual person. Therefore, they didn't require a policeman, or jail, or courts, or judges, because you are trained well.

That was the culture that existed before contact. When the contact came, we know about our way. But the newcomers understand only their own way, in writing. Maybe hard to admit it, but it has been. The results of the contact is the next important thing. It is very easy to recount them.

There are three major impacts in the Hudson Bay-James Bay area, James Bay Lowland. One is the fur trade. Quickly we will go through that. It changes the cultural conservation, the respect for environment, the respect to the animals, and respect of the human. It destroys the rule not to steal somebody's possession. When the fur trade came in, our people begin to steal furs from each other, as what the white people do. They see no reason not to do that. Also they begin to lose respect for the nature. They overkill, they kill animals, they kill beaver as many as they can, and leave carcass behind. That's the impact. And then they overkill, depopulate the animal, and nearly make them extinct. Beavers—it happened at least twice during the fur trade.

So that's not our culture, no it's not. It's caused from the fur trade. And then, people usually have what they call pride, almost extreme pride, amongst the First Nation, especially the Cree. When the fur trade people come in and understand the character of the Omushkegos, they take advantage of that nature. They encourage the hunters to compete with each other, to bring more fur than the next guy, so create some kind of hatred, and they resent each other. The sharing of the land begins to deteriorate and is not practised any more. That's the impact of the fur trade. The respect of the land is lost, because you've overused the land by doing many things.

During the fur trade, people were in such a hurry in the spring to try to catch as many beaver as they can, they never really cared to put the fire out, and there were lots of forest fires. And those people who were just rushing around to catch animals, they forgot to follow the old tradition, that is, to leave land as naturally as possible and to help fish—to lower the dam, the beaver dam each spring, so the fish can go up. That was forgotten, because there was such a hurry to travel and catch more beaver. This rule was, before the contact, the people in the territory—when there are lots of beavers, they dam the creeks, and they block the fish. Sometimes the fish can go over up the river in the spring when there's lots of water; they stay up on the lake for a little while. But when they come back, the water has lowered, right down to the dam; they could not pass the dam. They begin to die and rot, cause the water to be polluted and also the beaver cache begin to deteriorate the water. The most civilized animal, the most intelligent animal is a beaver—how clean is the house and the dam—but this also endangered the environment itself. The Native people before that time, they used to have a system; they used to release the water in the spring when there were beaver, so they discourage the beaver from coming in and damming the river, so those fish can swim easily. So they were sort of looking after them, the environment, by doing that. The men did that. These are the things that begin to not be practised after the European came—the impact of the fur trade.

So many other things that I could not mention here happened, and also when the Hudson's Bay Company begin to organize the goose hunting, there were lots of geese that were killed. And the population went down at one point, 1912, I think, because of this, because of the nature, also, and the weather. Also at that time, that's when the people begin to change the hunting habit, when the Hudson's Bay Company establish the goose hunting camps. So the people begin to compete, who's going to shoot many geese. The hunting practice was changed, deteriorated, [like] many things that were organized well before contact. These are the impacts, after contact. That's the fur trade impact.

What else about that? It changes the habit of the people, also. Because the fur trade bring in the items. Our people begin to lose their self-sufficiency because they buy the items—they buy the steel ax, they buy the guns—and their skills of creating their own tools were diminished, not used any more. The way they hunt changes, too. They begin to change the habit of the birds and animals, after that time. Then also, the hunting style. People used to have the deadfalls to catch the beavers and other animals and kill them right away, but when the white men came, they brought the steel traps, and many animals lost one foot, one leg. Many animals were wounded because of the steel trap. Also, time came that the wires begin to be available to snare the beaver at the entrance to his house. But when you wire the beaver, sometimes they pull loose and carry the wire away with them, and then it cuts through their body. Sometimes people find the beaver so suffering in an inhumane way, sitting on the riverbank, being cut through the skin with this wire, and slowly dying.

There is a strong story about cruelty to animals and how sometimes it got worse after the fur trade. One winter, a young man was trying to trap white foxes on the shore of Hudson Bay but he never succeeded. He was angry because the white fox skin was very valuable. The next summer, he and his two friends were hunting on the Bay shore. They saw a fox, and he swore he would punish her for getting away last winter. His friends helped him catch her in her den, and then he skinned her alive and let her go, she ran away like that. Even his friends were stunned but they didn't stop him. The next winter, all three, they disappeared in a terrible storm. That summer, around the same place, one of their relatives found a family of foxes playing with human bones like a hand and arm, not very old. The abuse caught up with those young men—their great sin, kische-pa-sta-ho-win, blaspheme act.

These were some things that were made worse from the fur trade impact. They are only a few examples. We change the state of the culture that was well-organized before. I don't mean to say the First Nation culture was perfect before the European, I'm not saying that. And the fur trade brings many useful things. But it just adds some more after.

Now we are going to talk about the next cultural impact, the Christianity impact on the Omushkego people. We have already talked about the Omushkego spiritual beliefs and practices before the European arrived. So after the fur trade, the next impact that happens to the Omushkego is the Christianization. It is just as important as the fur trade, maybe more important. The spiritual practice of the First Nation was the additional strength for the cultural survival. So when the Christianity came in and converted the Omushkegos in James Bay Lowland, they sort of denied the last resort for their survival. Denying them their own spiritual practice, it's just like almost taking the tools away for their survival.

That was the first impact of the Christianity. Later on, as if in preparation, as we know it today, the government worked with the missionaries to convert the James Bay Lowland to Christianity. The Omushkego people finally succumb, or submit to Christianity, some of them reluctantly and some of them willingly, some in recent years. Around late 1800s to early 1900s is a time that the missionary workers were so powerful that they convinced the Omushkego people that they should change by using a skillful approach and fear and [there were] very dedicated missionaries like Father François-Xavier Fafard, who were able to convince the Omushkego people to stop their traditional spiritual practices and beliefs, so they would join to Christianity.[6] As far as I could remember, the way they approached them was to convince the women first. Then the women, once they have been converted, they can easily make their husbands join to Christianity. As a result, the men became totally dependent on the white men. They didn't have much power any more. They just have to submit. After this happened, without them knowing why actually, so comes the treaty, Treaty 9 in 1905–06 around James Bay and then Winisk adhesion to it in 1930; I talk more about that in Chapter 9. So the treaty was done, which finalized dislodging the Native people from the land. Taking the land away from them. First taking their spiritual connection with the land, finally taking the land.

So that's an impact of Christianity. It has been abused. I am not condemning the Christian teaching or anything, because I am a Christian. I was brought up, baptized in Christianity, in a Catholic denomination. I believe that the good man, Jesus Christ, was a very honest man, and he never teach anyone to kill or to fornicate or anything like that; he always try to tell people to live right, his teaching. And one thing that this man did was, he discouraged the accumulation of wealth by his disciples. He said, do not take money, do not take the wallet, don't take two sets of clothes, just walk what you are, and then you will be fit. But that's not the way it turns out to be. The Christian leaders abuse the power, it seems to me, to gain much material things and power, and that is the resentment I have. But the church itself, the Christian teaching is very beautiful; I think it's one of the highest, well-taught and well-designed and well-intentioned. The man they call Jesus was truly a very holy person. And his teaching was great, I must admit. Anyway, as a historian, I like to say that it was the next most powerful impact that ever happened in James Bay, because it makes our ancestors, our forefathers submit, not willingly, but to give in. I cannot say if they knew what they did. They must have been in a situation which forced them to just simply give up.

The church teach them to obey the law, to obey the leaders, to obey the servants that come from the government, because they represent government and government represents God. That was a strong statement for our people to listen to. They didn't have much chance to question anything. So they lost their livelihood. They lost the land, they lost their spiritual practice, which give them strength on the land, and now they are

---

6 See Fulford with Bird 2003. Chapter 8 tells a story of strife between Louis's great-grandmother, a Christian, and a mi-tew whose practice she disrupted.

FIGURE 3: *St. Anne's Residential School in winter, Fort Albany, Ontario, 1932. The chapel (1); the priests' residence (2); workshop (3); the school under construction(4); shed to protect construction materials (5). Credit: Archives Deschâtelets, Fonds Diocèse de Moosonee, Dossier Albany.*

totally under the mercy, the hands of the white man. That was the Christian impact, Christianization.

The next one, which totally alienates the people from the land, is to put the children into residential school. This blocks them from their parents and mothers and love and everything, and causes lots of pain. But that is not the final act. There is another act that happens today continuously in the modern times. I have just mentioned two impacts, the fur trade and the Christianization. The third one is the residential school and the white man education. First, our people had to go to high school away from home. Today, they are at home to have a high school education, in promise that they will have a job when they grow up, which is not true at all. It doesn't work that way. And it's not going to work that way either, for the time being; there are very few jobs where they live.

I want to continue a little bit about the impact of the Christianity and education. They blend. The education was given to the people in James Bay and Hudson Bay. When our children were sent to school, they were taught the Christianity, to pray three times a day, once in the morning, and at lunch, and also at the evening. And to pray, a written prayer, a book, and also to say the rosaries, as it was then. At the same time, they were denied to speak their language. In the classroom, they were taught to read and write in Cree syllabics, to read the prayer book and everything, and times of the prayer. But right away they were told not to speak their language in front of the Oblate brothers who couldn't speak it. They could only use their language outside when they played. But never to laugh and scream, because they would annoy the people who do not understand the Cree language. I think that was what concerned our guardians, like the nun that was keeping us. I was not actually told to deny myself my language in school, but I was asked not to speak Cree in front of the people who don't speak the language. For some reason, it was insulting or annoying to them, so the sister, the nun, told us not to do that. In school, when we learned the English language in the classroom, we were told to speak in English as best as we can, because our teacher speaks in English only. But in the next minute, when we have another session or another classroom in which we were to learn the Catechism, then we used the Cree book to study the Catechism, and there we were okay to speak the Cree, but we were learning the religion. Not our culture, but the religion. Of course, we were young; we don't know anything about that, but that was the training system that was there. I didn't know anything about [it], I did not concern much about it, I just followed the orders, and follow what I am told, and never ask questions.

Even today, I don't think it was wrong; I still think, well, that was the best they can do. I am not resentful so much about that, and I don't hate those people who did that, but I hate what they did. Not what they do to us, but how they abuse the religion. They abused the power over us, and I resent that. The religion they teach was the best, very good. But the way they use it is what I resent very much from them.

But I don't hate. I have forgiven those people a long time ago, and I still use the religion that they have taught me, as much as I can. Try to follow its rules, try to live by it. I shall add a little bit about a certain negative effect upon other young people that I went to school with, especially the women, and also the ones who have got mad at the residential schools, they have denied their Catholic church, they went to join the other churches or tried to go back to the traditional practices. Totally opposite. But I didn't get that way. I stayed with my upbringing. I was blessed to marry an Anglican and she decided to join the Catholic church to avoid trouble over raising the children. So we did not argue over religion.

Today the young people are questioning everything. These old stories teach about Omushkego custom and what the life was like. One can learn from them by hearing, by imagining, listening. Maybe the stories can help the young people to learn our own history and find a place to stand.

A Quotation Story:
"It Must Be Your Thigh Bone that You Hear"

This is a very old quotation story; it happens a long time before the European came, because you cannot hear any manufacturing item by the European. It's an old man who speaks. And what he says is this. It's a very nasty way to say. He says, "It must be your thigh bone that you hear." Ki-ka-sii-pas-skwa-ta-pie-yan—"squeaking tight" [between your legs], used in conjunction with an-ni-ka-i-ti-ta-man [is what you hear]. That's all he says. Thigh bone, you know, the legs, the thigh bone? And that's what he says. So he uses this word to insult a lady. That's the quotation. It's very short.

Then the story opens by saying, long time before the European arrived, there was a terrible period in time, that sometimes in very poor years or sometimes when there's a famine, the First Nation people experience starvation, things like that. And there were times also that the extraordinary thing would happen. Sometimes the animals would get sick. Sometimes the beavers will get sick and die off. Sometimes the animals, for example, like sometimes polar bear, will be found to be out of its mind, actually crazy, and it was very dangerous to be near to such animal. And there were times the wolves became very crazy, and very dangerous, and they were called wih-ti-go wolves, wih-ti-go ma-hi-ka-nak. Wih-ti-go means other than ordinary beast or human. So this was a time in that year there were such stories in that area, the territory of the Omushkego people, that the wolves seem to have a crazy sickness, or whatever it was happening, and they were very dangerous. There were stories that wolves would kill a man by himself when he hunt. The wolf would hunt the human instead of being hunted. And it was very dangerous.

It was at this time this family group, this man and his wife, were living in the wilderness and they have an elder, the man's father, but there's no mention about the children. So the man would go out hunting all day, and he will return at home at the usual time, sometimes very late. And the old man, who was very old, would stay home and just exist because he cannot do anything any more much outside. And the lady, the wife, would look after the old man and cook for him and wash for him and everything, you know, care for him; at least it was company for an elder. For her it was a protection.

It was this time that she heard the story that the wolves were very dangerous, and she worried. There were times her husband would be not returning after the sunset, his usual time, and she worried, and she would go outside and listen if she can hear the sound of her husband coming home. In the wintertime you can hear a person walking with the snowshoes, so she can hear; that's what she was waiting for. So she went outside, she was worried, and she keep going outside in the evening, and the old man finally went to lay down to rest and sleep. And every time she opened the door flap the wind would rush in and give the old man chill again. And he got mad at her and says, "Why don't you stop going out and in?" he says. "Why don't you just stay and wait and sleep?" But the lady didn't· want to argue and she just say, "I'm sorry," and then she would go out and listen, and she would pretend to bring the wood in.

Later on, late at night, this time unusual late, it was very quiet night and was moonlight, clear sky, no wind, and she knows she can hear a distance. So she went out again, very late, and she stood there and listened very carefully, and all of a sudden, she can hear a sound that sounds very strange. It sounds just like a crunching of bones by someone eating. So she listen and listen for a long time, she was so sure that's what she hear. It cannot be the trees moving against, rubbing each other which the old man quoted as saying,[7] and then she went in and she wake up the old man, she says, "Listen, listen, I think my husband has been killed by the wolves because I can hear the crunching sound of the bones, somebody eating something." And the old man was very mad at this time, and that's when he says, "Why don't you leave me alone! There's nothing there, it is your thigh bone that you hear, the crunching sound because you don't rest!"

So she gave up. She didn't want to bother him because he was mad at her, bothering him so much. And so she went out again later, and she was so sure that her husband has been killed. She took the rope out, and there were some large trees around, so she climb up with her blanket and sit there and tie herself on a limb halfway up the tree and wait. And a moment later as she finished, she can hear the sound; then there was no more crunching sound. This time she hear some noise in the snow which sounds like an animal is running towards the camp. So she sat very care-

---

7 The Cree quotation phrase evokes the sound of bones creaking and implies a comparison to the sound of trees rubbing against one another in the wind—but there was no wind.

fully. She looked towards the trail where her husband should have come home from, and there with the moonlight came the wolf, a large wolf, and he has been totally stuffed himself, she can still see that he has been eating something. This was towards midnight now. So she just froze there, just sit, and she don't move. But the fortunate thing was that there was no wind, she was downwind from the camp, and also the wolf didn't smell.

So the wolf came, and it sort of rush back, and then just jump into the door of this teepee and find his way in. And the lady just barely able to keep herself from screaming. The wolf jump right in, and the next thing she hear was this growling of the wolf, fighting, and also hear the old man screaming, and he was calling for help and everything, and he says, "The wolf is here and attacking me." But the lady can't do anything, she just sat there. And then finally the old man's voice faded away, and the next moment, the lady can hear the sound of the wolf eating the person, again hear that crunching sound, and all night she stay there. She sit there, she didn't sleep; she just sit there, near frozen to death.

Then finally towards the dawn, the wolf finally came out all stuffed, and he drags a bit of meat here and there, bones, and followed the trail away from the camp, a long distance. And usually the wolf sometimes would carry the leftover food for him to go bury it away from where he eat, and this is the natural understanding. She understands that, the lady, and she knows as soon as he disappears into the bush, I will get down and run, and she did that. She waited for the wolf to disappear into the distance, and then she came down and run, run anywhere at all. And she left home, and then with the snowshoes she left, went to look for some other human beings and finally able to find them. There were some families were living not far away. And that's where she tell the story.

So this is a quotation story which started off with this word, ki-ka-sii-pas-skwa-ta-pie-yan … "It must be your thigh bone that you hear." That's the quotation. That's the end of the story. So quotation stories can be very short, they can be very long, they can be humorous, they can be sad, tragic, and horror stories. That's it, quotation story.

2

"Now, the Question of Creation"
Stories About Beginnings and the World Before We Came

Introduction
PAUL W. DEPASQUALE

Many Indigenous peoples continue to tell creation stories as a way to explain the greatest mysteries of life: how were the celestial and other heavenly objects, the waters, and lands created, and by what god or gods and powers? What are the origins of the natural world, plants, animals, and creatures of the land and sea? Who were the first humans on earth, and what kind of world did they emerge into and inhabit? Creation stories, observes Virginia Hamilton, "relate events that seem outside of time and even beyond time itself. Creation myths take place before the 'once upon a time' of fairy tales. They go *back beyond anything that ever was* and begin *before* anything has happened" (Hamilton 1988: x, her emphasis).[1]

As Louis Bird explains in Chapter 1, he has been recording his people's stories for about four decades. In all this time he has not heard any Omushkego legend that explains the primary origins of the land and water (Bird, Louis Bird on Cree Creation Stories, 2001: 5). He has not heard an Omushkego story, for example, like the Iroquois legend of Sky Woman, who fell to this world from above and, with the help of several animals, created Turtle Island (Earth or, in some versions, North America) by walking in circles on the back of a giant sea turtle. "Unfortunately," says Louis, "we the Omushkego tribe do not have the very beginning how the earth was created.... [Some of] the other tribes of Canada, they call it a 'Turtle

1 I would like to thank Kelly Burns for her research assistance and help transcribing several of the oral recordings used in this chapter (see References). This work was undertaken with the support of the Social Sciences and Humanities Research Council of Canada and the University of Winnipeg.

Island.' The Omushkego tribe, they don't have that. It may have existed, but I never personally ever heard it" (Bird, Louis Bird on Cree Creation Stories, 2001: 5).[2] Louis has recorded stories about the famous trickster/culture hero Wi-sa-kay-chak that explain the origins of several distinctive geographical formations along Hudson and James Bays, such as large, coloured rocks apparently created by Wi-sa-kay-chak as he journeyed from the East to the West, interacting with various peoples and animals along the way (Bird, Winter Territories 1999: 3).[3] Such narratives, however, do not attempt to explain the earliest beginnings of the world.

Louis has also observed that Omushkego people did not traditionally catalogue or order their creation stories. He explains:

> The Omushkego ... have not actually specifically outlined [catalogued or ordered] their creation stories. But they have many, many stories, concepts, theories of the possible answer to the question of where did the First Nation come from? How the beginning of the world did happen. Our Omushkego tribe did not have a creation story such as the Jewish people. We do not have any Genesis which says that God made man in six days. No, not that well-organized. But they did have stories that answered some of the questions of this kind. The problem is, they were never told or written in an orderly manner. Shall we say, what story comes first? (Bird, Louis Bird on Cree Creation Stories, 2001: 1)

Omushkego creation stories are O-mush-ke-go-wi. kis-ski-no-ha-ma-ke-wii-na, or "traditional Omushkego teachings," and are examples of a-ta-

---

2 There are numerous stories found among the Swampy Cree, Rock Cree, Woods Cree, and Plains Cree in which Wi-sa-kay-chak remakes the world from mud or moss brought by "Earth Diver" (see Brown and Brightman, eds., 1988: 132–33). One such story was told by Omushkego elder Simeon Scott (d. 1979) between 1955 and 1957 while he was living in Fort Albany and close to retirement. In Scott's "The legend of Weesakechahk and the flood," Weesakechahk enlists the aid of a beaver, muskrat, and wolverine to help him create land on a raft from a small bit of earth found at the bottom of deep water. Although the narrative tells "where this land on which we are living came from," the land in Scott's legend, as in other Earth Diver stories, existed prior to the flood and is recreated in the story (see Scott 1995).

3 See, for example, Bird, Winter Territories, 1999 and Bird, Legend of Wiisahceechak, 2002. Wi-sa-kay-chak is a complex figure, sometimes human, sometimes animal or spirit, so powerful that "he" (Wi-sa-kay-chak is of animate gender in Cree [which does not make a grammatical distinction between masculine and feminine], but always male in Louis's English translations) can even substitute for Creator, as we see below in "Creator Talks to the Animals About the Emergence of the Humans." On this central figure of Cree and Saulteaux oral literature, see Brown and Brightman, eds., 1988: 125–28. On Louis's understanding of Wi-sa-kay-chak, see DePasquale and Bird, in press, 2005.

noo-ka-nak, "legends." Having discussed these stories with many elders,[4] Louis orders them according to how they were traditionally taught, based on a "chronology" of narratives that tell "the story of the emergence of humans from a world in which only animals previously existed." An Omushkego theory of creation or evolution includes stories familiar to many Cree people of the Hudson and James Bay Lowlands: "Giant Animals," about creatures who once roamed the earth, believed to be dinosaurs; stories featuring Mi-she-shek-kak or "Giant Skunk," about animals with the abilities of mi-tew (or "shamans"), who conspired to slay Giant Skunk and predicted the arrival of humans; legends about the diving bird Sink-i-pis, who was dull and homely unlike his handsome brother the loon; and narratives about E-hep, which relate the arrival of the first humans, lowered in a basket to this world by a giant spider from the world above.[5]

This chapter presents several variations of three of these traditional Omushkego stories: "Giant Animals," Mi-she-shek-kak or "Giant Skunk," and "E-hep." Also included is another important legend, "Creator Talks to the Animals About the Emergence of the Humans." This story is not listed in the above chronology but would appear before "E-hep," since it antici-pates the arrival of humans.[6] These narratives belong to an oral tradition that is at least six generations old and are remembered by few people today. Once used to teach important life lessons, these stories about human expe-riences were told so long ago in the past "that the individual who have experienced it—his name and his relatives—have been forgotten. Therefore the story have become a legend" (Bird, Louis Bird on Cree Creation Stories, 2001: 8). As a device to aid in the remembrance and retelling of these nar-ratives, the elders "coded" them by repeating or quoting important words that had been used for ages. These ma-ka-aa-it-tway-koo-pa-ney or "quo-tation stories," as Louis calls them in Chapter 1, begin with a familiar line intended as a starting point for the storyteller and a way to heighten the interest of his or her audience. For example, the first version of "Giant Animals" below begins with the famous quotation, "Ki-it-ta-wa-ku-pun-mi-shi-ha-way-ya-shi-shuak. Ka-ki-pi–mo-ta–chik-has-kik-ki-na-hi-wak-

---

4 The closest Omushkego word to the English word "elder" is ki-shay-ya-how, meaning "older person, respected person; oldest of the people" (Bird interview, 2004).

5 For Louis's fuller "chronology," taking into account the Omushkego legends known to him, see DePasquale and Bird, in press, 2005.

6 Louis discusses the story of Sink-i-pis briefly at the beginning of "Creator Talks to the Animals About the Emergence of the Humans." We could not include the full version here because it is quite lengthy. See Bird, "Legend of Sinkepish."

ma-ka. Mi-na-ma-ku-ka-ta-pi–moo-ta-wak-at-ti-ish-skwa-ska-mi-ka-kay," which Louis translates as: "There were some giant animals that roamed the earth a long time ago and somehow they went into hibernation and these animals will roam the earth again at the end of time."

Describing his earliest reactions to "Giant Animals," Louis states that as a boy he didn't find anything particularly remarkable about the story, nothing worth giving a lot of thought to it; he simply enjoyed the experience of hearing a well-told story. The legend was retold often by his mother Scholastique, grandmother Maggie Bird, and grandmother's brother, David Sutherland (ca. 1880–1963), an elder and storyteller whom Louis cherished. Louis learned the quotation from Xavier Chookomoolin (ca. 1884–1957), a well-known elder who lived and traded goods about sixty miles south of Winisk. As Louis heard the legend repeated, the quotation's fantastic image of giant animals roaming the land was what most excited his interest and curiosity: "That's the one that catches my attention. I asked many elders, I said, 'What does it mean? Where does this quotation story start? Is it there in these story readings?' So wherever I went, I hear the same quotation, and nobody has extended explanation or anything. They're just quoted." Finally, in about 1960 Louis met an elder in York Factory who, when Louis repeated the quotation to him, said, "Ah, yes, we hear that too when we were young. Yes, it was the man who came from the prairie or visit this area in the early fur trade who have mention about a place west [where] they found bones that were big. And that's why the story is" (Bird interview, 2004).[7] "And then," recalls Louis, remembering how he discovered more details about the legend of Mi-she-shek-kak or "Giant Skunk,"

> I told him about the giant skunk story. "Do you know about the giant skunk story?" He says, "Oh, yeah, we all have." And he says this giant skunk came from the idea. It came because of those bones that were found. It could be real, there were some large animals, they could have been in the past. But maybe that was a leftover thing. And then he says it [the Giant Skunk] didn't fit into the modern size of animals. And the other animals didn't want him. So they tried to get rid of him. That's as far as this old man explained to me, the story-teller. Because we talk about these things. I was beginning to

---

7 This elder's surname was Spence; Louis thinks his first name was Jarvis.

ask questions. That was in 1960. Long time ago. I was very curious about this because I wanted to place those stories somewhere it would make sense. Whether if it's just a make-up stories or whether if it's real. And it was later, it was 1960, when I hear that, when I was in Churchill, Manitoba. So ten years later, I never thought about this one and the magazines where they talk about dinosaurs. But again, I thought it was just imagination. When I went to Edmonton in 1972, I went to the Provincial Museum in Edmonton, you know, where they show the dinosaurs. I went in there and you could touch the story there and you could sit there and look at those things in the picture. And that comes to my mind. You see this thing, that's what they were talking about, I thought. So I begin to think, my way of thinking is that our people understand there were animals first. Animals live on the land first and then human. (Bird interview, 2004)

Louis credits his mother Scholastique and his great-uncle David Sutherland for the story "Creator Talking to the Animals About the Emergence of the Humans." He heard parts of "E-hep" from Simeon Scott (see note 2), but adds that David Sutherland was "more precise" in his use of details. David would often tell stories with his eyes closed, smoking a pipe, "as if he was seeing a picture," says Louis. "We liked him when he's mysterious, when he's in that story." Part of the appeal of David's version is that he heightened the story's suspense by withholding the information that E-hep was a giant spider, encouraging his listeners to participate by asking questions about the nature of this creature. Sometimes David would not want to be interrupted—or would pretend not to want to be interrupted—when telling a story. He would sometimes tease the children by pretending to forget his way if interrupted; and then his wife would say, "Come on, don't be mean, tell the story to the kids," and David would continue (Bird interview, 2004).

Louis has recorded several versions of all these creation stories except "Creator Talks to the Animals About the Emergence of the Humans," which exists only in the recorded version presented here. Both "Giant Animals" and "E-hep" exist in three different versions. Because each is fairly short and gives information, details, and nuances not available in the others, we have included all of them below. Mi-she-shek-kak or

"Giant Skunk" exists in five different recorded versions, from which we have selected two that are representative of the narrative yet convey ideas and images not found in the other. Unlike creation stories told in Western print traditions, such as the biblical account in Genesis, no single version of Aboriginal oral narratives is dogmatically perceived as authoritative, although some communities still follow traditions about which families and individuals can pass on traditional stories and about how these should be told. Hopefully the variety and range of texts presented below will help to show that stories told in Native oral traditions are not fixed, static, inflexible, or always consistent, but that they vary according to the context of the telling and the background, intentions, and even mood of the storyteller.[8]

The process of translating oral recordings into print raises a number of issues and challenges so that even the seemingly straightforward task of producing a transcription of an oral recording is potentially difficult and open to debate.[9] Working with verbatim transcriptions, I have edited the texts following Louis's editorial suggestions, deleting false starts and repetitions and retaining his English usage, including grammar, diction, and idiom. This wording has been checked and corrected by Louis. In another publication of his traditional stories (see DePasquale and Bird, in press, 2005), I arranged Louis's words on the page in the form of narrative poetry, using line breaks to indicate a pause or breath and a line space to denote a longer pause, according to conventions practised by Dell Hymes, Dennis Tedlock, Julie Cruikshank, Wendy Wickwire, and others. An "ethnopoetic" line presentation seems appropriate for Louis's a-ta-noo-ka-nak ("legends"), perhaps not for his ti-pa-chi-moo-wi-nan (stories about more recent historical events), because it offers textures and nuances of the original storytelling performance not easily conveyed in prose format. Louis isn't much concerned with the arrangement of his printed English words and has therefore left decisions about presentation largely up to me. While considering how to arrange his trickster and cannibal narratives, I found stylistic and structural similarities between Louis's storytelling and that of Harry Robinson, an Okanagan storyteller whose oral recordings were worked into print by Wendy Wickwire. Describing the loss of dramatic quality of

---

8 On the ways that oral literature can be viewed contextually and ethnographically in order to learn how social, cultural, and individual factors give it shape and meaning, see Bauman 1986: 1–10.

9 For a good introduction to the theoretical and ethical issues involved in editing Aboriginal oral texts, see Murray and Rice, eds., 1999.

Robinson's oral voice when presented as narrative prose, Wickwire explains that her decision to use narrative poetry instead was based on this form's better ability to emphasize the unique features of Robinson's style: the frequent repetition, pauses, and sentence structure (1992: 17). For the stories presented in this chapter, I have used a prose rather than poetry format in order to maintain consistency in length and appearance with the other chapters in this book. Although Louis's distinctive manner of speaking, characteristic repetition, and dramatic pauses may not be entirely translatable to prose, this presentation still gives the reader a strong sense of his colourful and vibrant speaking voice.[10]

I have heard many authors and scholars express concern that the process of translating stories from oral traditions into print potentially transforms them into something fixed or rigid, lacking their oral qualities.[11] But in order for many of these stories to be retold again, not as in times past but in a modern era, they need to be relearned or learned by peoples who have lost or never known them because of years of colonial processes. Their stories told in print today are already enabling Aboriginal peoples to engage again—or for the first time—with meaningful aspects of their cultural traditions and histories. The ways that these stories will be performed and interpreted in the future, and retold to others, will be as imaginative, varied, and individual in their printed (or electronic) forms as they always have been for Aboriginal peoples.

---

10 Anthony Mattina's characterization of "Red English" is helpful in the context of Louis's English usage. Mattina explains that this pan-Indian phenomenon includes a lack of subject-verb agreement, expressions that could be construed by some as "substandard," ungrammatical conjunctions and elliptical sentences. Often Red English is judged as "impoverished and inferior" to English, and its use perpetuates a stereotype of "the backward Indian." Mattina counters that the problem really lies with people who judge Native people by their speech habits (1987: 140). His view that the arrangement of the text on the page is ultimately less important than the voice of the storyteller is perhaps also relevant here: "Let the texts come forth, in whatever typographic arrangement the editor deems appropriate. Given an understanding of the tradition and context of the text, I expect that the worthiest texts will require the least architectural support. And because it is a good narrator who tells good texts, let him be foregrounded" (1987: 143).

11 For a useful discussion of the ways that Aboriginal writing "moves beyond the mere imitation or reproduction of a European, or mainstream North American literary style" in order to "translate the genre conventions of Native oral tradition into written forms," see Schorcht 2003: 5.

Giant Animals

"ABOUT THE BEGINNING AND END OF TIME"[12]

I just call this legend "Giant Animals." I only use a quotation. Quotation is what I use for that one. It goes like this: Ki-it-ta-wa-ku-pun-mi-shi-ha-way-ya-shi-shuak. Ka-ki-pi–mo-ta–chik-has-kik-ki-na-hi-wak-ma-ka. Mi-na-ma-ku-ka-ta-pi–moo-ta-wak-at-ti-ish-skwa-ska-mi-ka-kay. That's it. That's as far as it goes. And it says: "There were some giant animals that roamed the earth a long time ago and somehow they went into hiberna-tion and these animals will roam the earth again at the end of time." That's a quotation, you know. And then the story doesn't come out like a beginning at all, it just open the subject to ask the question. If you ever start off with that kind of a quotation, a guy would say, "But where are the animals? Where do you find the evidence that they once existed?" That's usually the question. And if anyone remembers, he or she would say right away, "From the West." And then the next person would say, "Who brought the story?" Long time ago, they say, some kind of a man came, work his way through here in the Omushkego-land, and he was a fantas-tic storyteller—a liar, whatever he was. So, one of his stories is about the giant animals that once existed. He says, "There are bones. The bones have been found. Huge bones, you know, like thighbones and everything. And those animals must have walked on four legs." And he says, "They must have been very large." And he described the places where those bones are found. He says, "On the river, somewhere." That's where they see those bones, and they say they are buried under the ground. And so he says, "The idea is that the animals went into hibernation like a bear, but they have never come out." So the idea was that the animals just went to sleep for awhile, and then they will wake up sometime in the future, or at the end of time. They call it the "end of time." Apparently, they know there is going to be the end, those people who create the stories.

So that's about the beginning of time. That's our stories. And the next thing that came out is about the Giant Skunk.

---

12 From Bird interview, 2003.

"SOON THE WORLD IS GOING TO SHAKE"[13]

A long time ago when I was a young boy, I used to get so scared when I listened to the elders saying—especially when we would go to sleep—they would say to us (maybe just to scare us to sleep): "You better go to bed now. Soon the world is going to shake when the giant animals roam again." And so we cuddle to our mother's chest and then just go to sleep. And that's exactly what they used the stories for.

So in the morning or the next day, we would ask our grandfathers, "Is there really giant animals?"

So they said, "Um ... not really" [laughs].

We were disappointed. So anyway, they begin to tell us a little bit. And they said there was a story one time, in that area. Okay, the stories that I get are from the west coast of James Bay and southwest coast of Hudson Bay, in that area. A place called Omushkego-aski. So that's where all these stories came from. But long time ago people used to visit each other from a distance. Some people brought stories from the west, people who talk about mountains that touch the sky and beyond. They were great stories. Our people didn't believe that. They didn't believe those things. They said, "It's impossible"—you know, for the mountains to touch the sky. But we heard them. So somewhere around this land, somebody came in and brought the story that was extraordinary. And they say they have seen a place where the giant animals hibernate. So they say, "There were some giant animals that roamed the land, time before man, time before the animals we see. And those animals, they hibernate. And in time past, in the future, they will come again, they will roam the earth again, towards the end of the earth." That's what they say. That's as far as the story goes, the quotation.

And then we begin to hear the giggles here and there. "What did he mean by that?" So we had a story that comes up sometimes, like stories I hear in other places I go.

I've travelled in James Bay. I have travelled up to York Factory and across the land. And I hear the same quotation come up here and there a little bit different and little bit extended to my knowledge. And so they say that a person that came to the west coast of James Bay, southwest coast, he talks about the place called the mush-koo-tew, a place where nothing grow, only grass, a prairie. So he says, "In that area, that is where they found the giant bones that were washed on the lake or on the river."

---

13 From Bird, "Questioning the Elders," 2001.

That's as far as the story goes. From that comes the idea for the story of the giant animals. At that time. Nobody can believe that. There is no such way that a thighbone of an animal can be this long [gestures, laughs]. It was an unbelievable story. Nobody wanted to believe that. They just say that the man is making the story up to scare us. But today, whenever you go to the museum you will see those things being put together and the bones that are bigger than this and also the tail of an animal about fifteen feet long [laughs]. So there it is. Our people did find and know about those things. So there it is, we have dinosaur stories. And also we have an idea about time as it has existed longtime ago before man.

"TO SATISFY THE CURIOSITY ABOUT THE FINDING OF THESE ANCIENT BONES"[14]

And now, I have interviewed many elders. I have asked them many times to tell me if we have any creation story at all. In doing this I have run into many elders who have tell me the stories which has been passed down to them orally by their fathers, their grandfathers, and great-grandfathers which existed at least six generations ago. Some of the stories are very old. They are not even remembered any more. The only way they can recall the story was by coding part of the story, repeating the word that has been used for ages. Somehow they have forgotten the definition or the meaning of the story. And this is how it goes.

This story is from the Omushkego tribes along the Hudson-James Bay Lowlands. So they said a long time ago, a long time before the European arrived into this land. The stories exist amongst the first Omushkegowak. The story that has been coded for ages which says there existed giant animals upon the land who roamed the land and someday in period in time went into hibernation and have not appeared ever since. And therefore it is believed that in time—towards the end of time—"these giant animals will walk again on the surface of the earth." That is a quotation.

Ever since then, many Cree people have tried to explain what these words may mean. Why isn't there an explanation? So some elders have said sometime in the past there were such animals who live and somehow—by mystery—are not here. But the bones have been seen somewhere along the earth. Some tribes have seen these bones which are so large that no such animal exists in the present time. And the story begin which has

14 From Bird, "Questioning the Elders," 2001.

been quoted. Just to satisfy the curiosity of the questioners about the finding of these ancient bones.

Out of this idea the First Nations tribes have also told the fairy tale story. The giant animal bones were considered myth, not true, not possible. One story that came later said there were large animals that were found somewhere on the land, which still has flesh on them because they have been covered by the snow. Freezed up north somewhere.

Again, this story came about in the area of the Hudson-James Bay Lowlands where the Omushkegowak live and have created this saying as a myth, not even a legend.[15] Because there is no link to it. There is no explanation. There is no completion of the story. There is the second one. According to our ancestors, the Cree tribes have begun to outline their theory that the animals lived on earth before humans. From these two quotations emerged the legend of the Giant Skunk—Mi-she-shek-kak. The Giant Skunk, they say, is the remaining of the first giant animals that exist on the land.

Mi-she-shek-kak (The Giant Skunk)

"THE OMUSHKEGO EVOLUTION STORY"[16]

Now, you wanted to know how the Omushkego evolution story begin. Well, we don't have any scientific equipment, we don't have any dating process that is used today to know those things or even to investigate any place, we don't. But we have stories that tell us that people do understand this a long time ago. That life begins somewhere and that animals did live on earth, but no humans. We have those stories. One of them is called— very unexpectedly, you wouldn't think—it's called "Giant Skunk." And it's supposedly the leftover of the giants on the land. The Giant Skunk was not very welcome amongst the animals at that time. And when you listen to

---

15 Unlike a legend, which is rooted in some actual physical experience, a myth, according to Louis, is "something that is totally created which doesn't even have no physical experience. It's the idea of a world beyond physical. People would try to understand where the something came from. So they think that there is a spiritual world and that spiritual world connected to this world.... People used to say there is god for thunder and all that stuff. There's a certain god that is there and it's not material, it's not physical. But he is there, and sometimes these beings that are not physical, sometimes they disagree with each other. That's what the [Omushkego] people say, so that's what we call it-twa-soo-win, it's a noun. This is not physical, it's only in the mind" (Bird interview, 2004).

16 From Bird, "Questioning the Elders," 2001.

the story, there were no humans, only animals. And one thing the animals fear most is this Giant Skunk, I guess because of its smell, or maybe because he was big. Anything that was large people used to get scared of. I guess they apply that story into that, the people who create the story.[17]

So they say that the Giant Skunk is the oldest animal and he was big and the animals of its time were also big. And then you hear a little bit of the idea that things are not exactly what we see.

And when you listen to this Giant Skunk story there is no humans, just animals, and they speak and they think, they plan, they struggle for a living just like us, just like humans. When you listen to the story you forget they are animals because they are just like humans. They even plan.

It was that time when Giant Skunk was a threat to their lives. And those animals, one day they decided they couldn't stand this big animal. So they all gathered together and said, "Let us get rid of this giant animal because it is no good for us." And then one time they got together, all animals that are leaders amongst their group, they get together, just like having a council, to talk about this Giant Skunk that is bothersome amongst them.

So they decided, "Yes, we should try to kill it. But how are we going to kill it?" So they said, "An opportunity will come, but we will prepare."

So what happened one time when they were getting together, they laid out the rules that all animals should follow because the Giant Skunk, not only is he big, he is also a mystical power. In our language we call it mitew. I guess in the English language they say "shaman," so, "powerful shaman." This guy, that's why he was so feared, because he has all this power, much more than the others. So it is hard to get rid of him and, besides, he eats animals.

So anyway, when the animals gather together they said, "No person should cross wherever he walks. Wherever he stays, every animal should stay away. Because he would know every time when you walk, when you touch his trail he would know and follow and kill the animal that does that." There was no way to avoid him. So finally they make that rule. Everybody, every animal, every kind, every kind of animal remember that rule in order to survive, because of this Giant Skunk.

So one day this tiny animal [laughs], one day this tiny animal called a weasel was hunting on his hunting territory. He knew the rule, that he

---

17 In another version of this legend recorded by Louis, he explains that "all other animals are naturally afraid of skunks, its spray, it's painful to any animal" (Bird 0136).

shouldn't cross the Giant Skunk's trail. One day in the wintertime, he was traveling a far distance in the day, the little animal, and on his way home towards the evening—he was very tired—he wanted to take a short cut straight to his home as he get there, halfway through, very close to his home, and there was this giant trail that looked snow-ploughed. And he saw it and he just stop and look at it. "Hopefully it is not him," weasel thought. But unfortunately it was the Giant Skunk. Look close at it, inspect it, and he saw. "It is the Giant Skunk." He even smell it.

So he was so tired. He didn't want to go all the way back to try to find where he can avoid the touching of that trail—even to touch, not supposed to touch it. So the lesson to this rule, in order for survival, he decided, "Maybe I should go around." He argued with himself a little while. And then finally he thought, "Why should I have to go all the way back there? Why can't I just do something?" So he decided to dive under the snow right down to the ground. He says, "He won't know anyway. How would he know?" He did that. So he dive into the snow, right under the trail, right at the bottom where the grass and moss don't even touch the snow. And far away at the other side he came up, he did pass. And from there on, so he run home.

The weasel got to his home late at night and when he got home he forgot all about crossing the Giant Skunk's trail. His wife just welcome him and his food was ready and everything. And just before he goes to sleep, his wife asks, "How was your day?"

So he says, "Fine. Fine." And before he fall asleep he just remember. And he shook his wife. "You know," he says, "you know, my dear, one thing I forgot to tell you: I crossed the Giant Skunk's trail."

So they all sit up and begin to think. "Why did you have to do it?" she says.

"Well, I was tired. It was close to our home, so I decided to take a shortcut and ran across the Giant Skunk's trail and so I dive under. I was so sure, I am very sure he's not going to know it."

So his wife says, "Don't count on it, because he knows." And then the story stopped there for a little while.[18]

When he was diving, you know, crawling under the ground, at that moment the Giant Skunk knew that somebody was touching his trail

---

18 In Bird 0136, weasel's transgression is revealed not to his wife but to a community of "elders and other wise animals" who interrogate him about his error and spread the news throughout the animal community.

when he was sitting at home because he is a person who knows something mysteriously because of his capability as a mi-tew [laughs]. So he knows.

So in the meantime the little weasel went home.

And the Giant Skunk begin to feel insulted. He knows he is the most powerful animal. He knows he is the most feared animal and he knows that nobody should dare insult him, because if somebody crosses his trail, he's insulted, and that's why he feel that. And so he begin to find a way to know, to visualize who crossed his trail. So he eat, he eat something, some special cooking in order to have a vision to look for the trail where he was crossed. And then he couldn't see anything, not a thing. He went to check the trail but there is nothing there. Finally he found it, then he follow the trail and at that time the weasel knows he has been followed. He begins to take off, run away from home with his wife and kids and tell everybody along the way, all the animals, and they all took off from the area.

Soon the days passed, there were many animals following the same way, running away from the Giant Skunk.

So they make a journey across the land to the west because there are mountains out there, that is where they hope to go. Took many days, even months to try to get away. They finally reached into the mountain areas where they hoped to get help from their friend Mi-shi-pis-shew, the Big Cat, who was supposed to live there. That's why they go there, to ask him to help them.

So it did happen. They found him, they said, "Can you help us, because the Giant Skunk is behind us?"

And the cat says, "Why bother me? I am resting." You know, the cats want to walk around at night, I mean the wintertime. But he did help.

To make a long story short, they did kill the Giant Skunk. There is a long, long stories that describe the land and how many animals get away. And then they make their stand where they gonna try and kill the Giant Skunk. So they finally make a place where they are going to trap him, and they were able to trap him. And they had one animal appointed to sort of hold his—how do you call this thing? [laughs]. To try to hold the spray, that smell, that skunk release. So they use Wolverine to hold that, not to let go.

So they finally manage to kill the Giant Skunk. And after they kill it, they cut it in pieces, in pieces so small. So they said, all the animals said, "Carry it all over across the way and let it be the size of the skunk when the humans come to exist on this land." And that's it, the statements say that.

All the animals knew that there will be humans appearing on the land and they will be preparing for them, the humans. This story shows that our people knew there were some animals before humans.

Our elders had a good memory and they teach our children when they are very young and when you hear the stories when you are so small in such a way, you don't forget them, you remember them, and as you grow, you too begin to tell your children and your grandchildren. That's the way it works in our culture.

"WIN-NI-PEG, DIRTY WATER"[19]

So the animals decided when they get to the mountains, after they got tired and they don't eat right because they don't hunt, you know, they just barely catch what to eat. And the kids were getting tired and the older people could not move.

So finally the leader says, "Well, we have to do something. We cannot keep on going like this." So one night when they stopped they hold council. The leaders of the animals and the lesser animals and the bears were there, involved.

So they sit around and they said, "What are we going to do?" They all know that this guy [Giant Skunk] is not going to give up. And there is one over there, I don't know, which one was it? I think it was the bear, who had a way to watch this Giant Skunk, you know.

He was asked, "Can you turn on your vision, see how far away he is?"

So the bear went to work and he says, "Oh, yes," he says, "he is still coming. He is not far from us, you know, he is going to reach us if we don't move."

So they said, "Well, we might as well make a stand. We will have to fight him or we die." So they decided to find the right place to make their stand.

So they find this valley that was very deep and there was a long water there, a long body of water. At the other end, at the outlet, usually there is less ice, there is open water. So they decided to wait for him there. He may fall in, that's what they hope. So they waited there. And also they pick up the place where there is a big cat is usually hibernating. But he was, I think, he was not walking around [laughs]. So he was there. So that's why they picked this place up. This particular place of long, long, long lake. Like one of those—you know, how the mountains are, eh?—big, long

19 From Bird interview, 2003.

stretch of lake, probably ten miles. So they did not try to hide their trail this time because they know for sure they going to be caught anyway. So they just make a wide open trail right there. And so they wait. And not that night, but the following day, that's when the Giant Skunk appeared at the other end of the lake [laughs], between the mountains, there he was. He is coming! Big. Sometimes we asked the storytellers, "How come he was big?" "Oh, that's a leftover from the giant animals that lived a long time ago" [laughs]. So the story is connected.

So anyway, they got ready. They say, "There he is! He's coming! He's coming!"

So they take the children and lead them away into the mountains and the elders and everything. And only the male animals are there, and the biggest animals are caribou and moose and black bears and bears that lived there, they call them mi-she-ma-sqwa, the big bears. So they are all waiting.

And finally they say, "We will ask the cat to come and help us as we attack." Of course, they send a messenger over there to go and tell him, to see if he will come and help.

But, of course, the cat didn't want to be bothered. He says, "Go away! Don't bother me! I'm resting."

Finally, he agrees. "Okay, I'll come, on one condition." He says, "Prepare for me where I can jump." That's all he asks, you know.

So anyway, the Giant Skunk finally approach this area and he was tired, you know, not in a very good mood. And so he said, "What is the big idea going to all these places that you're not supposed to go?"

And nobody can say anything, just try to pretend, you know, ignore him and just hoping that he could just turn away, you know: "Don't bother us."

But he was insisting. And he was just pretending to find a place to sit and, "I can't see the reason for this impassable places that have been traveled," he says to these animals. Finally, he was trying to provoke an argument to give him an excuse to attack and the animals know that, they don't say anything.

All they say is, "I don't know" [laughs].

Finally, the Wolverine—very foolish, not afraid of anything, eh?—the Wolverine says—what did he say? I forget exactly what he says: way-way-no-na-na-ye-wa. ki-mat-ta-e-pa-nuk. So he says, "Well, it's foolish of us, you know, to run away from something because they saw the track of the way-way-no-na-na-ye-wa. ki-mat-ta-e-pa-nuk. It's a very hard name to say. way-way-no-na-na-ye-wa. ki-mat-ta-e-pa-nuk. It means "the bulgey cheek." That's what he calls him. And that's totally insulting to Giant Skunk [laughs]. It's the Wolverine that says, way-way-no-na-na-ye-wa. ki-mat-ta-e-pa-nuk.[20]

The Giant Skunk repeated the words and said, "Who is way-way-no-na-na-ye-wa. ki-mat-ta-e-pa-nuk?"

Wolverine said, "Giant Skunk! That's who."

Giant Skunk was totally insulted, you know. So that's all he needed, that's all he needed to attack.

So Giant Skunk slowly turn around, and the Wolverine was instructed to do that, and the other animals say, "As soon as he turns his bum around, before his tail actually go up, that's when you jump on him. And you jump on him and you hold him tight. While we work on him and try to kill him."

And that's what Wolverine did. As soon as Giant Skunk lift his tail, and he jumps right into it and just hold the bum tight as he can, you know, where the spew comes from. So that's his job. It's a dirty job he's got. Because he's strong, eh? So the rest of them jump on Giant Skunk.

So the animals shout for the Mi-shi-pis-shew, the Big Cat, and somebody runs up and called, "Come down here, we can't get him down."

So the cat got up and stretch—a cat stretch, eh? He asks, "Why did you have to come and bother me, huh?" [laughs]. So he started to walk slowly down to them.

And they say, "Come on! Faster," they say.

"No, no." He didn't want to rush. And then finally he approach there and he says, "Why in the heck are you getting so excited about?" You know, he was not very happy.

So they say, "We can't kill this thing. We want you to help us."

So anyway, he gets up to this hill, up there and that's when he begin to—you know the way the cat does, you know that?—and they keep yelling, "Come on, stop wiggling your ass! Jump!" Then he stop for a little while, he was insulted [laughs].

---

20 Louis describes way-way-no-na-na-ye-wa as a kind of language training for children. "It teach you how to say things, that's where the word come out." It is a playful, silly-sounding word that "actually means something. It's just a descriptive word. You describe the person's face when you say that, but in order to do that to this feared person [Giant Skunk] it was a total insult. Actually, the word is not that bad, but the way he [Wolverine] applies it there is enough" (Bird interview, 2004).

Finally, finally he jumps. He flies right into the neck of this Giant Skunk, four legs right into its neck. And he just hold it like this and his big claws and feet and teeth right in there. And eventually the Giant Skunk began to sort of keel over, slowly, settle down into the bottom.

Finally, he just died, the Giant Skunk.

So everybody cheer and laugh and scream and everything.

And then the Wolverine was still holding the thing, and he speaks from there. "Is it okay to let go now?" And how does he speak, I don't know?

But they says, "Not yet, not yet!"

So, anyways, finally they say, "Okay, let go, but put the tail down quickly!"

But he was so tired. And he forgot to put the tail down, so he let go and it just puke into his face. All that stuff that has been pressurized, right into his face, right there. And he just scream and scream, run around and jump around. And everybody was sympathizing, but there is not much they can do.

So he says, "Lead me to the water so I can wash!"

They said, "Not into this fresh water! No, no! You can't pollute the water."

So he was suffering. Finally, the pain subsided a little bit and he couldn't open his eyes.

So the elders and everything said, "You know, we've got to do something about this poor guy, he's been helping us and all that." So they say, "We cannot allow him to wash here, in this fresh water lake, have to send him some other place. Why not into the, where we came from, you know, like James Bay, Hudson Bay? Why don't we send him over there so he can go wash himself?"

So the animals finally say, "Okay, let him go there."

So the poor Wolverine was just, still couldn't see a thing. The pain has now, what they call it, sort of get used to it, eh? But he still couldn't see, still couldn't open his eyes.

So they said, "We will send you over there."

Says Wolverine, "Why do you have to send me all the way out there? I can't see!"

So they say, "It's okay, don't worry, you will go there. But every time you bump into a tree, ask the tree where he stands. And it tells you how far you are going."

So he says, "Okay, okay." Then he went.

And every time he bump into something he talks to, you know, "Where are you? What are you?"

Sometimes a stone tells him exactly where he is.

And sometime a small tree says, "I am in the prairie, the tree that stand in the prairie, you know, halfway through."

Finally he keeps on bumping into the trees and they say, "I am in the boreal forest before the James Bay." That sort of thing, okay. He's getting there.

And then, finally, he comes to the last tree in the James Bay-Hudson Bay area, and Wolverine asks, "Where are you?"

And the little tree says, "I am the last tamarack that stand on the shore of the Hudson Bay."

That was no Hudson Bay yet then [laughs].

So he was very happy and he keep on running and just jumping around, bumped into a big stone and he was just almost knocked down, and he says, "Where are you? What are you?"

And the stone says, "I'm a stone that sits right at tide water."

And he says, "How far is tide water?"

"It's still out there. It's at low tide," the stone said. So he just went again.

Finally, he trip over the stone again and says, "Where are you?"

The stone says, "I am the stone that stays right at the edge of the water."

And he runs and runs and finally he has his feet in the water and keep on jumping and running, bumps into another big stone and is almost knocked down again. "Why are you sitting here for?"

And the stone says, "I didn't do a thing. You bumped into me" [laughs]. "I am the one that sits at the halfway tide water." There he was, he goes into the deeper water and he begins to wash and clean himself and soon he begins to see. It was a beautiful day.

And after he finish washing, then he sing, just like taking a shower, hums away, and he sings a song about being his heroic act of killing the Giant Skunk. And he says, "I have managed to hold the spew of the Giant Skunk." He sings that song, eh? "I am the only one who can hold the spew of the Giant Skunk." And he just keep on singing that. I don't know the tune.

So anyway, by that time, he was clean, he went back towards the shore. And so they say, that's the end of that part of that story. And when they finish this part, they say, "that is why the Hudson Bay and James Bay is dirty, you know, can't drink it, it's salty and everything, because of the

Wolverine, he wash his face there" [laughs]. So that is why that water is—win-ni-peg, win-ni-peg, it means "dirty (salted) water." That's why that water is dirty [laughs].

In the meantime, those people [the animals back in the West] will just get rid of the skunk. So what they say is, the wise man says, "We shall cut him into pieces, all small pieces. And then we will," the boss, the leader said, "Okay, now carry to all four corners of the world and let it be the size of the skunk when the humans emerge." See the words, "when the humans emerge." Just a little quotation.

The reason they keep on saying this is because they want to tell us there were no humans yet, there was just animals. All the stories [tell about] vividly thinking animals and planning animals and scheming and everything. Just like humans, and there are also shamans, many of them are shamans. So when you listen to the stories you just feel like you are just watching a human doing something, thinking and planning, but these are animals [laughs].

And so after that, that's what they did, so it was done. So they carried the animals as far as they could go to the four corners and that's the size of the skunk we have today, just that size, because that's an act of, a part of, the Creator's work, they say. The Creator was there, they know it was Creator. He was the one that spoke to the animals to do that, you know. The animals were cooperating with Creator.

Creator Talks to the Animals About the Emergence of the Humans[21]

Now, it seems like the animals were here, and it seems that there were no humans at that time. But they expected the humans to emerge upon the land.

In the story of Giant Skunk, when one listens to the legend, you will say, "Yes, there is a Giant Skunk and there is a wolf and there is a bear and there is a caribou and there is all animals we know." They're all forced to congregate and stand to kill the Giant Skunk. And these animals speak as humans, think like humans, experience life as humans and plan as humans—think for the future, even think like humans. So that's the Giant Skunk story there. I'm just briefly outlining how the legends work.

---

21 From Bird, "Louis Bird on Cree Creation Stories," 2001.

And then after that, when these people [animals], as quoted before, why do they say, "Let this be the size of the skunk when the human emerge upon the land?" So the next story came in the time of these animals.

There was a story about the animals and also there was a story about the birds. They came together at this place where they arrive at a certain season. They congregate, they meet, they get re-acquainted. Just like humans, they have games, they have reunions. And they plan for the big feast for the ceremonies. And amongst them was the duck, and his name is Sink-i-pis in the Ojibwe accent. He is a diving duck who is very dull in colour and very small. He's from the family of the loon. He was the smallest and dullest. But he was the star in this story. And therefore when these birds have this activity there was no human. Only these birds. And when you listen to this story you forget they were birds. One forgets they were birds. They were humans more like. They think, they play, they celebrate, they plan for the feast, just like humans. Again, it shows us there were no humans, that there were just birds. After this legend ends, which is very lengthy, there comes a time when the animals and the birds congregate somewhere. To come together. Animals and birds. With this character in the place of the Creator.[22]

The Creator came to meet the animals, to speak to them and to say, "Do you know that the human is going to be on the land? He's going to be here."

[Animals:] "We came to ask you what you think."

[Creator:] "He [the human] is going to be dependent on many things. He's going to be totally different from you, the birds and animals. He's not going to fly, he's not going to have no feathers or fur. He's going to walk on two legs and he's going to have arms and no clothes—no covering, just skin. And therefore the question that is put to you is that the seasons has to be established. There has to be a winter and there has to be a summer and a season between."

So the animals begin to discuss the matter. They were asked to give suggestions.

Finally, many of them willingly gave the advice to this person. The best they can. How they think the seasons should be. And they used their

---

22 Louis explains that this character was Wi-sa-kay-chak, the trickster, who "can be everything, he can play God. He can play big things in our legends." Further, "We talk about a thing that we do not have name. So we throw Wi-sa-kay-chak in there. You see what I mean? You can manoeuvre Wi-sa-kay-chak, you can put him in the mystery, you can put him in human form, where there is a question of everything so you put him there. He's a very flexible thing, you know, he's a mix, he can change" (Bird interview, 2004).

bodies to number the months that has to exist. But none of those animals' suggestions fit the purpose of the human who is going to emerge and live on the land.[23]

When finally there was one person who did not say much. He just sat there and listened. And he is the frog.

And then finally they asked him.

And he said that there should be twelve months. "Just like the fingers of my hands. And also my feet. They each has three toes each. That will be the number of the months in one year for the purpose of this man, in order to survive."

His suggestion fit exactly, and therefore his suggestion was taken and agreed upon. And from then on the twelve months of a one-year term was created by this representative of Creator. Nobody identifies this person who is the Creator. But there is a person there who act like one (see notes 3 and 22). And therefore it had been decided that there should have been twelve months in one year. And when the human emerged, he was able to withstand the seasons. Not too long winter and not too long summer. And the seasons between. And it was agreed at that moment that all animals will have to contribute for the sake of the humans' existence. All animals have agreed. And for that reason the human can only be alive in the world by using the animals' help—their body, their furs, their feathers and everything—which gives the human a living condition to survive.

So that is the second story which shows us that the animals did actually exist before the human emerged. And in between time, the time existed amongst those animals and birds and waterfowl. Nobody says exactly how long it existed until one day the story again emerge which has been created amongst the people. And they say that there were two people in another dimension who wanted to be so much to be by themselves because they were young lovers.

---

23 In a recent interview, Louis added the following details: "So the animals they just listen, they just sit there. They all listening, this creature that is going to come, won't bother us if he's going to be different. So some said, 'Okay.' This person, Wi-sa-kay-chak, we call him, he says, 'There has to be a certain amount of seasons for this guy, there's got to be a season because he's this way. They have to get a certain amount of cold weather, in the summer they have to have seasons. So what we need is: how long is a season?' For many of them, they say, 'Well, why should we have something?' Some say okay. The beaver says, 'Let it be so many months of the year, as many as the scales in my tail.' And so they all of them argue with it, and he [Wi-sa-kay-chak] says, 'Just a minute, look at the scales of your tail. If it were that much cold weather, you would freeze to death.' So all of them tried to find, the caribou says, 'As many as my hair.' 'No it can't be, too many, too cold, too long, he won't survive.' Everybody contributed and when there was no answer, then Wi-sa-kay-chak says, 'we can't just leave it.' And the frog was there sitting and listening. 'Why don't you say anything?' And the frog says, 'But you didn't ask me anything yet'" [laughs] (Bird interview, 2004).

E-hep

"HOW HUMANS ARRIVED WITH THE HELP OF THE ANIMALS"[24]

So they [the young lovers] say they should find a place to stay by them-selves. And as they say that, a booming powerful voice spoke to their mind and says, "ARE YOU TRULY WISHING TO BE BY YOURSELF AND FIND A PLACE?"

And they said yes.

So the instruction says: "You go at the edge of this place. At the edge of this place, you shall find a person who is going to help you to go down to where you want to go." Apparently it was down there.

When they go to this place at the end of this place they found E-hep, which the voice had just mentioned. E-hep was ready to help them. And he says, "Give me time. I shall prepare to help you."

As they glimpsed at this place they have to go, they could not wait. They were so impatient. They keep asking Mr. E-hep: "Please, be fast."

But E-hep says, "You have to give me time. I will have to prepare how to get you there, otherwise I will have to help without completion of my preparation." It seems like E-hep was creating a string to lower them someplace. It sounds that way. Since the two people were so impatient, he agreed. He said, "Okay. I will create a basket and I will lower you down there on condition that you should not look down when you get closer."

So they promised and they went down.

As they get lower, the basket gets slower and slower because E-hep has to create the line that he lowers. And later when they were on top of the trees and they were so eager to look down, they forgot and they both look down. And they got stuck there. And then they found they'd been stranded in the top of a very tall tree. And no way for them to get down. Because they were so helpless. So they found animals walking down there. They called them to help. But not too many can help. Except the bear. They call him. And the bear says, "I need help."

So the wolf came out and he agreed to help him. So the bear lowered the two people down to the ground with the help of the wolf. And that's how the human begin to stay on the earth with the help of the animals. And therefore in time past, the First Nations began to have a dream quest.

---

24 From Bird, "Louis Bird on Cree Creation Stories," 2001.

Usually they have the bear as their helper spirit. And also the wolf. And from there came the Wolf clan and the Bear clan.

.... And there we are. We have outlined partially the idea of Creation. And from there on after two people existed upon the land and the population of the land begin. Time was not mentioned. There was no measuring time. Only all of a sudden it emerges that there is people.[25]

"IF THEY SHOULD LOOK DOWN THEY WOULD NOT BE HAPPY ON THAT LAND"[26]

We don't know for sure exactly where the first humans were from, but they noticed that there is a land down there, the land that is so beautiful. And they so wished to go and see that land. So there was a giant spider who noticed that they were longing to go there. So he said to them, "Do you wish to go and see and live in that land?"

So the people say, "Yes, I wish we could go there and see that land."

So E-hep, a giant spider, says, "I will help you if you do what I say. I will lower you down with my string. But you will have to sit in here in this sort of basket." But it is actually like a nest. He says, "I will lower you down in this nest. But even when you think you are getting closer to land, you must not look down until you touch down. Because if you look at the ground before you land, you will not be happy. You will have to suffer to live in that land, even though it's beautiful."

And so they got in the nest, and agreed not to look.

So E-hep, the giant spider, lowered them with his nest. And so it goes down and down, we don't know how far, but it seems to be far away and it took some time to lower them into this land. It's more like the earth, sort of. So they're so eager, so excited. And when they got closer they wondered what it looks like. So as they went down, they look over the side and notice the land. And it was just at that moment that the string that holds them up sort of let go, and they landed on the ground forcefully. They didn't get hurt really. But E-hep said to them that if they should look down, they would not be happy on that land, that they would suffer in order to live there. And that was the end of the story.

---

25 Interpreting the E-hep legend in an interview with George Fulford, Louis explains that the story is a metaphor for childbirth to help explain the mystery of human creation: "When you come to this world, you are actually separated from that world into the material world ... In this story, the mother is the creator that was descended from the creator, that mystery ... [The story is] not rigid, it's very flexible ... When I was little I didn't know [where babies came from] so the elders explain that to us. Just make it into small E-hep sort of story" (Bird 0024: 5).
26 From Bird 0024.

"AN OMUSHKEGO ROMANCE STORY"[27]

Now, how did the humans get here? [laughs]. That's another question people ask, "How did we get here?"

In the modern world there are intellectuals who say we came across [the Bering Strait] and walk across the ice and begin to inhabit this land, but our people don't remember that. They don't remember this. But they do remember their own stories. Where did the man come from? How was man created? How did he stay here? How did he come to be in the land? So we have to make up a story to satisfy the curiosity. I guess many times many children have asked—or anybody else asked—"Where did we come from? Where did the humans come from?"

So for that reason our elders, our ancestors, found a way to satisfy this mystery about how we became to be here. So there's one little story that has answered the question for us in our tribes. That is a story called "E-hep." E-hep [laughs]. It's a very easy name, easy to remember. So when our grandfathers say that, you know, there was E-hep, some say, "Who is he?" And they don't tell us, they just start a story. So this is the way it goes.

First, I'm going to tell you one thing: our Omushkego tribes, they are not very romantic. We have very few romance stories, but they are very powerful [laughs]. And sometimes forbidden.

So anyway, this story is to do with this, where did we come from? Where did the first men come from, humans? They say there were young people, teenagers, they say, not babies, living in the place—they don't say where. These teenagers, a boy and a girl, were deeply in love with each other and wanted to live by themselves. They don't want to live where there are so many rules, they want to be by themselves. They live in this place where everybody else live, and they usually walk out a little ways just to be themselves. One day as they were together, they looked down and they see a beautiful land. So they were saying, "I wish we could live there, just the two of us, we would be happy just two of us." All that sort of imagination.[28]

As they were talking that way a voice boomed from somewhere: "DO YOU REALLY WANT TO LIVE THERE?" [laughs]

---

27 From Bird, "Questioning the Elders," 2001.
28 Louis refers to the couple as a "man and his wife" in Bird 0024. Their desire to live in the world below is not the product of raging hormones and teenage rebellion but—much less romantically—the simple wish to "see what it [the world below] feels like—because it was so beautiful" (Bird 0024: 4).

They say, you know, "Yes, yes." They don't even know where the voice came from. And so they say, "Yes, we want to stay there, truly, yes."

And the voice says, "YOU SHALL BE THERE" [laughs]. Later on the voice say, "Okay, if you really want to stay there you can. If you try to live properly, then you will be there. But before you get there, you're gonna need some help." So the voice says, "Walk towards this direction. When you come to the edge or somewhere you will find E-hep who will help you to get there."

So they went. The two of them were so happy. They would find a place for them to stay. So they walked the distance and they are so happy they are going to have their own place.

Once they get there, they should find E-hep. He knows that they are going to appear, so he says, "You the two that want to go away?"

So they say, "Yes, we want to go there."

So E-hep says, "Wait, you got to wait awhile." He says, "I don't have a way to take you down. I will have to create something to lower you." So he begin to work, begin to have something to lower them. And the two lovers, you know, they couldn't wait. They want to get there because that's gonna be their place.

So they said, "How long will it take you to create this thing?"

So E-hep said, "It will take time. If you can be patient, I'll get it."

But they said, "Please!"

So finally, E-hep said, "Okay, since you are so impatient you are going to have to wait for me, but I will lower you as much as I can, but as much as I can and as fast as I can produce my mechanism."

So he created a basket—you know, for them to sit—and he lowered them with some form of string into the land, and the two lovers were so happy, but because they rush him they have certain rules to follow.

E-hep says, "Since you have been rushing me to lower you down, there is one thing I will tell you that you should not do. When you begin to see the land where you want to go, don't look down, not both of you, just one at a time. If you both look down, you may not get there." So they promised: "No, we are not going to do that. One at a time only." They promise.

So they going down slowly and soon they begin to see this very beautiful place. The flowers, the land, the lakes, the rivers, everything was there and also the birds that sing. So they really happy when they get there, couldn't wait. So next they begin to hear, to see, to smell also the flowers. They forgot their promise and both look down. Then all of a sudden they stop, they don't get lower any more. They remember the guy, the person who told them not to look down. So they find themselves stuck on top of a tree. They have landed on the place that look like a nest and they couldn't get down. So that's where they are, stuck in the air!

So they don't know what to do, they just sit there and they call to that person who lowered them, and he says, "I told you, I can't lower it anymore."

And later on, as they sit trying to figure out how to get down, some animal walks by. A fox walk by, look at them, and they said, "Hey, down there! What's your name?"

And the animal says, "I'm Fox."

And they say, "Can you help us to come down?"

And the fox says, "No, no. I never climb a tree. I can't climb. Sorry." He walks by into the forest.

And soon the caribou appear. So they called the caribou: "Hey there! Come and help us down!"

So the caribou went over and look at them and he says, "No, I can't. See my hoof? I can't climb up. I can't help you, sorry." So he walks away.

And then after that another one came, another animals, many animals came, but none of them could help because they didn't have the claws or anything to be able to climb. But they all said, "There is a friend of ours, our brother. He might be able to help you."

So soon there was a wolf, the wolf came around. So they said, "Hey there! Can you help us to come down?"

So the wolf says, "I could if I could climb. My brother's behind. He might help you. We'll wait for him."

So the wolf hang around for a while and soon the black bear appear from the bush, walks by minding his own business. Then they call him, they said, "Hey there, black guy!" [laughs]....

Anyway, so the bear says, "Yes?"

"Could you take us down?" they said.

And the bear says, "I'm so lazy, I just finished eating, I can't go up there," he says.

"Please!" they say, "take us down!"

So finally, the wolf says, "Go ahead, I will help you."

So the wolf helped the bear.

So the bear helped them down and gave the people to the wolf, first one and then the other one, slowly down. Finally they reach the land that they wanted to live.

And that is how the first people appear on this land. So that's the end of the story, that one. So that's how we came to be here in this land, because we have been lowered with the help of the animals and also E-hep.

3

Mi-te-wi-win

Stories of Shamanism and Survival

Mi-tew, that is the word we use. It is translated very roughly
as shaman ... or medicine man.... Mi-tew means a person who
has acquired certain powers or [the] capability to overcome
physical limits.... The higher the shaman's power ..., the more
impossibilities he could overcome.... The shaman could travel
[a far] distance in a very short time ... accomplishing things
that are not possible for the ordinary man.... (Bird 0028,
2003: 12)[1]

Introduction
MARK F. RUML

From the Omushkego perspective, mi-te-wi-win has existed for a very
long time, even before the creation of human beings. The old stories in
Louis Bird's collection of oral history are full of characters with mi-tew
power, such as the Giant Skunk (Mi-she-shek-kak), We-mis-shoosh, Cha-
ka-pesh, E-hep, Wi-sa-kay-chak, and I-yas. They provide vivid examples
of the proper use or misuse of this power and the concomitant results.
Louis's collection reveals that stories of individuals with mi-tew power
have persisted over time. Recent narratives about such personages (mi-te-

---

1 Note that there were also women mi-te-wak (see below in this chapter). The word that Louis
Bird typically uses (when speaking in English) for the Omushkego word mi-tew is "shaman"
and "shamanism" when speaking about mi-te-wi-win. The word "shaman" is derived from the
language of the Tunguz people of Siberia but is widely used by academics to refer cross-cultur-
ally to individuals similar to the Siberian prototype. The classic work on Siberian shamanism
is Eliade 1964. For a brief summary of Eliade's work on shamanism see Eliade 1987: 202–08.
For a general introductory summary of Native American shamanism, see Gill 1987: 216–19.
For a critique of Eliade, see Kehoe 2000.

wak) can be distinguished from older stories by their incorporation of European technology and characters, such as Hudson's Bay Company (HBC) employees.[2] Chapter 4 will illustrate the distinction between older and more recent narratives through two of Louis's stories about mi-tew power. This chapter discusses the dream quest, mi-te-wi-win, the extra senses possessed by mi-tew, and the shaking tent ceremony.

> Ok, I am trying to portray how the mi-te-wi-win was. And the way I have heard it, it is said that mi-te-wi-win is not a church, not like Christianity, no. Mi-te-wi-win was not created as a social spiritual practice. Mi-te-wi-win was developed individually. A person would develop it for his own capability as much as he can acquire. And sometimes when he has his own power he doesn't share it, what he knows he doesn't preach like Christianity does. He does not teach people how to say, "this is how you live, this is the way I show you, this is the way you are going to live, and this is the way you are going to practise." No … they didn't have that kind of instruction. (Bird 0104: 10)

The Omushkego mi-te-wi-win that Louis tells about for the Cree of the Hudson and James Bay region differs from the Anishinaabe (Ojibway) midewiwin or "Grand Medicine Society" discussed by Hoffman and others (Hoffman 1885–86: 143–300; Angel 2002). The Anishinaabe midewiwin is an organized society with initiation ceremonies to admit new members and to acknowledge their subsequent graduations to higher grades or degrees. Each degree reflects their attainment of increasing knowledge and spiritual power, and the ability to live in an exemplary way, incorporating cultural values. The Anishinaabe mide members meet as a society or group in midewiwin lodges at regularly scheduled gatherings throughout the seasonal ceremonial cycle. The organizational structure is the main distinguishing feature of the Anishinaabe midewiwin. Otherwise, for both Anishinaabe and Omushkego peoples, the mi-te-wak are individuals who live mi-te-wi-win as a way of life, are gifted with spiritual powers developed through the dream quest and other ceremonies, and can give life and take it away. The difference is that, in the case of the Anishinaabeg, in addition to the dream quest and other ceremonies, the midewiwin lodge provides a

---

2 Doug Hamm did a wonderful job finding elements of Louis's story of A-moe and Shee-wee-phan that were documented in the HBC Archives. See Hamm and Bird 2000: 144–60.

social structure in which to develop their spiritual gifts.[3] The Omushkego mi-te-wak, in contrast, develop their spiritual gifts individually through the dream quest, reflecting, according to Louis, the more individualistic, less communal nature of Omushkego society. The mi-te-wi-win worldview sees the created world as a source of knowledge and power (spiritual, physical, mental, and emotional). Through the dream quest process, an individual is able to access that knowledge and power. Children begin this training when their parents or grandparents recognize that they are gifted to be mi-tew. The mi-tew who has attained a high level of mi-te-wi-win can then use the very powerful "shaking tent" (koo-saa-pa-chi-kan) to access knowledge and power from the spirit beings. The shaking tent is central to a discussion of mi-te-wi-win, and an introduction to this ceremony will follow a discussion of the dream quest.

The stories that Louis has collected show that the mi-tew and mi-te-wi-win have been fundamental to the physical, emotional, mental, and spiritual existence of the Omushkego people since time immemorial. Since the mid-1800s, however, their lives have been seriously impacted by the colonial enterprise and especially by missionization and the residential school system.[4] Mi-te-wi-win and the mi-te-wak were the primary targets of the Christianizers, especially the Roman Catholic Oblate priests who came to the Omushkego homeland beginning in the 1840s.[5] The Oblates saw the mi-te-wak as being in league with the devil and condemned as evil their spiritual beliefs and practices, including feasting, drumming, singing, dream quests, and especially the shaking tent.[6] On tape 0035 (Bird 0035) Louis provides an English translation of the Oblates' Cree version of the catechism (the so-called Black Book, named for the colour of its cover) that was used to instruct Omushkego people in the Catholic faith. It clearly states that participating in traditional beliefs and practices is a violation of the first commandment ("Thou shalt have no other gods before me.").[7] Louis

---

3 It should be noted that not all Anishinaabe people who are mide are members of a midewiwin lodge. I have heard some say that an individual is born mide and no person can initiate someone to be mide; for this reason, these people do not join a particular lodge.
4 See Louis's discussions in Chapters 1 and 9.
5 For an excellent examination of the encounter, see Fulford and Bird 2003.
6 Louis Bird documents this perspective in his tape collection. See: Bird 0035; 0123; 0125; 0132; 0133; 0134; 0135.
7 Fulford and Bird note that in the Black Book one of the Oblate priests, Father Fafard, posed the question, "Who is breaking the First Commandment?" His answer was "First, he who worships devils, animals, the sun, stars, false idols. Second, he who does drumming, shaking tent, evil singing, evil feasting, evil smoking and dream quests because these are the Devil's creations." See Fulford and Bird 301. Also see Fafard 1924: 138–39.

documents how overt and systematic the condemnation of the mi-te-wak and mi-te-wi-win was and the traumatic consequences for the mi-te-wak themselves—depression, suicide, insanity, alcoholism, and other sicknesses.[8] He helps us to understand the dilemmas of young Aboriginal people who today wish to return to their traditional spiritual beliefs and practices,[9] but who often hesitate to do so out of respect for the wishes and fears of their Christian grandparents, many of whom are survivors of the residential schools and had Christianity forced upon them and even, in many cases, beaten into them. The old people remember when it was illegal to practice traditional spiritual ways.[10] They do not want their grandchildren to experience the same persecution and trauma.[11]

Louis himself was raised in the Catholic faith and was discouraged by his parents and grandparents from following Omushkego spiritual beliefs and practices.[12] At the same time, however, they taught him the old stories and teachings, establishing him as a living link to his pre-Christian past. Louis does not reject the Christian tradition in which he was raised. Rather, his Christianity is enriched by his lifelong dedication to understanding, documenting, and preserving his own Omushkego religious tradition. He respects and acknowledges the beauty and profundity of his traditional culture and history. Listening to his stories and talking with him gives one the impression that he believes that his Omushkego culture can rival any culture or civilization in human history. His work pays tribute to his ancestors, and he hopes that some day the young people of the

---

8 See especially Bird 0123.
9 An Omushkego student once came to my office and began to cry over the deep personal turmoil she was undergoing. She had enrolled in my Aboriginal Spirituality course because she wanted to learn something about the traditional spiritual beliefs and practices of her people. Her Christian grandmother, who had been taught that the old ways were evil, disapproved, even though the course is academic, taught from an historical perspective. She even sent the ministers from her northern Manitoba community to come and have a prayer meeting for her granddaughter, to pray for her soul.
10 In Canada the Potlatch Law of 1884 and subsequent amendments to the Indian Act outlawed the Aboriginal ceremonies. The law was dropped from the revised Act in 1951. The video, "Potlatch: A Strict Law Bids Us Dance," re-enacts a notorious trial at Alert Bay, British Columbia, in which people who participated in a potlatch were sentenced for "dancing," "drumming," "singing," "giving gifts," "accepting gifts," etc.
11 Some Aboriginal people who are Christian maintain that they have become Christian freely and willingly, finding "salvation" through Christianity. They believe that it is the "true" religion. They dissuade people from following the traditional beliefs and practices because they believe that the traditional ways are evil. On the other hand, many non-Christian Aboriginal people think that those who are Christian have been brainwashed and wonder how someone can be both Aboriginal and Christian, given the history of colonization. For an introduction to the burgeoning literature on Aboriginal and Christian identity, see Treat 1996.
12 In Chapter 9, Louis narrates his own great grandmother's story, Grand Sophia, who almost lost her life to a mi-tew for practising Christianity.

future will want to know about their old ways and traditional teachings; this is what motivates him. Louis is truly a remarkable and gifted man. Given his intellectual and other gifts, including his storytelling abilities, I have no doubt that had Louis been born in pre-Christian times he would have been singled out to be instructed as a mi-tew.

The Dream Quest and Mi-te-wi-win[13]

And so we shall begin. What I usually start off with this procedure is this: first of all, I want to say, the stories about this subject only covers the area of the Omushkegowak land and the Omushkegowak themself. We are not talking about other tribes. Not even Oji-Cree people. They have their own system. And so do other people west from the Hudson and James Bay and also the Native people that are to the east of James Bay and Hudson Bay.

This is not an instruction how to become a practitioner of traditional spiritual belief and practices. In English they say "shamanism." But the shamanism is not enough to describe this subject. Let us call it "the First Nations traditional beliefs and practices." Or in other words, we can say "the First Nations spiritual ideas or beliefs." One of the First Nation tribes are the Omushkegowak who live on the west coast of James Bay and on southwest coast of Hudson Bay. That is where the Omushkegowak live— in English translation, "Swampy Cree." Now let me begin.

I did not receive any instruction to begin to be a mi-tew or to practise mi-te-wi-win as I was born in Christianity. To make the story short, I do not wish to talk about myself, but I want to talk about only the stories that I have heard from our elders in the Omushkego land. I will begin by saying I will not be able to teach you this subject by speaking to you through this mechanism we call tape recorder. It will only give you ideas in the ways of the subject. Because, in time past when our people used this kind of belief and practice, they have a system in which they follow.

---

13 Except where otherwise indicated, the following transcript is from Bird 0104.

Guidance and Instruction From an Older Relative

It has been said the parents would first recognize their children, especially their son, who can be developed into such practice and belief. Once they find out that their child, their son, is gifted on something, by listening to his dreams, they will recommend this child to his grandfather, grandparents, either one, to be his personal guardian and teacher for this development. And usually the young person must start in a very early age, preferably at the age of five and thereafter, but not later than fifteen years of age. For the reason is that they believed, our ancestors, the sooner you get introduced to this subject and practice the better for your body to develop along with it. Because when you develop your mind, your body also has to be strong and in good health. And when your body is in good health, your mind also functions much perfectly. That's their teaching.

And then the child is now set to receive some guidance and instruction from his personal guide, preferably his own grandfather; if not it will be his uncle and if not the next of kin of the elder man. The grandmothers can do that also, they can be a very perfect guardian to do this, as long as the grandmother knows the subject or have seen or have watched and understands how it works. Most of the time in the past, all the elders used to know this thing and therefore automatically became the guide and also the instructors. For that reason, the youngster who is to be developed into such practice is appointed to a teacher, and he has to listen to his grandfather [the teacher], whatever he recommends and suggests, that he will have to follow.

Dream Quest

Now, the first level of this development, they say, it's that you must obtain dreams. In order to obtain the dreams that may be useful to you, as a young kid you must get over your fears first. The first fear any child can have is fear of being alone, and that is the first thing a person has to try to overcome. Once a youngster can overcome this first fear of being alone, especially the darkness, then he is ready to further develop himself how to learn. Usually about six years—it takes about one year for the child of five to get over his fears of being alone at night inside the home; that means to be able to sleep alone. Then after that, the following year, if it's possible, he has to try to sleep outside, away from home. Or at the same time, during that time, he is supposed to go with his grandfather or a teacher to go spend the night together. And the instructor, the guide, would watch over the young person. If, by any reason, this young person is having a difficulty enduring the dream, dream vision, dream quest or something, he is there, he has his own grandfather, the instructor, right close by, of which he can or she can approach and ask for the calming effect for his instruction, and it usually happens.

Once that is overcome, then the child can be on his own and use the guidance of the instructor to try to condition himself to sleep and also to have thought of positive ideas that he wants to find out. If he is to get over all his fear of things in his life he must try to contact them in his sleep and he must condition himself to sleep half only. He is instructed by his guide that he should not have full protection or full comfort when he is sleeping. He must have minimum of covering. He must have a minimum of comfort so he conditions himself to sleep only half and half awake at the same time. At that state of mind is where the dream is actually almost real. And that is where he has to put himself to. And sometimes it can be very terrifying and he must understand that this is not real, this is a dream.

Once he gets to control that he is on his way, and he can almost call or command any kind of dream that he wants to involve in that condition. If it has to do with the animal that he fears, he must summon the dream and then have in his dream a vision of the animal that he fears.[14] And then he must have the power enough to speak to the animal in his dream and then he would win a friendship to this animal, instead of being to fear of him, that he would be winning its trust, in fact being as one of his helpers. The word we use in our language is o-pa-wa-chi-ka-nak—his dream helpers or his spirit helpers, they say, but that doesn't really cover what it means.

Once he gets this state and is able to communicate such thing in that form, if it's an animal, then he is on his way. All he has to do is develop and maintain the same thing during his development to this stage. Once you get over one item and then the next, what else does he have that he is mystified and feared? He has to summon that subject, and he must deal with it in a state of quest of dream. Once he has, shall we say, overcome all its danger-

---

14 Louis has identified two types of dream quest. One is specific or intentional, focusing on a specific thing that you are looking for, for example, the "animal that he fears." The second one is non-specific: "you can dream of anything … you can accumulate things … you don't particularly want one particular thing." The first one is called na-ta-wi-pa-waa-mo-win and the second is shii-shii-kwa-ni-pa-wa-mo-win (personal communication).

ous possibilities and have now approach for such a friendship into such that he is afraid of, he is on his way. He has to acquire those things first, all kinds of subjects that he wants to understand. And then every animal that he is afraid of he must summon in during this dream quest. This would take about five years. During the five years, he would have been able to get all the things in the earth that he is afraid of and that he is mystified by. He would now be comfortable to be thinking about [them].

Let us say, supposing in the area of the Omushkego land, picture the kinds of the animals that are dangerous. One of them in the land, the most feared, dangerous, is the polar bear, and then the black bear, and the wolf is dangerous, and then some other animals, they can be dangerous. Even moose can be dangerous in the special season [mating]. There is also the smaller animals that can be dangerous for your health. Then there is other animals that are there around the saltwater [Hudson] bay. Some mammals that are there are not necessarily dangerous, but mystical beings because no human can go into the water, nobody understands readily what the whale is like, what the walrus can be. And how many other mammals are there in the water. Even in the rivers, the fish. There are some fish that we don't understand how they are and how they live. And we know every fish is even cannibalistic. They eat each other. And that is not a very nice thing to know. Some of the fish are not eatable, sometimes they can make you sick. And any other thing that lives under water and also on the ground. The birds that fly. There are certain birds that can be dangerous in certain seasons. For example, the hawks, different hawks can be dangerous during their nesting season. They can kill. All these things a child must understand and summon in his dream. And all these animals that are potentially dangerous for the human, he must dream about them, he must tame them in his dream quest.

Then also, the next thing is the element. Now, the element is something else. The element—I mean the atmosphere, the air, and also water itself— is dangerous. No one can live there who is an ordinary person. And one must understand how to live, how to deal with that. And the four directions of winds. One must have in his development state during the dream quest, must solidify these elements that are not solid, for example, the four directions of wind. There are times when the wind will be very destructive, and people have to be very careful of those things, because they can kill you, if you don't watch, if you don't know how to look after yourself with them. Therefore, usually some people, some develop[ing their powers], will dream of the north wind and north direction as a being, a very powerful being. And we in the James Bay and Hudson Bay area, the elders that we talk to have said, [that] the most fearsome strongest direction of wind, the being called ki-way-ti-ni-siew [north], it is like a person. As if having its own mind, just like a human, and very dangerous. And the dreamer, a quest for dreamer, must [be able to] visualize the north as a being, a human form, so he can speak to it, and also he can turn it into his favour, so he can use it during his lifetime if it's possible. Or it can help him and also be kind to him during his lifetime. All four directions of wind, he must—in his own power, in his own mind, in his dream quest—he must turn these into a human form that he could summon or contact as a person.

Now, after being able to do that in a dream quest, also he has to go into the further destructiveness of the wind, that is, when it's a whip-out storm. When the wind becomes too strong, that he must dream, in [a] different form of this wind. To say: when you see a changing atmosphere with the wind, like a thunder, which creates a thunderstorm and lightning and everything. The lightning and the thunder goes together. People in time past have not [been] able to describe scientifically what it is, so they approach it by a dream in a dream; in a quest for dream, they do the same thing and try to form it in their mind as a being. Thus we hear generally the term called "thunderbird." It is mostly people who have formed this element, this power, into a form of bird. And what do we have in the species that are dangerous in the air? The most powerful one we know is an eagle. So eagle plays the type of bird that this thunderbird that has been formed into; it's similar to the eagle. But it depends to [on] the individual, how, in what way can he use this as one of his helpers. Or how much is he able to gain during his dream quest, to win these powerful forces, that he has turned it into a being and able to summon it whenever he wants. Or that he is able to avoid its dangers. These are the things that a person has to do. That is why many Native people when they speak about thunder and also other stuff, they usually say "thunderbird" as if it's a living being. But we know today, thunder and a lightning is not a bird. But in those days in the past, it is in their mind power that they have visualized this thing as a bird, a most powerful predator. And for that reason, to associate things as a real substance, they form in their dream as if they could create it.[15]

---

15 For further documentation of beliefs related to thunderbirds, predominantly among Manitoba Anishinaabe, see the CBC Ideas episode, "Thunderbirds," Matthews 1995.

And now we turn to each direction of the wind. They also have to have a meaning, as if every wind direction has its potential benefit to man, and it also has potential danger to human. And all these, they have to dream, and to be able to win its favours rather than a destructive association with them.

All these things have been told to me by the elders who have understand. And that's the basic development about what I call "dream quest," the quest for dream. You're trying to create the dream for you to understand, you try to contact things by your mind.

And they've said, there are also many other things, almost every living thing on earth, the person who has methodically developed this during his dream quest will overcome anything: the elements, the animals, the birds, the fish. The fire is also what a person can form into and understand as a human form or even in a physical form, and can communicate with it and also have a command over it. This is the reason why the people we call mi-tew can overcome these things even if the odds are against them. This is the reason that a person developed to be a mi-tew, to survive. And it has been said in our area, the Omushkegowak, that every head of the family must have this kind of thing. Every man must have certain amount of these things. Not every man have everything, but at least some level.

Now, we are going to have a little bit more about the dream quest. Some people will have to dream about the man themself, to understand its [his] potential danger to each other and also what is the benefit to have humans around. Now it seems we are going into the human form, the actual human. Some people who have developed the shamanism, or should I say are in a dream quest, [a] quest for dream ... some young people have heard the question about things that are mystery to them. Let us say, in time past, people fear the women activity. The man is mystified by the woman, its [her] created way. Woman has menstruation every month. And sometimes man tries to understand what is that. Because they're trying to understand, they try to form it in the woman form. And that is a very dangerous thing to do. Many men who are going to be a fully grown man, they dream this stuff because their body demand some desire, and some wanted to know what it is. So they dream. They dream this particular stuff, that menstrual blood, and they dream it as a woman, sometimes the most beautiful woman. And only that woman they can win its [her] love, and then they think they have acquired something. Sometimes this kind of dream can be very negative and destructive for such an individual. I personally have seen a person who have make a mistake. I will not speak about this person for now. I want to continue on, what does the dream quest do.

So it has been said, a person who is healthy, by the time he has been able to acquire the dream quest of all these things, he is now fully grown man. He will be about thirty years old. By this time his body would have stopped growing, and his body can withstand all these pressures of mind, knowledge, and everything. When he stops this dream stuff, this quest for dream, it is now as if he had accumulated the power within his mind and that he could command any one of those things that he had dreamt, as accumulation of benefit for his life. He could summon any one of those things that he had dreamt or he could face it without fear because he will be able to have understood—he would have known these things already and then he was not afraid. There is a story about that. There is a story that says some individuals, some men, even women, have only a few or the minimum ... of dreams during their quest for dream. And thus that is enough, sometimes that's all they need.

WOMEN AS MI-TEW

The women do not have to do that. The woman, usually they say, is gifted. She could acquire those things very easily. Because the woman has been treated so less then man, because of that conditioning, they didn't have to induce themselves into condition, because they were already treated less than a man. Therefore, they didn't have to go out in separate ways to quest for dream. And they were different, the women were differently developed. Not like as a man. A man usually is developed for physical power and also usually with the great mind control. Very vaguely, I'm trying to say what I have heard. There is so much about this thing.

Extra Senses—Mind Power[16]

Then during their process of dream quest they also sharpen their readily available, instinctually grown-up senses. We all have five senses which has been created within us. We can use the smell, the sound, we can have a feeling, and also the seeing ... five anyway, we have five of those that are

---

16 See also Bird 0035: 11–13.

readily available for us. They say, when a person have acquired such dreams, he is able to develop extra, at least seven other senses. That exercising a proper dream quest would have sharpened their senses of seven other kinds. Which is more like, you know, five of those magnified into the branch of other things. That is what it means.

Actually, what the man does is that: he exercise the mind. There is an elder who had tried to explain these things to me, because he had seen it himself when he was young. And he had listened to the elder who was explaining those things. So he said, when you have at least very close completed your dream quest, when you have at least halfway through the highest achievement of development, you are able to summon those dreams when you need it. He also said, when you have get to the most of the things that has to be done, you can accomplish impossible things. You have trained yourself to use your mind power because the mind has three levels of this activities. One that is never stopped, that is the one that you use. You use that as a primary source of dreaming, the mind that never stops, that goes anywhere, that can do anything. The second one is the one that you use when you are fully awake. That is the one that is creative, physically creates things, plus using the mind to be creative. These are readily there, they come automatically with your five senses and also the needs. But the extra senses that you have sharpened and developed is what is called "the extra-sensory perception."

It's also the other one that in our language is called pi-moo-ta-hi-go-si-win. It means to be able to project yourself where you want to be instantly. And then also to be able to summon other beings to assist you. That means the most powerful mind, the third mind. I think they call this in English (English people understand this, doctors and everything), "subconscious mind," that one doesn't use often. That is what you are using, [what you are] able to use it when you have went to the quest for dream.

It is the third level of your mind that you awaken when you sleep. When you want to dream something, when you want to know something, you can summon these two: the one that it can do anything and the one that you use when you are actually awake. They can help you to dream something that you want, to actually see it in your mind. And the third level of mind, subconscious, is the one that you use to be able to accomplish almost anything that you want, of which you have dreamt when you were young. Your subconscious know these things, and they could come out and activate your mind to the way you want. That

means, if you want to do something that is impossible in ordinary physical thing. In other words we say, you could perform the impossible thing.
Another way of saying is that you could perform a miracle that is not
possible in ordinary man. For example, you could command things, you
could command the element, you could make it happen the way you
want, and also you could overcome things that you cannot do otherwise
as an ordinary person. You could walk on water, you can even walk on
air, or travel on air. Or even travel instantly in your mind to go and see
where you want to see—not going there physically, your body can stay
behind—that's what I mean. Also you could do something with your
mind only, to be able to move things and to make a person do things,
without their knowledge. You could make a human do something by
your mind power and they won't even know it. So this is what I mean to
develop the extra power of your mind, and this is what our ancestors use
which is called the mi-te-wi-win.

LIMITS OF THE MIND

Ok. I have gone that far, but there are still many things yet, that our ancestors—somehow, my own grandfather has said—there are certain things
that a human mind cannot do. There is certain level of this that cannot be
overcome. Where the Great Spirit is located. Whatever that means, I don't
know. But it seems to say that there is a Great Spirit who can overcome
every power on the earth and the atmosphere, in any place. The Great
Spirit who has created everything that we see, everything on earth. This is
a Great Spirit who has its mind power that can create anything, and this
is what they were saying.

Some elders who have developed this sort of thing, some were gifted to
act controllably, also, to exercise their given power with morality, rather
than immorality. Our ancestors may not have developed an institution
because they did not live communally, they did not live in community.
They did not establish a larger society, more than a clanship. Therefore,
they did not require to have any more than that. That is what my ancestors have told me. And these are the things as far as I understand. But,
unfortunately, I was not allowed to do this—allowed to understand at
least, allowed to listen, but discouraged to try to do it.

Now, to go back to what the certain kind of a mind power can do.
Our ancestors use or moderately use this power of mind, they were able

to use animals to see things, any time when they want to if it's justifiable. What I mean to say is, they can use the animal to see things ahead. They can use the hawks, they can use the birds that fly, to see what's out there ahead where they want to go, just by using that power. Not distracting the bird or anything. They would even be able to do that with the fish. They used fish eyes and fish senses to know under water. And they also can do that in the wilderness, they can do that to the different animals. But they were not allowed to be able to do a few things, that is, to instantly know where the animals are that they hunt. That is something that has not worked so well. These are the things, some of the things that our ancestors were able to do.[17]

Mi-te-wak Fights[18]

Every time when a person acquires the power as a mi-tew, there is always another mi-tew who challenges him. And therefore the powerful mi-tew never have peace, because there's always a challenger, to prove themself, to find out if they have enough power to beat the powerful mi-tew. That has been the repetitious activity amongst the Omushkegos.

So it was not nice to have that kind of situation for mi-te-wak to challenge each other all the time, because it doesn't give any pleasure or any peace to the family people. If one mi-tew is so powerful, he never rest, and his family is always on guard. They're always being bothered by something mi-tew use for their challenge to each other. It is not peaceful. Some mi-tew that actually have the power do not bother anyone, even though they are bothered. But it is their loved ones that is suffering. That is one thing I have been told from my own ancestors and their ancestors, that is one way this mi-te-wi-win is not it's not really as good as it sounds. It is good when people use it properly. When they use it for their benefit, for their health, and to be able to cure themselves, to treat themselves when they are sick. And also to defend themselves for anything or sometimes

---

17 At this point in the recording Louis breaks into a discussion of other First Nation groups attacking the Omushkegowak. He talks about the positive aspect of mi-te-wi-win and how it could be used to sense the coming of an enemy. As he says, "The thing is shamanism, I mean mi-te-wi-win is sometimes not very nice. Sometimes it's very bad. But sometimes it is very good. Sometimes a shaman, a person who has the power, can be very useful to guard his people, to have this power for the successful hunt, and so people will not starve. And sometimes the shaman will be protecting the groups."

18 For more on mi-te-wak fights, see Bird 0036.

against nature, against the element and therefore also against the human if they are bothered. But sometimes it always happen in summertime that the visitors from the distance came to kill them.

Ok, I am trying to portray how the mi-te-wi-win was. And the way I have heard it, it is said that mi-te-wi-win is not a church, not as a Christianity, no. Mi-te-wi-win was not created as a social spiritual practice. Mi-te-wi-win was developed individually. A person would develop it for his own capability, as much as he can acquire. And sometimes when he has his own power, he doesn't share it. What he knows he doesn't preach like a Christianity does. He does not teach people how to say, "This is how you live, this is the way I show you. This is the way you going to live and this is the way you going to practise." No, they didn't have that kind of instruction. But they have it only the way they have experienced it; they guide the next generation if they [the next generation] know they were gifted or if they know if they want to be one. All they do is guide and support and stand guard for them, for the learners or for those who want to develop their own shamanism.

And when, as I said before, when the person is fully shaman he is automatically looked at as a leader and looked at as a supporter or defender. That's the way it was. There were some good shaman, there were good mitew who guide or guard their own people, their family, their clan, and sometimes in some of the tribes, when they get together. And in those days that is why the elders were always looked up to, because they have accumulated a lot of knowledge how to survive on the land. Most of them have accumulated a lot of mi-te-wi-win power. The skill, the knowledge, and the control and understanding of things that require to understand in a lifetime. So they became automatically advisors, they became automatically decision makers. Automatically they became protectors of the tribe, because they have a wisdom. So that's one part of explaining what shamanism is all about in the Omushkego country.

FIGURE 4: *A shaking tent at Waskaganish, Quebec, on James Bay, 1965. This kwashapshigan (the East Cree term varies slightly from the Omushkego), shown in early evening before a performance, was used by Joseph Cheezo and built at his request by Mark Blackned. Photographer, Richard Preston, who also provided the photo.*

Introduction to the Shaking Tent
MARK F. RUML

Louis says, "We have not heard any person who has (openly) used the shaking tent ever since the last one died somewhere around 1935" (Bird 0015, 2003: 3). On the other hand, the Anishinaabeg in Manitoba have continued the shaking tent (jiissakaan) to this day. Their reasons for holding the shaking tent and their way of constructing the lodges are basically identical to what Louis has said of the Omushkegowak. Briefly, four or more poles are stuck deep in the ground in a circle perhaps two or three feet in diameter, and rings made from small trees are slipped horizontally over the poles, reinforcing the structure, which is further reinforced with rope. The structure is then covered with a tarpaulin, blankets, or birch bark, and bells are strung together and tied at the top.[19] The shaking tent man (jiisakiiwinini) or shaking tent woman (jiisakiiwikwe) enters the lodge, and he/she or someone else sitting outside the lodge begins to sing special shaking tent songs, calling the spirits to the lodge. The arrival of the spirits is signified by the often violent shaking of the lodge, hence the name "shaking tent." People who attend the shaking tent ceremony bring tobacco, food, and gifts. Those seeking help or advice will approach the shaking tent, individually or with a friend or family member, kneel down, and place their tobacco under the lodge. The individual will then explain why he/she is there, what he/she is asking for. If they are speaking the English language, one of the shaking tent man's/woman's helpers will translate into the Anishinaabe language. The jiisakiiwinini/jiisakiiwikwe will then begin to call in the spirits and will ask them for the answers to the person's question or solution to their problem.

The current ceremony among the Anishinaabeg is typically set up as a healing ceremony. People want to know why they are sick and want to be cured of their sickness; it is through the shaking tent that the jiisakiiwinini/jiisakiiwikwe is able to find out the cause of the sickness and the cure. The ceremony is also used to find out information from afar, find lost articles, get protection "medicine," and many other things. The shaking tent can also be used to fight other jiisakiiwininiwag/jiisakiiwikwewag (shaking tent men/women), although this does not seem to be as common among the Manitoba Anishinaabeg as it was for the Omushkegowak in Louis's area.

---

19 I have been to several of these ceremonies and helped to construct the shaking tent lodge on three occasions. The number of poles used, the type of trees, the covering, and other details vary among the shaking tents I have seen, but the basic structure remains the same.

There is so much more to this ceremony that, based on what I have seen and heard, more unpublished than published information exists.[20]

The Shaking Tent

Dream quest is just the beginning. The next item is "dream vision." Someone when he is able to do the dream, now he can have a vision when he wants to, as a dream. So dream vision is the next, and then after that he has a power to create things by his mind power. This is a shaman, a certain level of shamanism. The first level a person can do that minimum, and then the second level he can do it not as high a power, but the third level is the highest, where a person once he gets there, he doesn't have to do anything at all—all he has to do is use his mind. He can make things happen with his mind. Doesn't have to have an object to do it or anything. But those people who began to branch off into the specialization of shaking tent, then that's how they do it. They have to have shaking tent in order to do so. That is specialty communication.[21] Koo-saa-pa-chi-kan, that is the shaking tent, can be used in many ways. Koo-saa-pa-chi-kan is a very multiple purpose practice. You can tell the future, and you can communicate instantly to the people you know. It's just more like a radio or a telephone amongst the tribes. It can also be used to predict the good hunting and also be used to scan the area where people wants to go hunting, and it [is] also used like radar scan to sort of watch if there is any danger coming, either by the beast or by the human. Another level of scanning is, the mi-tew uses that to see if anybody is physically near to try to hurt you, [your] family, or yourself.

Then also the shaking tent is also used offensively; that is bad, really. When you use it for just watching things, or telling future, that is not considered [a] "sin" for this culture, but the one that is considered bad amongst the people, amongst the Natives themself, is when you use the shaking tent offensively, when you know when you have been bothered by some other shaman, and then you set up the shaking tent to find out who and why. And once you find out that there is actually another shaman that is bugging you and really cause you problem, you use the shaking tent

---

20 Nevertheless, an excellent place to begin is with Hallowell 1942. See also Brown and Brightman 1988). A related ceremony among the Lakota is the yuwipi ceremony. See Powers 1982. Powers notes the connection to the shaking tent and includes a bibliography of related sources.
21 Bird 0012: 12.

to retaliate to the other shaman who is bothering you. And you are allowed to use other people outside to witness and even invite them to give you advice and then you destroy the other person on the other side who bothers you, and that is bad. Of course, one should use [it] as a defence, you defend yourself, you know, self-defence. It's justifiable, I know, it can be justifiable. But if you do it on purpose or just to see how powerful you are, that's no good.

One other thing that you can use that shaking tent [for] is to curse someone. You find out that somebody has done you wrong and you contact him with the shaking tent and you tell him that he is going to be having problems, because he hurt you personally, and that is a bad use. You're not supposed to use the shaking tent offensively, but you must only use for your self-protection and also for your wellbeing, and most of all communication.[22]

A man told me he had witnessed a shaking tent operation in the offensive way. Mark this statement: there is a shaking tent that you can use to benefit people for communication purpose originally set for this sort of thing. But there are people who use the shaking tents offensively when they are bothered by other shaman. These Omushkegos used to use shaking tent to defend themselves, and this is exactly what he saw, this man when he was just five years old. He just barely remembers, only scary part of it, not the rest. But as he grows up to be about near ten or whatever, his father was still alive, and he asked him: "What was that happening?" and his father says: "Well, I didn't think you'd remember." So he told him that was a time when the three Omushkego families were bothered by [an]other shaman from the distant land and had to defend themselves with the use of the shaking tent. So this is the first witness who have told me this, and I am the second person to hear. He saw it, and he tells me the story.[23]

22 Bird 0035: 5.
23 Bird 0036: 9.

4

Mi-tew Power

Stories of Shamanic Showdowns

Introduction

MARK F. RUML

This chapter presents two stories about the use of mi-tew power. The We-mis-shoosh story is an old legend. The story of the orphan boy and the Kische Mi-tew (Great Shaman) is more recent, as revealed by the incorporation of European technology. Both stories tell of the defeat of a powerful senior shaman by a young mi-tew: in the first case a son-in-law, and in the second an orphan boy. In both cases, the older man is a Kische Mi-tew, a very powerful and "feared shaman" (koo-chi-kan).[1]

The Legend of We-mis-shoosh[2]

Hello, tan-shi. I am going to punch right into the legend, it's a story about a person. I will tell you a legend just like the way I've told to my audience at home, my children and my grandchildren.

A little bit of an introduction about this We-mis-shoosh. It means, it teaches morality. It teaches you to respect things that we have in our life. So it begins. You will catch on later.

---

1 These transcripts are from Louis's English language tapes. He has continually emphasized that the English material is extremely simplified, however, and that the most detailed information is contained in the Cree versions. He also maintains that many Cree concepts and knowledge either cannot be translated adequately or get lost in the translation process. Both stories are presented here with very little editorial interruption.

2 This is a transcript of a story told by Louis at the University of Winnipeg on October 2, 1998 (Bird 0022). For other versions in his collection, see Bird 0055; 0057; 0065. Louis says that there are five different versions: one for children, one for youth, one for adults, one for the old, and one for the very old. The Bird 0057 version is the adult version. It begins with the story of the boy as a five-year-old living with his mother and father and details how the boy became an orphan.

There was this man by the name of We-mis-shoosh who was a very proud person. He was also a very, very powerful man. He had acquired a lot of powers through this procedure of dream quest, dream vision, and training to be a shaman. So he had acquired a lot of that and he had passed through many, many tests and he was able to begin to be the most powerful one. And he abuses this power, and misuse and misapplied and for that reason, at the end, it was not very nice. It was very tragic for him. So what he did is—in that place where we came from, there were people who believe that you could extend your life if you had the power of shamanism. And this guy had that. He thinks that in his dream quest, he had dreamed that he could extend his life on earth if he takes another life of a person. So that's what he dreamt. He believed that.

He tried, he begin to practise it after he had exhausted all of his training. And he tried to apply that. Before he begin to actually realize that he had acquired some power, he misused his powers once in a while. Just to see if he has actually acquired the power. So he made a mistake and he gets so proud of himself, and thinks so highly of himself, and he doesn't care about anybody else. In the meantime he had married, he had a wife, and he had a son. [At this point in the story] the son is only mentioned; I guess he must have had also daughters. I guess in our culture at that time the boys were more respected than the girls.

Anyway, his son was only about twelve years old when he [the father] begin to sort of look for another woman. Interested in other women. Because he didn't respect his wife as much as he used to when he first got married. So he started to get interested in young women, and he did find a young woman. It was about this time that he was really thinking about, you know, he should begin to worry about his age. He should live a bit longer. So he had dreamed many things, many ways to do anything that he wants to. And apparently his wife passed away and he had two daughters, but his son also is there. But his son didn't stay with him; only he stays with his daughters.

He begin to use his magic powers. He begin to exercise, and he uses also his daughters, two of them. He begin to be ageless by using this method that he had dreamed. What he did was, he used his daughters to get the new man all the time, a younger man. And each time they had a son-in-law, he kills them by using all kinds of measures to kill. Just an excuse to kill. And he has many ways to kill. So he was feared. And he was despised because he was misusing his powers and he was humiliating the humanity. Something like that. So he was gone all over the land and people wanted to kill him. They wanted to get rid of him but they couldn't because he is so powerful. Nobody could touch him. And he took advantage of that.

Once in a while he had killed his son-in-law and he would pick another one. Trick him into marrying his daughters, and his daughters are beautiful. One is very beautiful. He always uses the daughters to catch the man, and then every time when they get married, he find an excuse to kill them. Again, his daughters remain the same as young ladies. In the years past, at least ten, he had killed ten young men. Those were his son-in-laws. By this time he was known as the most mean, vicious, and very bad person to everyone in that country. But he was feared by everyone.

Then one day this young man was born, and he had this strange gift that he was able to acquire such training such as what you call the spirituality or shamanism. But anyway, he was gifted.[3] And the elders were watching him grow and they say, "That is a gifted young man." [So the young man reached the time when he was to begin his training—he doesn't require much training—] so he was trained to have some knowledge about the powers of that shaman; I hate to use that, "shaman," it's a mi-tew. The right word, mi-tew.

So he had all the gifts to develop and have a higher power and higher level of that. He was trained and raised by his grandfather and trained by his uncle and encouraged by many people around him and he was known to be a very good person. Kind, but very powerful. He was the one that says, "I could get rid of that man for you, no problem." He promise. And everybody says, "No! You're too young. You would never get near to that guy." So he says, "Give me a try. If you don't like him, I'll get rid of him." So all the people, the elders, gather together and say, "If this boy's gift, if we can actually trust him that he could kill this mean person," because the old man is really giving a bad example to the rest of the people. So they say, "He should get rid of." They said, "Okay, we will give the authority of this young man to, if he can kill him." So the young man was given the okay to go ahead and get rid of the old man if he can. He had developed himself, he had learned, he had dream, he had vision that he was going to do this. He knew he was going to succeed. So he had the okay and he went out.

---

3 In the version of We-mis-shoosh from Nathaniel Queskekapow (a Cree Elder from Norway House, Manitoba), gathered by Gary Granzberg, the young man is identified as I-yas. See Granzberg and Queskekapow 1999: 242.

So the first thing to do is try to deceive the old man, to try to beat him in his mind. So what the young man did is, you know, he studied the old man for a long time, many years, his behaviours, his actions, his ... what does he do to hunt, where does he fish, what does he do when he kill his son-in-laws, what kind of method he use? What does he do? Does he have a pleasure of first, you know, torturing them, or what tricks does he use to do that? So he studied the old man for some years, until he knew exactly the moves that he used and where does he take his son-in-laws to kill them. He studied the man very thoroughly, and he know for sure he can beat him. Finally, he said, "Okay, I'm ready."

So when he's ready, they said "great!" So he went to visit his territory. The old man's territory is big. It's large and nobody dared to go there. So he went in there. And where he usually traveled, he usually canoed, the old man usually canoed for his pleasure and everything. His assurance that nobody is going to bother him. And it was one of those days that he found the little boy on the shore. Abandoned, the little baby boy. He says, "Look at this little baby boy, laying there crying," and he thought, why did they throw out the nice little boy? So he went ashore, beached his boat, and reach out of his canoe, I mean with his paddle, put the boy in the canoe, and went on home in the evening. The boy went to sleep and it didn't bother him. Almost forgot about the little boy. When he got home and beached his boat into his camp, daughters in there, he forgot the little boy in his canoe. Went into the camp and, as usual, [was] treated with respect and fed and given drink, whatever it is. Two daughters would be always there. So he says, "Oh, I have almost forgot, I have found a little boy. One of you girls go pick him up and bring him."

So the older girl, the one that is a bit too proud of herself, went out. Quickly get up and went down to the boat, the canoe, and look at the little boy. But the little boy was very dirty, been crying and all of that, never been cleaned for a long time. It looks starving. So she thought, "Aah, that dirty-looking little baby, I wouldn't touch it." So she went back up home and the old man says, "Where is the little boy?" "Oh," she says, "ugly! The baby's ugly and I don't like it, that's it." But the younger sister was more humble and very nice. And the old man says to his daughter, "You go pick up the little boy and clean him, he's going to be nice."

So the young girl went down and found the little boy sleeping, sleeping nicely in the canoe. She pick up the little boy and bring it in. First, she went in the river and cleaned it a little bit and bring it into the teepee. As she walks in, the boy has changed. He was very, actually, nice. It was nice little boy. And then she begin to clean it right in front of her sister. Wash it and all that stuff, lovingly. And the little boy just begin to be so beautiful and lovely, and the older sister begin to be jealous. She says, "I should have had the boy, I went there first." But the young girl says, "No way, you had your chance, this is mine." So they fight for the little boy for a little while. Finally they give it up, but the older sister always trying to get a chance to hold the little boy. The younger sister doesn't want her to touch it.

So the years pass. Many years pass, I guess that boy begin to grow very fast and very wise. Very easily taught and trained. Really very active and very strong. Soon, fifteen years it seems to be, he was already a man. A very strong, powerful young man, and very handsome, and the older sister is now really jealous. She would like to have him. Because now, the law in that camp, in that family, was that if you could raise the little man, he would be yours and for life, even to marry that little boy. So that's why the older sister gets so jealous. She would have that pleasure, to marry the young man. Now she lost her chance. Only the younger girl has that chance because she has been kind to the little boy.

And now the little boy is a big handsome man. So time pass and the boy begin to gain all the manhood and knowledge and powers, like an ordinary trained mi-tew.

So he catch onto many things, and he traveled with his father-in-law-to-be. Anyways, he's not yet father-in-law, but he was trained by him. Already the old man was looking at the young man as a good challenge. Very best challenge he ever had if this young man's powerful enough. He was eager to try to trick him or something. But he always failed to trick him, because the boy seemed to know everything. So that was a great challenge for him, and soon enough he really get to be jealous of the man himself. He says, "This guy's getting to be powerful. I should get rid of him before it's too late, you know, otherwise I'm not going to live." So one day, he waited for the chance to have a chance to try to kill the young man. That was after they got married. Finally they got married. The little girl who picked up the boy, now it's her husband.

By this time years pass and there were two children already from them. So they were really good families amongst them, this young man and young lady. But the old man started to worry. He says, "I should have taken chance before they have the children." So he began to worry. He begin to think, "What system should I use to kill this man, to take his life?" It's not because he hate him, it's because he has to fulfill his dream. But the more challenged the man is, the more powerful he will be, and that's what he wants to get.

Anyway, one day comes, and the young man knows that that guy's eager to kill him. So he says one day—he never talks to his father directly, he always talk to his father through his wife. And also the man, the old man, never talks to him directly because he respects him.[4] Talks to him through his daughter and that way the communication goes like this, never directly. So one day the young man says, "I wonder if we can go out, and I like to eat beaver, I like to have it." He describes exactly the cooking he likes, and the old man was told, and he says, "What does he say?" to his daughter. "Well," she says, "you know, he would like to have a taste of beaver now, it's been a long time." So he, the old man, says, "Oh, I got the exact spot where we are going to get the beaver. I will take him there tomorrow." So the young man says, "Sure."

So early morning they left and they went to this place where there's a beaver house and a beaver dam and everything and it's a beautiful place. They started to make all kinds of traps and they make camp there. This was winter time, it was January, cold, very cold outside. So they make camp. Usually after working on the ice and water, your moccasins get wet and your leggings get wet, you have to dry them, so that's the procedure. And they get into their makeshift camp. They hang up the sticks where they can hang up their leggings and moccasins. So on his side the old man hangs his and on the young man's side he hangs his stuff. There's a fire. And the old man plans. He knows what he's going to do. This is one of his tricks.

So as soon as they lay down, finally they settle down, and the young man pretends to be sleeping. A bit snoring [laughs]. The old man begins with, "He's sleeping! Better move now before he wakes." He got up and take a stick and took all his leggings, moccasins, and put it one by one in the fire. It started to smell. It's a terrible smell [laughs], the leggings and everything. So, he says, "Phew, phew, something smells!" And he tried to wake his young son-in-law. Young man knows that, he hears that, he knows, he saw him with one eye open, what he is doing, eh? So he just lies down as if he's still sleeping. Finally, he goes, "Oh yeah, yeah, what happened?" And the old man says, "Something is burning! Is it not your leggings that have been dropped?" So the young man just turns around and

---

4 This avoidance pattern is an old custom. Similar avoidance behaviour is found in other First Nations societies, for example, the strict mother-in-law avoidance among the Dakota. A son-in-law would never talk directly to his mother-in-law.

he says, "No," he says, "My leggings and moccasins are okay!" "But look, it's on your side! Look at that, they are gone," the old man says. So the young man says, "No way," he says, "these are yours! Mine are on your side. I put them there." He [the old man] says, "Oh no!" and he woke up and checked. That was not his on his side, that was his that he put in the fire. Anyway, he had caught himself, he destroyed his own leggings and moccasins and it's cold outside. So he begin to think, "Ohhh, how did I ever make a mistake? Now, what is going to happen?" How is he going to go home without leggings and moccasins in the below zero weather? So he thought, "I got to do something, something I have to do," too ashamed to apologize, too proud to apologize to the young man. So he thought about it: "Suppose I make up a good story. Suppose I talk to him nicely, he might give in, to give me some of his clothes." Because he didn't have much on, only leggings and all that [which got burned in the fire]. So he knows he's going to freeze if he doesn't have any fire. So he decided, "Okay"; he talks to him, the young man asleep.

So he begins to tell a story to him. He says, "There was one time that old man and his son-in-law were traveling into the bush and they camped and that foolish old man pretend to accidentally drop his leggings into the fire. And the young man woke up and he find out that his father-in-law has lost his leggings and moccasins." So he tells the story to him. "And the nice, pitiful young man, he is so pitiful towards the old man who had destroyed his leggings. With this nice-hearted good feeling, he lend some of his clothes so that he can go." All this beautiful words and all that stuff, pity and everything, eh? Sounds so great. And the young man didn't move, he just lays down there. And then [the old man says to the young man], "Did you hear?"—the old man says to him, because he didn't move. So the young man says, "Sure I hear, yeah." So he says, "So what you think?" The young man says, "It's a good riddance to the old guy who was trying to kill his son-in-law!" He didn't receive any pity. That's how he answered. So then he went to sleep and the old man just kept the fire going all night, so he couldn't sleep. Even if they camped the next day, because it's time to go, you know. He begged his son-in-law to give him some of his clothes or something that he has. But the young man did not want to give him. He says, "You did it. I could be freezing to death if my leggings and everything was gone. You wouldn't give me anything, so no mercy there." So he was left behind. Nothing, just a little clothes on his body, a little shirt.

So he decided, "I gotta to do something. I have the power to do things, why not apply them now?" This is where I need to apply these powers that I have." So he had dreamed during the dream quest that he had many dreams how to save himself. So he decided to use the stones first, dream-stones and warm stones to make a trail for him. Commanded them, "Go!" So the stones say, "gooaaaa," like that in the hole [snow?] and then he followed step by step. Goes a little ways but soon the stone began to get cold and they began to move slowly. Wait for another step and it gets cold, then he says, "No, I can't take this!" he says, and he runs back to the camp and stands in the fire and says, "No, it didn't work now." So he warm himself up and put more fire. He scratch his head and says, "what am I going to do next?" Tried to recall his dream. "What am I going to do this time?" I think he has about five different tries and it didn't work.

Finally, he tries again; it's the last one. He has to have this powerful magic in his mind, to turn his self into a caribou. So he says, "Caribou can travel in the snow very fast. I can get home very fast if I turn myself into a caribou." In order to do that, he has to make himself look like a caribou. So he had a little bit of tree branches, puts the stick into his head. Turns into a caribou head and paint himself black in his legs and everything. There stood a caribou. Right now, now it's ready. Then he goes on and jumps into the snow and off goes the caribou very fast. Then all of a sudden he begin to doubt himself and he turn again into a human. And he almost freeze to death. Rushed back into the camp and into the fire. Make a fire again. He says, "How did that fail?" So he sat there for a long time. "What am I going to do now? Why did I dream about this stuff, what could I do?" So he says, "There's not much to do, not much left."

Anyway as the last resort, he decided that he might as well try this, so he went as far as he could run into the bush and grab the little moss hanging and dig up a little bit of moss and a little bit of tree roots, the fine roots and all that stuff. And then he begin to tie moss onto his body and his legs and his feet and all that. It was warm enough, sure, but would it stay there? So finally he decided it should stay, so he took off slowly, not too much. Doesn't want to lose anything. So he walks and he walks and he walks. Sure enough he was half way, he was getting close to his home, then he says, "Maybe I'll make it!" So he began to run. [And he was inside the camp] and he was going to make it. But he started to run and everything all started to fall off. He just barely make it into his tent and he was stark naked. He has to run in like that to cover his ass. Total shameful.

So his daughter says, "It serves you right because you always do that to your son-in-laws, you always kill them that way. And for this time, you have met your match." He was so full of shame, he didn't say anything; he just went to his place. And then he had his own extra clothing and he was all right for a time. So it taught him a lesson for it. He says, "This young man is tough, not easy to take."

So he waited for maybe a year or so. Had built up his courage again to try it again. "But this time I'm not going to fail." One day the young man knows he's going to try it again, so he says, "I wonder if there is any place that I can go sturgeon fishing?" So the old man says, "What did he say?" And the young wife says, "He says he was wondering where he could find the sturgeon fishing." He says, "Oh yeah, I know the place, the exact spot I know. I'll take him there tomorrow." So the young man says, "Okay." So they took off the next morning with the boat and everything and go up the river this far distance. And they finally find this spot, there is the rapids, really fast water. At the bottom there is a nice, nice shallow and deep spot too. And that's where he saw these sturgeons. They're spawning. Usually they spear them when they're spawning. So they had made the spears and all of that, and the boat is a dugout boat I think, because it has a narrow point where you can stand. So the young man wants to grab his spear to spear the fish right there. And he [the old man] says, "No, no, no you don't do that. You have to go up there and stand there right in front and that's where you spear them." So the young man did that and went up to the bow, that little place there, and that's where he stands. And he says, "Now, now, spear them!" So as soon as the boy is ready to throw the spear, he [the old man] floods the boat, he move it, like this, and the boy just fell backwards. And these are the big fish, they were big fish that were there, they were not actually sturgeon. They were just a flesh-eating fish, some kind of a thing. They were not the proper fish, they just seemed to be. And this is the dream of the old man what does that, the way to kill the man. Trick him that way. So the young man fell in among them, these fish, and [they] grab him. And they just swallow him. What they say, they say it was a giant northern pike. A giant northern pike, you know how the teeth are with this thing.

So he was swallowed whole by these giant northern pike. And the old man says, "There! I got him, got him this time! Hurray, hurray, I knew I could do it!" But anyway, he turned back, and he went back home very proud of himself that now he had extended his life for sure, because the

man was hard to get. So he was just laying there and sort of guiding his
boat. So sure he had got rid of him, killed him, the young man. When he
reached to his camp, his grandchildren run back, the young man's children. Grandchildren, two boys, run back to the beach to welcome him.
And they were holding the fish stick, you know, oil fish stick. So he look
at this, he says, "Where did you get the fish?" to the boys. And the boys
say, "Our dad brought the fish." "YOUR DAD!?—Your dad must be now
digested by big fish." He says, "Oh no, no, he brought the fish to us and
this is what we eat." Didn't believe it. He says, "This is not possible, I'm
sure I killed him." But he didn't say that to the kids, he just said that to
himself. So he started thinking about it, could it be? He went into the
teepee and lifted the teepee flap and there sit his son-in-law. Sort of open
[his] mouth and look at him, and his daughter says, "What are you star-
ing at?" "Oh I thought I saw a bug on his head." So anyway, he never did
that before, it was just an excuse.

So he went back to sleep and started to thinking about, "What is this
guy, how come? I never had a problem, you know, killing a person." He
began to think, "How am I going to do this? This is something strange."
Never has he failed to do that. "Hmm, maybe there's another chance. I
might have a chance yet." So the days pass. Maybe another year pass and
the young man know that that guy's eager to kill him. So he allow him to
suffer for a little while, just for the sake of torturing him because he's
been killing people. So one day in the spring time, I think in the summertime, people used to have in the springtime games and playing games
together and all that, you know, the leisure hours. So he says to his wife,
"I wonder if there is any place I can find to build a swing so I can swing,
you know, I feel like having a swing." And the old man, he was just across
the way, he says, "What did he say?" And the young wife knows that, you
know, he's after him again. "Oh, nothing, no, he was just saying, he was
wondering where he could find a place where [he] could build a swing so
he could have a fun."

"I know just the place," he [the old man] says, "I know the place! I'll
take him there tomorrow." He's really eager. And the young man says,
"Oh sure, we'll go there tomorrow." So morning came and they prepared
and off they go. Some distance away. It says that they traveled in a strange
way, I don't know, it's with the shaman power stuff. So they find a place
where there is a high mountain and there's a quartz there, that is, like [a]
cutting where there's a stone, dried river bed. And that's where he takes

him, right up the mountain there. And he says, "This is where I used to come to do my swinging, you know, when I feel like it." So the young man says, "Okay, here we are."

So they went to take some roots, you know, the very long tree roots and make a braid-like sort of thing. Make it long anyway, go way down. So they make that. They work together fine, as if nothing happened. Then they finish it, way down there halfway down to the top or somewhere, they make the seat. And the old man says, "There you go, your turn." So the young man says, "Sure," and he slides down there with one side of the rope and he grab onto the other one and he sits. And, "I'll swing you," said the old man, "swing until you say stop." So he started swinging. Swing far out until almost one hundred and ninety degrees. Then he says, "Now you get up, you stand up instead of sitting." So the young man just got up and stand up and he swing him. When he was in one of those extreme swings, he just pulled the rope like this and the young man just slipped and went down. But he managed to grab a hold of one of those hanging trees, there is a little tree roots there. Managed to grab that and hang onto it and catch his fall. One, maybe three-quarters of the way down. But he looks like as if he went straight down, by the old man, and he says, "I'm sure that that man is gone."

But the young boy did not, he's safe. Saved himself. So, he climb up, climb up right away, and the old man was ready to go. So by the time he climbs up, the old man pick up all his stuff to go home. You know, with pride, "I did get him, I did beat him." But the young man, he says, "Just a minute, old man, I'm here!" So he says, "How did he survive?" He didn't say that, but he said it in his mind. So the young man says, "It's your turn, where you gonna go away? No, no, it's your turn now." So the old man says, "No, but I, I don't feel up to it. I'm too old for that stuff." So he says, "Well, just do as I do. I did what you tell me." He says, "You can't run away from it." So anyway, he says, "Okay." Reluctantly he grabbed the rope and went down, same way as the young man. And when he [the young man] swing him, and as soon as he swing so far out, he says, "Now stand up." Just like the way he [the old man] told him. And the old man barely get up and stand up there shaking and swung, very hard, not that way, but this way. The young man pull the swing. Then the old man just tumble down screaming. And the young man listened. Thump, that's all he heard. Actually he hit the ground down there, somewhere down in the gorge, stones and everything. Way down, no one could survive that fall. So the young man said, "Well, he should be finished. That's it, my job is to get rid of him." So he walked back home.

So he got home and it's all right. His wife didn't mind, they didn't mind much, his daughters, they didn't say anything. They just thought that the old man was way behind a little bit. And it's getting darker, getting darker at night. And the older girl says, "Where is our father, is he coming?" He says, "I don't know." So she says, "What happened to our father anyway, he should have been home by now?" So the young man says, "Well the last time I saw him he was on his way down to the gorge. I don't think he's going to make it." So the young lady says, "Well, he's been doing that to our husbands and he's always killing them." "Well, surely this time he has met his match. It's amazing, I don't think anyone could survive that fall." So they went to bed.

Somewhere after midnight they were sleeping and they hear this noise outside, "hhhhhhhhhmmm, hhhhhhmmmmm." That was the old man coming home. So they opened the door and he crawls in and his head was tied with the tree roots and everything, bit of the brains sticking out of there. He had survived the fall. So he had made it home. So the girl says, so pitiful, they started to know it's him. They nurse him with all kinds of medicine they know. And the old man did heal. He passed the critical point. He began to heal and he's all right, he passed. So they tell him, "Don't ever do that again because why bother?" He admit now he has been trying to kill his son-in-law and says, "I won't do it again. Promise."

So the years pass again. A few years pass. The children now are getting big. And he couldn't resist. He says, "I should be able to beat this guy. I should. I shouldn't fail any more." So the young man knows, he knows what he's thinking. He's just taking a chance when he's going to ask again. You know, when he's going to be so eager to try to kill him. So one day this young man says, "You know it's been a long time since I had eat sea gull eggs" in that season. "I wonder if there is any place I can find sea gull eggs?" He was talking to his wife. And the old man was listening the same way. So he goes and leans to his daughter and says, "What did he say?" And his daughter says, "Nothing, he was just wondering if there is any place he can pick up the sea gull eggs." "I know! I know just the place. I know just the spot, it's not too far from here." It was a large lake or water, whatever it is, if it's salt water, I don't know. And there was a large body of water and there was some islands that you can see sign of beaches and it was there. About there's where the sea gulls usually lay eggs. Lots of them, plenty, all kinds. All sizes too. So he exaggerated, there is a place to find eggs. So the boy says, "Sure, I'll go tomorrow."

So early the next morning, they were very eager to go, he was, but the boy, no, he just takes his time. Finally, before lunch, before midday, so they finally made it to the boat and they were ready to go. They shove off right out into open water and that's where he pointed. He says, "That way, beyond the horizon there. There's an island there with all kinds of sea gulls a nesting. Some are very big too," he says. So the boy says, "Sure, let's just go." So they went. They paddled across and finally they see way out in the horizon, they see the sand beach, really beautiful. And they can see the sea gulls flying around, some of them sitting on the egg, on the nest. He says, "That's the place I'm talking about."

Actually, there's no such thing. It's just the mind and power of the old man that created that vision. These are guys who are struggling with the mi-tew. You know, the two mi-tew fighting each other in their mind. That's what they're doing. That's what the story is about. The man is very strong, the old guy is very powerful. So he created the illusion that there is an island, sea gulls and everything. And the young man knows that. But he went along there anyway. So they beached their craft, their boat and everything. And the old man just barely get up and says, "I don't feel like walking, you go ahead." So he pick up his own basket and pick up eggs not too far away. He told his son-in-law, "Beyond that ridge, there is another type of sea gulls that are there. They have very tasty eggs." So he says, "Okay." He goes out there and all that. He knows what's going to happen. While he was there, he pick up his eggs and filled his basket and decided, "I should take these back." He knows what's going to happen, the young man.

So when he gets over this ridge, he saw there goes the old man way out in the distance, paddling out. And he yell, he says, "Hey," he says, "you leave me behind." The old man didn't even turn his head. He just kept going. So he [the old man] says, "Now for sure he's going to be eaten with those things," those beasts that he created for him to kill him. But the young man knows that. So he overpower the old man's power, and what he did is, he shot one of those giant sea gulls. And take the body off and jump into its skin. And grab a few eggs in the meantime for his young, and took off towards their camp. And slowly was gliding up, and there was an old man down there enjoying himself, he was singing, and he says, "I finally done it, I have beat my son-in-law in this game." He was laying on his back with a little paddle. Then the young man look at him and says, "Oh ya! Oh ya!" right over top of him and he let go. Right to his face you know. The old man just "Uuuph." He says, "This sea gull had digested my son-in-law so fast," he says, "It smells like human shit." He thought he was already digested in that shit. Actually it was him. It was his son-in-law, you know. Well anyway, the young man just went ahead and landed and bring the eggs to his home. And when he got there and his wife started boiling eggs and feed their kids. In the meantime the old man was arriving, towards the evening. Already the boys were running around and eating and playing outside. They saw their grandfather coming, arriving. So they run down to the shore to meet him, with the eggs in their hands, the partially eaten eggs. So he came and looked at them, "What are you eating?" They said, "Eggs!" "Where did you get the eggs?" He says, "Our dad brought some eggs." "Your dad!" So the boys just play and didn't even listen, just say hello to their grandfather and sort of keep on playing. And he says, "Your father and husband must have been digested a long time ago." He didn't say that to hear, he just said it to himself, he was so sure he had killed him. So he walks in thinking that he knows he's dead now.

So he had accomplished what he wanted to do. Now he's going to live longer. That's what he believed. Walks in, lifts the door flap, there sits his son-in-law, sitting there fitfully healthy and everything. He just couldn't believe it. "How does this man survive? What does he have that I don't have?" He knows now this man is tough to kill. So he didn't say much. He just went back to his seat and pretend there's nothing happening. And the young man never said anything. He never did, even when he comes in, he never mentioned what happened.

So anyway, years pass again. Same thing, his daughters still the same age and everything. Nobody seemed to get old at that point, and a time has passed, many years have passed. By this time the young man thought, "I should get rid of this guy now. You know, it's been a long time. I repaid him every way he has killed his son-in-laws. I have even given him a chance to kill me that way, but he hasn't. So there is only one way now, is to finish him off." So in thinking that, he begin to build a canoe, a cedar-strip canoe, a very beautiful thing. And cedar and bark, birch bark, covers it with a beautiful—decorated nicely, decorated and everything. As he built it during that summer, the old man look at it and couldn't resist. This canoe is the best that he ever saw. So he says, "I like to have that canoe. I am going to have that canoe, so I'm going to kill him first."

So summer went on and the boat seems to turn into such a beautiful boat. Sometimes he asks his daughter, he says, "Do you think you could let me have a little try of it once?" So the daughter went to her husband and says, "Do you think you could let him have it, you know, to try it?" So he says, "Sure, sure, anytime that he wants to. But it's not finished yet. It has to be finished." It was finished enough for this old man because it was so beautiful. And he [the young man] kept on making and make it so beautiful and decorate it and all that stuff. Then finally the old man couldn't resist and he says, "May I try his boat?" to his daughter. And his daughter relays his message, "The old man wants to try your boat, the canoe."

So he says, "Let him have it, let him try it." And this was early morning before lunch. The old man was so eager to get in it, he tip over the brand new canoe and carried it to the shore and he gets in. And he was looking for a paddle. So he says, "Where is the paddle?" The young man says, "No, he doesn't need no paddle. This is a special canoe. He doesn't need it." So the old man says, he understood, "Yeah, there must be something about this boat." So the young man says, "He doesn't need no paddle. He just has to hit it on one side, and it's going to go 'tap,' then the boat goes." He says, "You have to hit it lightly, then it will go in just ordinary speed. You have to hit it harder to make it faster. And the faster you want, you have to hit it much harder each time and it will go faster. But if you want to turn, you hit it to the left, then you turn to the left. Turn to the right, hit it on the right. You want to go straight, hit it lightly like this [both sides at the same time]. It will go straight, or it will stop. If you want, stop." So the old man says, "Ohh, great!"

"One condition," the young man says, "you shouldn't play around with it. You only have to turn when you want to turn. You only go fast if you have to. Not just to fool around in. That's the condition that you get to try it." So the old man says, "Sure, sure, of course, I'm not going to play with it." He'll be very careful, he said. So there he goes, off into the open water, whatever it is. Whether it's a sea or lake, or fresh water or salt water. You know where we come from it's salt water. 'Cause it's the Hudson Bay.

And off he goes into the water. Tap it a little bit, and it goes. When he was far from the shore, he wants to try it some more. "I wonder if it go any faster? What speed should I go in this thing?" So he tap it a little harder, it goes on, this boat just skimming on top of the water. "Now that's fast, really. I wonder if it go any faster?" Hit it some more, a bit harder. This time the canoe just touch the top of the water, just flying, all straight out into the open water. So he was enjoying and he says, "Well, I should hit it, I should try it anyways. I wonder if it turn to the right if I [Louis makes a noise like tapping the paddle on the side of the boat]?" And sure enough the boat just turn. Then after he hit it on the left and it turns to the left just like as if he was actually controlling it, just by touching it more like. So he does that, he play with it as he was out there and really enjoy himself, and he forget the warning, what he was not to do. He was totally lost in his own playing a game, playing with this boat.

While he was there, it usually happen during the summer that the great storm would hit that lake. Very quickly in the formation of thunderheads and all that stuff. That's what happened that afternoon. So he saw this cloud coming from the shore where he had left. Big puff of thunder or cloud and everything. And usually under there is a wind. A real powerful wind. So he looked at that dangerous-looking cloud coming. He thought, "Well, with this boat, hmm, I can go anywhere, no danger, I can hit the beach anywhere in no time." So he just enjoyed himself there going like that and all over the place in the open water. But the storm was coming, really thunder and lightning coming. Finally he decided to turn by now, make it to the shore before it gets here. So he hit the boat to turn it around. The boat didn't budge; it just went slowly. He hit it again; no, it didn't, it just went faster again. Try it out again; no, it didn't turn, it just goes a bit faster. He hit it again, and it goes a little straight to the storm, it has turned a bit but it went straight to the storm. And this storm was really coming fast, really a gust of wind in front was touching the water and black, blue-black, and lightning, very, very vicious storm coming. So he tried to turn this boat and it didn't want to obey him. And he begin to remember that's not supposed to be done. "I had played with this stuff," he says, "but I am going to force it."

So he began to hit it here and there, and it just goes full speed ahead into the storm. And now he is really—he went crazy. This thing is not obeying him and he got scared. He began to beat it and beat it and beat it, and soon the storm was upon him and it hit him full force. And the waves just take him upside down and everything and still he's pounding the boat trying to make it do something, but it didn't. So he went down. The boat and him being twisted, twisted around his body and his head sticking out, just dragged into the bottom of the lake. And the sea begins to be calm. And that's the end of the old man. That's it. He died. Being drowned, beaten, wrapped up in that beautiful canoe. He never made it to the shore; he died then, he was drowned.

And the children went down to the shore to watch for their grandfather. On the shore, they walk onto the shore of the lake to look for him to appear. But they did not see him. So they went back and said, "Our grandfather hasn't arrived yet, he must have went wrong." The son-in-law says, "Yeah, he must have, you might as well stop looking for him. Maybe you should look on the shore, he might have washed in." So the boys went walking along the shore, looking for their grandfather, maybe a sign of life or anything, maybe even a boat. And even the daughters went there to look for a sign if the boat could have been washed in there.

Finally they find a bug dragging itself on the shore, the head sticking out. It looks like a dragonfly. Pulling itself on the shore like this. And the kids say, "Look, look at this bug!" And the bug says, "Please, please, careful, careful!" he says. And that was the old man, he has turned into a, into the we-mis-shoosh. You know, the we-mis-shoosh is the name of this bug that we have on the water, it has a little [shell and it] drags the shell around its back, and that's him. That's We-mis-shoosh. He has turned into We-mis-shoosh because of the mistake he has made. That's the end of the story.[5]

---

5 In a discussion with Louis, George Fulford identified this as a caddis fly (Bird 0055). The caddis fly is also called a sedge fly. "Any member of about 7,000 species of mothlike aquatic insects (order Trichoptera) found worldwide, usually in freshwater habitats but sometimes in brackish and tidal waters. Generally dull brownish, caddis flies have long antennae and hairy wings that fold rooflike over the abdomen. They feed primarily on plant juices and flower nectar, though a few are predacious. Many caddis fly larvae construct a portable case from grains of sand, bits of shells, and plant debris glued together by a sticky substance they secrete. This case surrounds the larva's abdomen while it matures. Caddis flies are important to freshwater ecosystems because they clean the water by consuming plant and animal debris and serve, as larvae and adults, as an important food for fish, particularly trout." Encyclopedia Britannica <http://www.britannica.com/ebc/article?eu=384751>. Many thanks to Dr. Donna Giberson at the University of Prince Edward Island for her photograph and enlightening emails about caddis flies. Among other things, I found out that the caddis fly in Louis's area is of the genus/species *grammotaulius*. In addition, she informed me that "the sticky substance they use to hold things together is actually silk, the same stuff that moths use for their cocoons." For further information Dr. Giberson recommends Dr. Glen Wiggins's work on the Trichoptera of North America (Wiggins, 1998), "the 'bible' of caddis flies." See also Wiggins, 1977.

FIGURE 5: *We-mis-shoosh wrapped in his canoe. See the end of the story and footnote 5. Photo credit: Donna Giberson.*

The Young Orphan Boy Defeats a Powerful and Feared Mi-tew[6]

The story is like this: there was a powerful shaman who could do almost anything, who had the servant and had been very well-off because of his power. And also because he was so sure of himself that he would have whatever he needs. He begin to be [a] feared person because he is so powerful. So people tried to avoid him so they won't aggravate him.

As the Omushkegowak used to do after the European came, they used to gather into the outlet of one of the major rivers that flow into the Hudson and James Bay. Usually at this time, the European were trading at Kashechewan, Ontario, which is on the west coast of James Bay. And the people within the land, the Omushkego people and also Oji-Cree people used to congregate to Kashechewan at the mouth of the Kashechewan River, the second oldest settlement that was created by the Hudson Bay fur traders, the English people. It was one of those periods after the establishment, it could have been somewhere around 1700, maybe 1800. I guess we can fairly say, at the beginning of 1800s, because people used to have guns then. Not everybody has a gun, but there were quite a few. And they had this new established tradition they did after the European came. They always go into the Ekwan River from Winisk River, from Attawapiskat and way inland into the mouth of the Ekwan River, and they used to meet there, and every spring after the ice cleared off the rivers and then partially opened into the west coast of James Bay, they used to go there and they meet, in that Ekwan River, to the north side and right up about two miles

---

6 Bird 0107.

to the north. That was the famous campground and it was that time they used to have all those games, and competitive games and reunions and everything, before they push on to Kashechewan.[7] Besides that, they wait there for a week to have the James Bay shoreline open a little bit more so they can paddle along the shore, those who have canoes, and those who don't, they just walk on the shore.

So it was one of those gatherings that they were having games and competition games and shaman games, I mean shamans competing and showing off how much they can do. It was one of those things that happens in that story. There was this shaman who was, they called him "feared shaman," and in our language it says "koo-chi-kan." At the same time there was a young man who has been an orphan as a child and he was raised by his uncle. I don't know if it's his father's brother or if it's his mother's, I'm not too sure.

Anyway, as it was believed in those days, usually an orphan would acquire a powerful shamanism because he's not loved, he doesn't receive full love from parents because his parents are not there. So he's always in that state of loneliness and always in the state of needing, needs comfort and everything. He's always in a state of fear. He's always conditioned to be that way. It's just exactly the exact condition to be shaman when they are in the quest to dream, when they want to get dream. So the young person doesn't have to want to because he already have it. Usually these kind of people were extraordinary, very powerful. So this was the condition. The shaman that was there [was] feared, and the young person was, nobody knows, he's just nobody, he's just one of the young poor guys. He was around, but he was just a young person, perhaps maybe fifteen, eighteen. And he loves to play with people and likes to play the game that people play.

So that evening, one day, he was with the game with the other young people and some other grown-ups. They had a team and he was on one side. As they were playing so intensely they were really trying to win the game. They wanted to make more score than the other team, and he was really pushing, this young man. And that moment, that evening, the mitew happened to have this urge of trying to pick up a fight. He had a dream and he wants to try it out. So in order to attract attention he came

---

7 I recall Louis saying that there were so many people camped here and so many lodges that if you tried to look across the encampment, you would be unable to see through to the other side. In Chapter 6 he writes that the camp was "two miles long and about a mile wide." This location is the setting for "The Wailing Clouds" story in Chapter 6.

out all decked out, I mean dressed up. As if to say, in European term, "dressed to kill." So the highest prize that they thought it was, in those days, was otter skin. There is an otter who is totally black and inside the fur it's just like a silver lining. It's a very beautiful stuff. And it's blue-black outside. We don't find many of those, but this guy did, and he had enough pelts to make a jacket and the leggings. That's the way he dressed. And he came out all dressed up and bring out his stick. So people, those who were playing and those who were observing, who were sitting on the ground, they said, "Oh no, there comes the shaman," and they say, "Now we've had it, he's looking for a fight." So many elders just leave, they just didn't want to witness anything, and some people sticks on, but the team, they were so intense, they were just really trying to win the game and they forgot to look at him. And some of the people said, "There comes the shaman." But they said, "Hell with the shaman, let's win this game." So they really did ignore him.

And the shaman came in and joined one team, and then he began to play. And everybody forgot about him and they just play as hard as they can. It so happens some people were aware of the shaman; they just didn't want to tackle him, because this game, you really tackle someone, you shoulder your way and you fight, you kick—or not kick but you push him with your body. It's something like a hockey game but it's not the wintertime. But they have two balls that are tied together almost, and then there's string across and then they have a stick that looks like almost like a hockey stick except that it has the little notch in there where you can put your stick in between the balls, and you can throw them any way you want. So this is what they were doing. I forget the name of that. There was a name for it. But the name has to do with these two balls: pim-mi-tish-soo-way-ask-wa-hi-gan.[8]

So this intensive game was going on and that shaman was in amongst them, nobody really care, they were so intense, they would push him around and kick him around, and then finally he'd grab the ball and run away with it the other way, into the creek. The boys were so mad and they said, "Bring the ball back, what's the idea, this is the way we won," but he keep on running and the young boy, the orphan boy, run after him and push and shoulder him off and then grab the ball and bring it back, and the shaman catch up with him and grab the ball and throw it back into the

---

8 Louis defined "pim-mi-tish-soo-way-ask-wa-hi-gan" as "stickhook ball swing," in a personal communication, April 2, 2003. See also Chapter 5 and Chapter 6.

creek. And he did throw it back into the creek. There was a creek there. Not very deep, maybe up to your crotch area, muddy, and that's where he threw the ball. And the young boy was mad at him. He says, "What's the idea of throwing the ball, don't you know the goal is over there!" But the shaman just kept on going like that.

So the boy just run after the ball and the shaman behind, and they're trying to catch it under the water. The boy found it, but the old man caught it back again and shoved it under. By this time the young boy was very frustrated and he grabbed a hold of the old man on the neck, the back of his neck, and dunk him in. And he says, "Get the ball!" So he hold him there for a long time and the shaman ass end was sticking out and wiggling and everything, and he pulled him out, he says, "Did you catch it?" The old man didn't say a thing; he just spit out the water and everything. And then he [the orphan boy] says, "Find it!" and he dunk him in again as far back as he could, and the old man was just kicking the water. Finally he almost stopped, then the boy pulled him out again; he was actually falling in the water. The old man couldn't speak. So finally the boy catched the balls and bring them out and shoved the old man back into the water.

So he brought his ball back, [but] by this time everybody was aware that shaman has been totally insulted. Means death, the boy is going to be dead. So the game is forgotten. Nobody wants to play any more. The boy says, "Come on, come on, let's finish the game, to hell with the old guy, let's just finish the game, we were almost winning." But all of them just sort of dragged their feet back home and didn't want to play. And the old guy just came up and the other elders were sitting by the creek and they didn't want to look, they didn't want to comment anything. He came out and all totally, totally soaked, all his beautiful uniform. And his hair was braided in front of his head and dripping and everything. He came in and he muttered his way up and he says, "Truly he's a bad boy who has soaked my uniform, my best uniform." That's all he says, and he just walks away dripping into his tipi. The game is over and everybody just went home so certain that this old guy is mad and he's going to kill the boy. And no one dared to step up and defend the boy.

So anyway, the game's over. All the players went home, and so did the old man. And his [the boy's] uncle was there watching the game. So when he got home his uncle was there at home, and he scorned him right there. He says, "Are you tired of living? What is the idea, why did you have to do that to the old man?" The young boy didn't say anything. And his uncle keeps saying, "There is nothing I can do, I cannot defend you, that guy's powerful." So the boy says, "Well," he says, "I will not call your help if anything happens. I guess it will be just up to me." That's it. Still, his uncle just simply couldn't believe it. His aunt is crying, so sure that he's going to die. So they went to bed anyway. With sorrow and everything. But the boy didn't seem to care; he just went to bed as everybody went to bed. The uncle and the aunt were just laying huddling each other and just waiting for something to happen. Towards after midnight, there it is. All of a sudden the boy screams in agonizing pain. And it seems just to die off, struggling and screaming and yelling and talking as if he was fighting someone, but there is nobody there. And the uncle didn't move. He just didn't want to interfere, and so with his wife. So the screaming and painful yelling was still there. Finally it stopped, that was it. So the old couple just laid there and they said, "He's dead." So they said, whispering to each other, "We'll wait until morning, until dawn, we will give him a proper burial somewhere."

When the dawn came, the old lady make a fire just like as usual, tried to think that nothing really happened, except the death and everything. But to her surprise, the boy was there! Sleeping! Breathing! So she nudges her husband and says, "Get up, get up, look at this!" The old man get up and look; there is the young boy sleeping quietly as if nothing has happened. So they begin to get up. They make something to drink, breakfast. They begin to eat. Once they finished the breakfast, they talk to the young boy. They said, "Are you okay? Are you alive?" So the young boy stirs a little bit, he says, "Of course, of course I was just asleep." Says, "We heard your screaming last night." "Ooh yes, oh yes, yeah I did receive something from the old man, I guess." It was just early dawn, not yet, not yet quite daylight. So he got up. They gave him a drink of something. Then as he get up, his blanket is rolled aside, then he finally reached behind him and he come out with something, a large dandelion, you know the way the dandelion look like the one that blows in the wind, sharp things that looks very fluffy, that's what it looks like. And there were quills in there, porcupine quills and other stuff. And he says, "This is what he sends me." He holds it up; he says, "Look at it." I forget what is the parts that those quills are sticking into, I think there's animal parts that he has sticked those needles in, this old guy who wanted to kill the young boy. But the young boy says, "I survived."

Just before they finish, he drinks his tea or whatever it is, he says, "Auntie, could you give me a couple of your steel needles?" You know those beading needles that the white people use to give. So she says, "Why do you need the needles?" He says, "Just let me have them." So the aunt says, "Well, I have a few. How many do you want?" He says, "A couple will do." So she handed over the pincushion and she said, "Just pick the ones you want." So he picked two of those beading needles and one square, triangle sort of needle, the one that you use to sew the hide. He says, "Ok, these." So he handed over the rest. So it was done, it was done already. He says, "I shall send these things to this old man; I can't just hold on to his property." He put needles in it, three of them, then he went out and was gone for a few minutes, come back in. He says, "He shall receive it sometime today." Then he went to sit down and drink some more and have a little breakfast, and then he lays down as if nothing happened.

As the sun rises, everybody begins to rise and they look towards where the old man used to have his tipi, the old shaman. There was nothing there. The tipi is gone, only the poles are standing. And somebody said they went to look, everything was gone. So one guy said, "It was about before dawn that we heard the noise and we see them, very quietly loading the stuff in the canoe and they left, these two men and the shaman." Apparently they say that he's going to go away and then kill the boy from there. So they said, the boy just didn't even bother, they didn't even go there.

Now, let us pick up a story about the shaman's trip up the river as he goes away. What happens is that he had sent his power to this young man during the night, that night, and nothing happened. He knows that they [his power] didn't kill the boy. He knows that he is going to be beaten. So he instructed his servant to take him away as far away as he can and perhaps find something he can defend himself with. But fortunately it didn't turn out that way. They were going ahead and up the river and not far distance, and by the afternoon they were just going and going, and he says "Come on, come on, faster, faster"; he was trying to reach the place where he used to go to offensively, like a fort or something. He was trying to reach there. And the two men were straining, poling and paddling, and he was in the middle. He never did used to pick a paddle. This time he was picking a paddle and paddling as fast as he can. Then all of a sudden he break the paddle. He can hear the loud crack. The paddle is usually strong, but he breaks it in half. And he just crumbled on the bottom of the canoe. And crippled his legs and then dying. And then after [he started] jerking and everything.

The two men look at each other and says, "What happened?" So they beach the canoe, check him, roll him over on his side, or on his back, and then the blood came out from his nostrils, his mouth, his eyes, and then on top of his chest lay this pincushion full of pins, steel—cushion on top of his chest, sort of coming out. And they said, "That's what kill him." Never in their life have they seen such a powerful man to be so pitifully dead. At that moment they took an opportunity to say, "Well, good riddance. He has been ruling us too long. In fact, he enslaved us. Let's get rid of him." So they pulled the canoe right up into the bush, along with the old man and his stuff and everything, and filled the dry branches and everything from the tree and all the dead trees and piled them on top and set fire to it. From the distance, from the Bay shore, people can see this black smoke coming out from up the river. And they know, this was the end of the shaman. The young boy of the orphan age has beaten the great, powerful shaman.

So that is the sample of a story about shamanism. There is nothing pleasant or love in it, but pride and some bad things. Many stories are examples as that. Very few are beauty with kindness and love.

The thing is, this shaman was so proud. He was so confidence in himself, he forgot. Sometimes the giant can be killed by the smallest man. He had forgotten that, so he was beaten. And that's the end of the story.

This story is a lesson in life. The elders used to interpret this story to say, no matter how powerful you are, you should never show off. You should always consider other impossibilities because you are not the power. The power is the Creator, the Great Spirit is a power. You should always consider mostly an orphan child. Sometimes power and the greatest will come to the most humbled person. That is the lesson. The humble shall destroy the elite people or the powerful people. That's the teaching. So shamanism is not all perfect as it seems to be, when it's misused. But when it's used properly it is a good thing, it's beneficial to people. That's the end of the story. So that is the reason people trying to get the dream to be, to establish themself as a shaman. But there are few stories existing to talk about the good shamans, but many bad ones. But they are teaching us. They are teaching us to avoid these things in our life. The bad stories teach us to avoid similar situations, if we were to grow up, if we were to have such acquirement. If we were a shaman, it tells us not to do these things that are bad. That is why the stories are provided. That is why the stories existed. Any of the good stuff like the good life and everything, they don't actually stand out in the story; we don't hear much about the good thing, but bad things usually sticks out in our mind. That is the meaning. That is why the stories are told.

5

Omens, Mysteries,
and First Encounters

Introduction
JENNIFER S.H. BROWN

Some of the most powerful and intriguing themes of the old Omushkego stories concern glimpses of and interactions with outsiders, mystical, legendary, and historical. Some visitors were Europeans; others were not. During the making of this book, Louis Bird told a story about some strangers who came north to James Bay before the first Europeans settled there. They captured a young man and carried him off to their land far to the south; there he made a miraculous escape just before he was to be sacrificed and returned to tell the tale. "The Omushkego Captive and the Na-to-way-wak" comes first among the stories in this chapter. It exemplifies mi-te-win power, a theme found throughout this book. It also reminds us that Europeans were not the only exotics to find their way into Omushkego country; they were latecomers encountering people who knew they were not alone in the world.[1]

Then come several stories about early relations with Europeans that Louis recounted as a cluster in February 2002. Some offer retrospective foreshadowings of the newcomers, as sensed or found through dreams and mi-te-win power. One tells of a mysterious stranger who joined some

---

1 See Bruce Trigger (1976, vol. 1: 275, 283) on Huron and Nipissing trading visits to James Bay. In the decades after the destruction of Huronia in 1649, the Iroquois (or Na-to-way-wak in Cree, variously spelled) sometimes raided as far as James Bay; young men earned prestige for their bravery on such expeditions and honour for bringing captives home alive for adoption or sacrifice, in consolation for earlier losses of relatives in warfare (Richter 1992: 36). See Lytwyn 2002: 75, for a map of Iroquois war routes towards James Bay in the 1650s–70s. Lytwyn (77) states that the raids were made for complex reasons but "were aimed primarily at disrupting the flow of furs to the French." Bird 0077; Bird 0083; and Bird 0107 tell stories of other old hostilities with Inuit from across Hudson Bay.

Omushkego people on a caribou hunt; another records a first encounter with sailors and their grounded ship and evokes the circumspection and pragmatism that the Omushkegowak brought to the occasion. A final anecdote evokes humour as an old man and his wife discover the properties of mirrors. They all speak vividly of legendary and historical encounters with strangers who ventured by sea into Hudson or James Bay, and of how people dealt with them.[2]

TRACKING THE EUROPEANS

Written records document the European strangers to a limited extent. Several explorers found their way into Hudson Bay before the Hudson's Bay Company founders sent their first traders to winter at the mouth of the Rupert River in 1668–69. But only two early expeditions wintered in James Bay before 1668: Henry Hudson and his crew on the east coast in 1610–11 and Thomas James and his men on Charlton Island in 1631–32.

Captain James and one member of Hudson's crew, Abacuk Pricket, both wrote accounts that mentioned the Native people they met or did not meet. Their constructions of contact events offer vivid counterpoints to the Cree stories. Putting the Cree and English tales side by side, we learn how different peoples remembered different aspects of events as worthy of note and learned from them within their own frameworks of knowledge and values.[3] The stories offer clues about what the visitors and their observers thought they saw, looking through a clouded glass into worlds beyond. They also convey from both sides the sensory and emotional experience of contact and near-contact: the sighting of fires, human footprints, sharpened stakes, or sails; the strange taste and appearance of ship's biscuit; the sounds of distant voices or gunfire or the ring of a steel axe, so different from the duller sound of a stone axe on wood.

Hudson and his ill-fated search for the Northwest Passage are well known in colonial history. Most written accounts emphasize the mutiny of June 1611 in James Bay and the mutineers' abandoning of Hudson, his son, and seven other men in a shallop on the edge of the sea ice. As we shall see, a story that a Frenchman told, probably at third hand from an

---

2 This tape, entitled Early Contact (Omens and Stories) is Bird 0114, and was recorded in Winnipeg on 27 February 2002. Thanks to Donna Sutherland who transcribed it in December 2002. Louis Bird and Jennifer Brown then checked the text for accuracy and clarity, and to trim repetitions.

3 For a fine discussion of what becomes or does not become an "event," and for whom and why, see Fogelson 1989: 133–74.

Omushkego source, hints at their fate. But throughout the months before the mutiny, Hudson's men were finding Native traces and trying to interpret them, while leaving traces of their own. Somewhere on the northeast shore of Hudson Bay in summer 1610, the sailors found, as Pricket wrote, "some round Hills of stone, like to Grasse cockes, which at the first I tooke to be the work of some Christian." Pricket investigated one of them: "I turned off the uppermost stone, and found them hollow within, and full of Fowles hanged by their neckes." The men could not linger; "Our Master ... shot off some Peeces [guns] to call us aboord; for it was a fogge."[4] If the Inuit makers of the cache were watching the intruders, they kept out of sight. But they probably heard the ship's guns, for such sounds carry great distances over water.

In October, Hudson and his men hauled their ship ashore near the Rupert River, and by 10 November, they were frozen in.[5] During the winter, the Englishmen saw no one, though surely they were noticed as they set about hunting "Partridges [ptarmigan] as white as milke ... above an hundred dozen" (over twelve hundred, to feed twenty-two men over six months). By early spring, however, the birds disappeared, and the hungry men "went into the Woods, Hilles, and Valleyes, for all things that had any shew of substance in them, how vile soever: the mosse of the ground, then the which I take the powder of a post to bee much better, and the Frogge (in his ingendring time as loathsome as a Toade) was not spared." These excursions too were probably cautiously observed.[6]

Finally, as the ice began to break up in the bays, a lone "Savage" (who would have been Cree) came to the grounded ship, "as it were to see and to bee seene, being the first that we had seene in all this time." Pricket wrote that Hudson "made much of him, promising unto himself great matters by his means." The captain demanded knives and hatchets from his men to trade, but only Prickett and one other obliged. Hudson gave the visitor a knife, looking glass, and buttons, and the man "Made signes that after hee had slept hee would come againe, which he did." This time, he brought two "Deere" [caribou] skins and two beaver pelts on a sled. He laid the knife on one beaver skin and the mirror and buttons on the other, and gave the two pelts to the captain in silent trade. Hudson then "shewed

---

4 Pricket in Purchas 1906, vol. 13: 384–85.
5 Pricket in Purchas 1906, vol. 13: 387.
6 The Rupert River was part of an old trade route between Tadoussac and James Bay (Lytwyn 2002: 126). Lytwyn (Chapter 2) also cites archaeological finds indicating precontact habitation of Hudson Bay Lowland river areas, and the man who visited in early spring would hardly have been living alone.

him an Hatchet, for which hee would have given the Master one of his Deere skinnes, but our Master would have them both, and so hee had, although not willingly." After making signs that suggested to the English that he would come again, "he went his way, but never came more."[7] Hudson's hard bargaining may have offended him; or he may simply have had spring hunting and other things on his mind.[8]

When the water had sufficiently opened, Hudson decided to seek further contact with the local people. Taking the ship's longboat or shallop, he went southwest because "(that way) wee might see the Woods set on fire by them." Pricket wrote that Hudson "was perswaded, if he could meet with the people, he should have flesh of them, and that good store." However, "he returned worse then hee went forth. For, hee could by no meanes meete with the people, although they were neere them [him?], yet they would set the woods on fire in his sight."[9]

This episode has often been interpreted to mean that the Crees deliberately set the woods on fire to keep the English away.[10] But it appears that one fire already had been seen, and Hudson went in that direction, possibly reading it as a signal fire and hoping that he would find people there. Second, while Hudson saw people setting other fires and they did not come to meet him, Pricket did not say that they set fires to keep him away; indeed, they could readily have avoided a man offshore in a small boat or attacked him if he came too close. Third, an assumption that the Crees were simply reacting to Hudson probably overstates his importance to them and risks a subtle Eurocentrism. Finally, there is another explanation for the fires. The purposeful use of fire in the spring (when burns could be relatively controlled) to clear woods and underbrush and to create meadows was a significant Aboriginal means of managing landscape to encourage grasses and browsing for game, improve visibility, clear campsites,

7 Pricket in Purchas 1906, vol. 13: 391.
8 This encounter contrasts with the seemingly more substantial first contacts described in Cree oral stories of first meetings collected by Colin Scott at Wemindji, north of Rupert River; see Morantz 1984: 176, "Oral and Recorded History in James Bay." Morantz (2001: 49) has suggested that one of these episodes (in which some Cree visitors to a ship take off their fur clothing to trade and are given some different clothes to wear) corresponds to the encounter with Hudson. I suspect they are different; Pricket is explicit about a single man's brief visits, and the details do not correspond. On the challenges of comparing and linking Native oral and European written accounts of early ship-to-shore contacts, see, for example, Clayton 2003.
9 Pricket in Purchas 1906: 392. The wording of the passage is somewhat different in Christy 1894: 137: "and though the Inhabitants set the woods on fire before him, yet they would not come to him."
10 For example, Neatby stated, "the natives ... set the woods on fire to keep the unwelcome visitors at a distance" (1966: 376), and Francis and Morantz wrote (1983: 17), "they refused to be approached, setting fire to the grass and shrubbery to keep the Europeans away."

and the like, in the boreal forest and elsewhere.[11] In this instance as in others, actions and signs could be read very differently by people who did not know each other and by writers who later tried to interpret these alien encounters.

On 24 June 1611, Henry Hudson's crew mutinied. Hudson, his son John (aged about nineteen), and seven others were set adrift in the shallop somewhere near Charlton Island. Their fate was never positively known, but a French story set down in 1612 offers clues. In 1611, Samuel de Champlain arranged for a young man named Nicolas de Vignau to winter with a chief of the Kichesipirini, Tessouat, on the upper Ottawa River. In Paris in 1612, Vignau claimed he had traveled to the "northern sea" and had seen the wreckage of an English ship on the shore. The Native people were holding one boy or young man (the French garçon is ambiguous); they had killed the rest (written as eighty men, a clear error) for trying to steal their food and supplies.

Champlain visited Tessouat the next summer, hoping to repeat Vignau's voyage. But when he had Vignau repeat his story to Tessouat, the chief and his people strongly denied that Vignau had made such a trip, and he was obliged to recant. Yet the core of his story was plausible. Champlain's copyist certainly erred in writing that eighty seamen were killed; eight casualties and one survivor, however, would match the number in Hudson's shallop.[12] The likeliest interpretation is that Vignau had heard a true story from Native people trading with the James Bay Cree and appropriated it to impress his French superiors, assuming his deception would go undiscovered. The specific incident has not turned up in surviving Cree oral traditions. Louis, however, tells a story in this chapter that alludes intriguingly to a young English-speaking stranger turning up among his people long ago. Castaways and later HBC men (as a consequence of French attacks in the 1680s) could both find themselves living on their own among the Omushkegowak, at least for a time.

---

11 See Lewis 1982: 17, 35; Long 1986b: 32. Lewis (45) suggests that the "signal fires" reported by explorers often "seem to have been more of an afterthought of White observers than an ongoing practice of Indians"; outsiders would not have understood the functions of spring fires, in particular.

12 On Vignau, see Biggar, ed., *The Works of Samuel de Champlain*, vol. 2, 255–58; 288–96; 304–05. Vignau's biographer, Marcel Trudel (1966), found his story believable, allowing for eight rather than eighty casualties as the plausible figure (Hudson's entire crew had numbered twenty-two) and noting that the distance he said he traveled was too short to bring him to James Bay (suggesting Vignau's story was not first-hand). Trigger and others also have noted how Aboriginal people controlled river traffic and protected their middleman trade positions; the French could not travel freely without permission or guidance (on Vignau, see Trigger 1976, vol. 1: 275, 281–85).

In 1631–32, Thomas James wintered in the bay that his mapmaker labeled, "James his Baye." The next year, he published a narrative of his sojourn with a dramatic if wordy title: *The Strange and Dangerous Voyage of Captain Thomas James, in his intended Discovery of the Northwest Passage into the South Sea wherein the Miseries Indured, both Going, Wintering, Returning; & the Rarities observed, both Philosophicall and Mathematicall, are related in this Journall of it*. His voyage was a product of the rivalry between the ports of London and Bristol. A group of London merchants was about to send Captain Luke Fox to Hudson Bay in search of the Northwest Passage, and the Bristol Society of Merchant Venturers decided to send James on the same quest, to keep the Londoners from gaining a monopoly over any new trade routes discovered (Christy 1894; Cooke 1979: 384).

James left Bristol on 3 May 1631, but did not reach Hudson Bay till mid-July; severe storms and ice slowed his progress and led to his wintering in James Bay. Despite the length of his stay, he found only traces of "Salvages," as he called them; none came to "to see and to be seen." Still, his allusions to the unseen tell us how a Bristol sea captain construed the unknown regions he had entered; while never meeting real people, he had real fears about them, mingled with ambivalent wishes for their help and guidance.

On 26 August 1631, coasting along western Hudson Bay, James reached the mouth of a large river whose spreading estuary reminded him of home; he named it the New Severn after the river that flows through Bristol, England. A familiar name, however, could not deflect anxiety about the unknown. A boat went ashore, but did not return. Then the English saw a fire on the shore. The ship fired guns as signals, "but they did not answer our shots or false fires" (firing of blanks). The sailors feared the worst; "We thought withall that it had been the Salvages, who did now triumph in their conquest." But then the landing party safely returned, reporting "no signe of People" (Christy 1894: 487–88).

Three days later, the James and Fox expeditions met by chance. Fox, the more seasoned navigator, who was soon to turn north and head home, wrote that James told him that "hee was going to the Emperour of Japon, with letters from his Maiestie." Fox was not impressed: "'Keep it up then,' quoth I, 'but you are out of the way to Japon, for this is not it'" (Christy 1894: 359). James continued south, along "a most shoald and perilous coast, in which there is not one Harbour to be found." On 3

September, "we knew we were at a Cape Land, and named it Cape Henrietta Maria, by her Majesties name, who had before named our Ship" (Christy 1894: 490).[13]

The cape marked the entrance to James Bay, where the expedition had terrible times. Landing on a large wooded island, they built a "habitation" named Charles Town after the king (hence the later name, Charlton Island). Fears followed them. On 7 October, James and his men "wandered up and downe in the Woods, to see if we could discover any signe of Salvages, that so we might the better provide for our safeties against them. We found no appearance that there was any on this Iland, nor neere unto it." Further searching confirmed their absence "as farre as we could discover (which we further proved by the making of [signal] fires)." Deciding that once the extreme cold set in, "they could not come to us if there were any," James wrote, "we comforted and refreshed ourselves by sleeping the more securely" (Christy 1894: 509, 511).

After a dreadful winter, cranes and geese appeared in May, and the men "sowed pease" and ate green vetches to counter their scurvy. June brought "infinit abundance of bloud-thirsty Muskitoes," but the ship got refloated (Christy 1894: 546, 548, 557). On 24 June, James raised a cross on a hilltop above the graves of three men who had died that winter; fastened to it were the king's and queen's pictures "drawne to the life and doubly wrapped in lead," the king's arms, and the arms of the city of Bristol, along with a shilling and sixpence.[14] Then on the highest spot, he lit a fire such as he "had formerly made, to have knowledge if there were any Salvages on the maine or the Ilands about us"—a clue that, at some level, he would have welcomed their information and aid. But his fire got out of control and spread to the "towne," and the Englishmen quickly had to salvage their goods and leave (Christy 1894: 558–560).

On two further landfalls, James imagined encountering Native residents. Stopping on Danby Island to get wood, he saw two thick stakes driven into the ground and "firebrands" cut with a hatchet or other iron tool: "This did augment my desire to speake with the Salvages; for without doubt, they

---

13 Henrietta Maria was the wife of King Charles I. The Omushkegowak have their own name for the cape, ki-ni-ki-moo-sha-wow, which means a barren or treeless headland. Aboriginal place names typically describe a place or allude to an event that happened there; European explorers, in contrast, honoured remote patrons, nobility, saints, and the like, in their naming practices, or transported names from home, as also in the case of the Severn River and James's name for the west James Bay region—New South Wales.

14 On the English uses and purposes of such crosses and the diverse practices and symbolic meanings that the French and other Europeans associated with the raising of crosses, see Seed 1995.

could have given notice of some Christians with whom they had some commerce" [and by extension, information about the elusive "passage into the South Sea"]. But none appeared (Christy 1894: 567–68).[15]

Finally, heading out of James Bay, the ship reached Cape Henrietta Maria on 22 July. James and some of his men went ashore in the ship's boat, and "upon the most eminent place" of that low coastline, they again erected a cross with the king's arms and the arms of the city of Bristol. They also brought two greyhounds that they had maintained through the winter in hopes of their usefulness for hunting. Here, indeed, they saw some "Deere" [caribou]. "We stole to them with the best skill we had, and then put our Dogs on them; but the Deere ranne cleere away from them at pleasure. We tyred the Dogs, and wearied our selves, but to no purpose; neither could we come to shoote at them." Then, as the dogs had not been of service all winter and would not be now, James "caused them to be left ashoare." Evocatively, he imagined that a relic of them might sometime be found: the male "had a collar about his necke, which, it may be hereafter, may come to light." Once again no local residents appeared: "I did see no signe at all of any Salvages" (Christy 1894: 571–72). Four months later, his ship limped into Bristol, not having found "any hope of a [Northwest] passage this way" (Cooke 1979: 385; Christy 1894: 603).

Thomas James was the only European before the 1670s to traverse the Omushkego Cree coastline from the Severn River to the islands of James Bay—the region of Louis's stories. No one can prove that the Omushkegowak saw or heard his ship, but the *Henrietta Maria* was the earliest of many vessels to appear on their horizons in western James Bay. Its captain vividly set in print his experiences in the bay that he named— part of a sea for which the Cree had their own name (n. 27).[16] He earned a small niche in English history, but never imagined how he and his countrymen might be recalled in another people's stories. Coming to see, the English were seen and heard by eyes and ears beyond their ken.

---

15 Christy (1894: 568, n. 1) speculated that since Hudson and his companions may have been abandoned less than twenty miles from Danby Island, the cut stakes and firewood could be relics of their presence. But the man who had traded with Hudson also had received a hatchet, and Cree people were also probably trading iron tools from the south. The Cree may also have salvaged equipment left by the lost men. Nicolas Vignau's story of 1612 mentioned earlier (note 12) is the best clue to the fate of Hudson and his men despite the problems presented by his account.

16 See Davies 2003 for a detailed study and appreciation of James's narrative. Davies does not, however, look into Hudson Bay Native contexts or views to any extent.

OMUSHKEGO VOICES

Louis's stories of strangers in Hudson and James Bays convey a long history of Omushkego thinking and prophecy about them.[17] They embody both mythic elements that seem very old and echoes of lived experience that surely reach back to the era of Hudson and James. Some stories that foreshadow the coming of strangers have a strong spiritual or, in Cree, mitew or shamanistic element. The first story below tells of a magical escape from the Na-to-way-wak. Another tells of Cha-ka-pesh, a very small man but one possessed of strong shamanic powers, in short, a mi-tew. He lived with his wise older sister who tried her best to keep him out of trouble— a difficult chore as he was always testing his limits and her control. She could not keep him from traveling across time and space to find a ship on the saltwater sea.

Other stories tell of a mysterious stranger helping with a caribou hunt and of an encounter between Omushkegowak and sailors whose ship (the first these Cree had seen) had gone hard aground on Akimiski Island in the northwestern corner of James Bay. It is tempting to try to link this ship with an event recorded in writing; in September 1631, somewhere near Akimiski Island, Thomas James's ship indeed got grounded "amongst great stones, as bigge as a man's head, where she did beate for the space of five hours most fearfully."[18] But that mishap involved no meeting with local people, whereas the ship in the Cree story was grounded for several days in calmer weather. In any case, the oral story does not aim to pin names or dates on Europeans, but to supply implicit advice about how strangers met, how the situation was handled, and what it meant for the future.[19] The story probably also represents convergent retellings of recurring "first contacts" between various Crees and Europeans whose ships were always getting stuck on the shallow tidal mudflats of Hudson Bay.

Thomas James's narrative was printed in 1633. Louis recorded his "contact" stories in 2002 to be written down about 370 years later. A quality of immediacy might be expected in James's account, but the same

---

17 Bird 0114.
18 James in Christy, ed. 1894: 598.
19 John Long recorded from James Wesley a story with some similar motifs; Wesley located it at the Churchill River (1986b: 39–40). Compare Cruikshank's points (2003: 435) about the Aboriginal stories about Skookum Jim and the discovery of gold in the Klondike in the 1890s: "the question of which versions are 'correct' may be less interesting than what each story reveals about the cultural values of its narrator." See also Cruikshank 2003: 454.

quality endures in the old oral stories; their tellers' attention to detail and sense of place have kept them alive for nearly four centuries. The Cree stories come from a vibrant tradition that has spoken meaningfully to many generations. James's story, in contrast, would hardly have survived if it had not been attractively written and published. In England, the significance of his voyage was slight except for the gaps it filled in for mapmakers, and his mission, like those of all his contemporaries who sought the South Sea by a northern route, failed miserably, discouraging further seekers for almost a century (Cooke 1979: 385).

The juxtaposing of the English and Cree stories highlights contrasts in the roles of English and Native agency—the relative ability of the parties to initiate action and control events and outcomes. James, in the English style of his times, took credit for the discovery of "his Baye," setting up crosses on behalf of his king and the city of Bristol. But he moved at the mercy of the winds, waves, ice, and storms, losing hope of delivering his king's letters to the Emperor of Japan and, at times, almost all hope of survival alone "in this so unknowne a place" (Christy 1894: 490).

In contrast, the people who lived along the shores of the Bay and regularly visited the islands to harvest waterfowl and fish were skilled survivors, travelers, and observers. They heard the English guns, saw their signal fires, watched their ships pass, and would have salvaged any useful items the travelers left at "Charles Towne" and other stopping places. Maybe they even met the two greyhounds abandoned on Cape Henrietta Maria. But with one exception, they did not come forward to meet Hudson or James. Being at home in a land they knew, they had more choices than the English and probably less fear. When some of them did approach the grounded ship of Louis's story, they did so deliberately and with care, balancing the odds and establishing a new if brief relationship in which their hospitality and helpfulness yielded some reciprocal benefits. Among this story's other teachings (caution, close observation, circumspection), the resulting exchanges of furs and metal tools offered, in memory and in the hindsight of the story, a model for future trade and reciprocity.

The stories of encounter are not all serious. Louis ends his series of "contact" stories with a short one, both startling and partly humorous, about a trade good that made a striking impression—the looking glass. Its reflective quality, literal and figurative, reminds us how stories cast light back upon the people from whom they come, as well as on various versions of history. The Cree word for "mirror" is wa-pa-mo-win, literally, "seeing yourself"—your face comes back at you (Bird, 25 November 2003). We cannot tell what Henry Hudson's Cree visitor did with the looking glass he received for his beaver pelt. But Louis's final story suggests one of many ways in which such a new and remarkable item might become lodged in Cree domestic life and gender relations. It offers a closing metaphor for reflections on encounters with others and how they have been diversely seen and interpreted over the years.

The Omushkego Captive and the Na-to-way-wak: A Remarkable Escape[20]

It happens many times in Hudson Bay and James Bay before the European came, and it happen after they arrive—I don't know exactly how many years ago that it happened the last time—that some other tribes have arrived in this area and came sometimes to simply take the humans away with them, captives. And some tribes would arrive in this area, mostly very innocently, to look for women or a young man, and there is a tribal story about that. There's two kinds of stories. The people who look for the women usually are not raiders, they are not attackers. But they decided sometimes just forcefully come into the community and take the women they want, and if they find any resistance—of course there will be a resistance—so turns into ugly massacre, killing, so usually these people who came from the distance from somewhere would kill off the children, the elders, and anyone that stand in their way and take what they want. They would take the young lady, and then they would take a man if they want, and then take him home.

These are not raiders, they are not attacking to kill, but they are forced to kill, because there is this resistance. And they take the young men home, they take the young women home for their relatives to marry, to avoid, what do they call this thing, not to marry their relatives too closely, to avoid the weakness that involve when that happens. In inner marriages, the relationship marriages, usually develop the very bad effect, deformation or weaknesses or some disease, so to avoid that they would find a fresh blood, different kind of blood to mix into their line. So this is the reason why it's important for them, it's so important that it may involve

20 Recorded by Louis Bird, 21 March 2004, Winnipeg; transcribed by Jennifer S.H. Brown in consultation with Louis Bird. Lytwyn (2002: 74–79) summarizes other accounts, Cree and European, of hostilities involving the Na-to-way-wak; see note 1.

killing. So their idea, it's a right thing, it's a survival thing. But to those who are attacked, it's a very bad thing.

Then there is another kind that I would consider raid. Raid means they attack the camp of the Omushkego people and then they will take women, especially the young teenagers, the young men, and sometimes even the elderly lady who is skilful in repairing and everything, for their servant. These tribes and these kinds of people, they were called in our language, we could say, a-to-way-wak.[21] A-to-way-wak, I think they used to call them, which just mean something like the raiders, or kidnappers, that nature, because that's the way they do.

The story that I wanted to tell was about this young man—he probably would have been twenty when he was kidnapped and carried away to captivity. And he tells the story. This has happened many times before the European came, and this particular story happens to be this young man, who is not a teenager but a man, a young man. He was taken down south by these captors, way south somewhere where the people lived together, and their houses seems to be big, not like the tepees that the Omushkego use and the way they live. These people live differently, it's more like community, and this is where he was taken. And he tells a story about other captives that were with him. He observe during his captivity other members or captives were being killed in a certain season, and they were made sacrificial offerings sort of thing. Actually what happens in that camp, they would pick the season, and then kill this being in sacrificial order and then after they kill this innocent person and then they would ... cook it as sacrificial offering. But they don't burn it right out into a crisp, they just cook it more like, in rituality. After it's cooked or, I believe, if it's boiled, if it's cooked by boiling or stew, they cut it into small pieces, and each member of the band would be circularly sitting around the big enclosure, and each will have a piece, and then they will have this. And their belief is that they will extend their life.[22] That's their belief. So this was the sacrificial offering.

---

21 At the end of this story, the term used is "Na-to-way-wak," and in discussion, Louis decided it was his preferred term. An old term, *na'towe'wa, was widely used in Algonquian languages to refer to various Iroquoian groups. Some have translated it as "snake," but Ives Goddard believes that this is a later extension and that it "should instead be compared to the verbal element *-a'towe—'speak a foreign language', to which it can be related by regular grammatical processes" (1978: 320). Both variants, then, with and without the initial n, have validity. See also note 1.

22 An Omushkego comparison is the reasoning of We-mis-shoosh for killing his sons-in-law in Chapter 3. On Iroquois views and ritual practices surrounding captives, anthropophagy, and the symbolism of the "boiling war kettle," see Richter 1992: 35–37.

This man told a story about that. And his time was arrived too; he knows that he will be probably next. But the person that he was kept by as his guard, as a captive, was friendly. The family that he was kept in, the older lady or some elder have trained him to try to save himself as they get to know him and begin to love him as a friend. They decided, "Maybe you shouldn't be killed, maybe you should learn how to escape, you know, by your own cultural practice, probably if you have some gift; have you dream anything in your dream quest that you could apply for your safety or to survive?" So he remembered, yes, he remembered as a young boy he had dreamt something that he did not quite understand what that is. So his captors, the keepers, the elder said, "You go back to your dream. Go back to that dream and see, and try to apply it for yourself to save yourself." So it so happened; he dreamt. He dreamt a saviour for himself, and he kept it secret. And when the time comes for his turn to be killed, whatever reason, he willingly give in, otherwise he would never escape anyway, so he submit to it and they already prepared. You know he can escape by now, because he has trained himself.

So as the day approach then he was taken into a gathering place, where they usually kill a sacrificial offering. He was asked, in there amongst the group, amongst the tribe, he was asked what was his last wish, this is the last day of his life. So he said, "I do wish, I have one wish. I like to dance before I die, and I could dance seven times around this fireplace, and my seventh time, then I will give myself to you." So the leaders, the elder says, "It sounds innocent enough, it's right enough request"—says, "allow him to dance." Then they get the drummers and singers to sing and he begin to dance. He begin, around and around, lingers a time, and then he decided that he noticed one elder was sitting right on the edge, and every time when he passed there, the elder will hold the wooden spoon, and he noticed there was a big pot there where he's going to be cooked, this young man. He notice what the old man's sitting there for, because when he is killed and cooked into the pot, he want to dip the spoon at least, to have the soup. That's what his mind's about, this old guy, and he was too eager to do that, and he come very close to where this young man was dancing. Sort of give him an angry feeling towards the old man. So he dance.

On the last, sixth dance, he says, "May I, one more request?" The elder says, "Sure, what is it?" So he said, "I wish to dance my last round with a tomahawk." The elder says, "That's innocent enough, give him the tomahawk." Also the elders were very, very eager to finish off this process, so they gave him a tomahawk. And he received the tomahawk, and then he went to dance around for the last round. He had decided already what he would do with this tomahawk. As he passed by the elder who was eager to eat him, he just give him one quick whack over the head and knock the old man down dead. In doing so he jumped into the opening of the smoke area, the smoke hole of the structure, and he jump up into the roof. And everybody screamed in the inside, and some guards were running outside to see if they can catch him outside. As they see, the only thing they saw was the black raven flew away from the building, and off he goes, making that sound the raven makes. So that was his escape. He return home to tell us the story.

That is one of the stories that's included in what we call a-to-way-wuk or sometimes na-to-way-wuk stories, or all these kinds of different names of the people that did raid or attack the Omushkego people in James Bay and Hudson Bay area. That's the end.

Omens, Mysteries, and First Encounters with Europeans

Today is February 27, the year 2002, and time is about 6 a.m. I am recording this tape on the subject of the Hudson Bay area first contact of the Europeans of the Omushkego people on the shores of the Hudson Bay. There are many stories that have been told by our people, their experience of the first contact between the white people from distant land. It's going to be a very condense form of this recording because someplace in my collection this same subject had been recorded in my Cree language, and therefore these words are from many, many different elders who have heard the story in various ways, not very uniform. But in order to keep it on the record, I have decided at least to record a small part of each that it may be written down someday, and then perhaps in time, other part of information will be found by the First Nation people who remember this story so it can be written down in proper sequence. Now, I am going to do my style of telling story which usually I put things in a sequence. As a storyteller I have developed this kind of thing and now I want to start from the beginning.

There is a story that came down to us from our ancestors in time past, even before the European ever set foot on this land. I always try to emphasize, different stories have different names; different stories have different purposes. This kind of story is called "quotation story"—in our language we say like this: ma-ka-aa-it-tway-koo-pa-ney. So the last part is where it says exactly, end of quotation, that is what it actually mean. The person who speaks are repeating the words of a person who has said something and that's all there is—a statement is short. Then the story open. Sometimes the story is very long and somewhere along in the middle, there is that word of a person about the story who said something—his word has been kept alive for some good reason, or sometimes for the question—sometimes it's mystical, sometimes it's dramatic. For that reason it can be remembered and the story come to light. Sometimes the story doesn't come to light, but the story will be found in years to come to have been the prediction of something to happen in the future. This [story] is one of them.

"I Cannot Have Anything from these We-mis-ti-go-si-wak"

To make the story short, I am going to say there was a custom of the First Nation in Hudson Bay and James Bay area when an elder, especially a man or even an elder lady, when an elder became to be so old and became to be bothersome for the survival of the family, the elder will know when the time is up that he or she has to decide not to burden her/his family any further and would demand to bc left behind in a place upon the land in which they live.

So in this case, there was this old man who was blind and very frail and was not able to travel any more with the group, and in a time of famine, and also in the time when people should move to the next arriving food source, which they used to do. It was this time that this elder decided that he should be left behind, so that he believe for his kindness the rest of his family can survive before they get so hungry and too weak and unable to move. In order to avoid this situation, he demanded that he should [be] left behind. And he was left behind, in a place where he had requested and there to die by himself. This was done as he requested.

Then, whether it's unfortunate or fortunate for him, he survive; he survived the duration by some mystical reason which he could not explain, but said that he constantly found a piece of food and piece of water beside where he lay, which keeps him alive until the season should change into spring season, and then managed to crawl out from the wooden teepee structure where he was left. And he managed to crawl into the creek—the sound of the water. He went there to sit beside it—blind. Again he said he always found a piece of meat or some kind of a food item beside him, and the water that he can drink. This is a mystery that he did not understand, but he did understand it meant that his time was not up.

And where he sat is on the sunny side of the small creek. Also in that place there were plenty tall white poplar trees. It was amongst those trees that he was sitting. And it was in the afternoon—in the warm day—when he was sunning himself there, that someone heard him singing, a man who was wayfarer or person that was trapping by himself—a young man—who found him. And here is his quotation that we repeat. He [the old man] says, "I cannot, I cannot have anything from these We-mis-ti-go-si-wak"; he calls the trees We-mis-ti-go-si-wak, and that means the trees that sway at the top by the wind and have the white, white bark—so we call them We-mis-ti-go-si-wak. That was the word that the young man—first time he heard that word—remembers, and this was long time ago, long time before the European ever came. And the word that he said was remembered by this young man.

In time, some people arrive in their [Omushkego] territory and our people found a name for them and they call them We-mis-ti-go-si-wak. Why do they call them We-mis-ti-go-si-wak? Some elders have tried to break down his code word, We-mis-ti-go-si-wak—what does it mean? So We-mis-ti-go-si-wak means people who are—travel with the wind. Way-pas-ten is something that sails without control—that's what it means, way-pas-ten. Then, we-mis-ti-go-so: mis-tic means the wood, and a wooden boat.[23] So it was said. That was what the old man was saying, that these beings will be here with no help to us at all, at the beginning at least. So our ancestors have translated this word. That's the reason I picked this story at the beginning, and that was a long time before the European came to the Hudson Bay area as we call it today. In time past—nobody know how long the time went—before the European ever show in the Hudson Bay, James Bay area, there were many events, many stories came upon and gone in that area. Then one day again, amongst the tribes in the Hudson Bay area, the Omushkego people had been visited by many tribes, many different kind; they had been ambushed, and killed, and slaughtered, and they have sometimes stand against the other tribes who came to attack them. There are many stories and there were other stories

---

23 See also John Long citing the findings of linguist C. Douglas Ellis who notes the James Bay Cree use of this term for "white man," although his etymology varies slightly (Long 1985: 162, n. 62).

that were kinder and a bit more gentle. And some stories has been remembered that later in years came to recognize what happened in the past, that awaken a person's mind to remember the past, and this is the second story.

"In the Memory of the Wikeson I-skwe-o"

It so happened that during the time, maybe after the old man have been quoted of his word, then something happen to these Omushkegowak in their territory, something that is not really outstanding but just came out later to be quoted again. Again a person says something that was understood later. I begin to wonder, who was this person? So this was the story.

Amongst our Omushkego people on James Bay and Hudson Bay they have the hunting style which sometimes takes place in the late part of March and sometimes the whole month of April when the weather begin to change and warmer. In those days, the hunting tool was only bow and arrows, and sometimes what we call pe-mo-te-squan which means sling, sometimes the other one is pe-mi-ti-shway-hi-gan; it's something to do with the two weight that tied to the string, and this is what people used to have to hunt the caribou. Two heavy objects tied into a string that is maybe three feet long (I'm just guessing), so this is what people used to throw into the front legs of the caribou running, if it's ten feet or five feet from their distance.[24] And when they do that, they trip the caribou momentarily, and they were able to kill it with the spear, if they don't have the bow and arrow—but this was done only when they have a special cooperative hunting which they call funneling or corralling caribous—corral. But they don't have to have sticks or anything or wire, they only put objects on either side of the funnel shape or fencing thing, and chase the caribous into that and into the narrow end, there where the hunters concealed snow holes—like a trench—so maybe three hunters would be sitting there. And their idea is to get these caribou come close to them and stand up and while [the caribou are] momentarily forced to stop—that's when they hit them with the bow and arrows or throw the slings—I mean tripping slings at their legs—to trip them. So these stones that are attached to strings usually wrapped around in the caribou's front legs; if they do at the right times, they can catch all four legs and the caribou

---

24 This is reminiscent of the bolas traditionally used for game on the pampas of Argentina in South America.

would just simply drop momentarily while he is struggling to release him-self—to release the string, and then the people would jump at the caribou and stab it or pierce it with their tool. So this is what they were doing. But in this time, the sling was not used, but the bow and arrows, because it was warmer.[25]

And there was the man who was called—he had a strange name. They call him Wa-sha-hay-ni-goom—the only way I can say is, Cut-away Nose—whatever that is. That's what it sounds like. I cannot describe the nose, but that's what they call him. He was a strange person, nobody quite know exactly how he came to join the tribes and he was a strange guy. They say when he join those group of people, when he attached himself to them, he became one of them, one of the family in that family. There he was—he attached himself to a man who has three or two sons—very great hunters. And that family also has in-laws, and probably about three families, large families, with many young men and women. He was in that group of people, this man, and he was known as Wa-sha-hay-ni-goom.

And when the time come to hunt together with corralling caribous or funneling caribous, he was assigned, because he didn't know the hunting style, he was told to work with the women, the young women and also young boys who are fast runners. He was assigned to do that job. That is, to block the caribous as they go into the funnel—to block them from the large end which they run in. When they've been shot or been attacked or been shot at the other end, at the small end of the funnel, usually the cari-bous would turn back and speed back into the opening space in which end they had come in. It was here that this group of people will have to block those caribous who are rushing at about thirty-five miles an hour with their head hang up high, which usually they do, and blockers try to stop them. And these people—they're in front with their snowshoes—they are supposed to throw anything in the snow and scream as much as they can and try to turn these caribous back into the funnel. That was his job. And he was amongst those young ladies—16-year-old, maybe older—who were experts, I mean who were trained to do that. After successful hunting—after the caribous has been killed and the huntings end—then they begin to drag the caribous into one pile so the leader of the hunting party can divide the meat to the group. And this man, Wa-sha-hay-ni-goom, was

---

25 See Chapter 7, which explains that bows and arrows could not be used in the coldest weather because the bows would break.

there, and he was given one adult caribou and one last-year caribou; he had two because the hunt had been successful.

Then he remembered while they were working out there at the far end, there was a young girl beside him that he was close to that they were screaming their head off trying to turn the caribous round. And he noticed how hard she had worked and he sympathized [with] her. The women were not given separate share of animal—separate caribou—to these women who work so hard. For that purpose, he felt sorry for the young girl who had worked so hard with him. And when he was given the caribou and everything, when he skinned the caribou that he have, he gave one hind quarter to this young girl, and he said, "In the memory of the Wilkeson I-skwe-o." Wikeson I-skwe-o, so it sounds like Wilk-a-son when you want to repeat that and try to catch English sound. So what makes him say Wikason I-skwe-o?—it was a woman he remembers, in the memory of this woman, and he gave this young lady a piece. It was that word which he says, "wigkisan, Wikason I-skwe-o," that's what he says when he hand the meat over to the young girl. Of course the young girl protests, says no, no, you know, because she sees on the women's side. The women were considered a bit, I don't know, maybe a bit less than man—less of a person, because she was under maybe, under the other family and she was having her share from there. She protest a bit but he says, "No, you take it, you work as much as hard as I am and you must have yours." She accepted in that term, and the other people say, "OK, if you want to give away your food, that's fine."

So there's that quotation again that has been talked about, and nobody knew for sure exactly where this man is from. It has been said at times during his stay with this family group, he didn't stay with only one family, he stayed with other families in other times, but nobody says exactly how long—how many years that he mingled with the Omushkegos. People say at times when he is in a bad mood, or some accident happened to him that just hurt maybe his hand or anything, he would utter some word that he used which must have been a curse word. The word that they been saying is that quoting him, he says, "by gosh," it sounds like. He would utter that word when he's stubbed or startled or hurt accidentally. So that word has been used to imitate his word. But nobody knows what that is. He didn't explain.

And sometimes it's said, in a time when they were resting, or sometime when they sit around and someone has to entertain, to tell a story which has happened many times, maybe someone would be asked, "Tell us a

story" or "Tell us a legend"—to pass time. I guess he was asked one time
to tell a story, but he says, "No, I don't know any one of your stories.
Your stories are different than mine because I came only to visit." So
they ask him, "Where did you come from?" He says, "Far, far distance."
"How far?" they said, the Omushkegos, and he says, "No, no, it is a
distance that I cannot tell you exactly how far it would be." He says,
"The life there is different than it is here, the place where I came from, the
people have a large house, it's stone buildings and high. And in that place
also, it's a different climate, and in the rivers there is a different kind of
creatures, and the flying creatures are not the same as you have here."
And he described also the very thick forest, like different trees, and that
was all. There was nothing else that he could explain. That's three strange
things that he has been known to remember by this man. And that was
the end of that one.[26]

Cha-ka-pesh and the Sailors

Now, I have missed the very old story. It was in time before any memories
can be remembered. Now, I'm going back, even further back where our
legends were created from. The things that happened before—a time when
one could not recall when did it happen. A time where the legends came
from. It was one of those legends, that we called Cha-ka-pesh. This character, the little guy, plays a great part in one of the famous legends.

Cha-ka-pesh was a mystical man, he was a powerful shaman; and small
as he may be, like a midget, he was a man, nevertheless, who possess all
kinds of cultural powers and spiritual things and shaman—powerful mi-
tew, that is. He was a person that usually challenge anything. Anything
that is not supposed to be done. He lives with his sister. And his sister was
the wisest woman that ever lived, who has knowledge about everything—
any question that he has, this little man would only bring it to his sister,
and then he would get some answer. Sometimes some very good sound

---

26 A name like Wilkeson surfaces once in Abacuk Pricket's account of Hudson's voyage. One
   Wilkinson, according to Llewelyn Powys, was possibly an early member of the crew, but if so,
   Powys believed he was let go before the ship sailed (1927: 126). No Wilkinson was listed
   among those on board at the time of the mutiny. Wa-sha-hay-ni-goom could be an English survivor of Hudson's shallop, the young captive mentioned in de Vignau's story above, but that
   leaves "Wilkeson" unexplained. A more plausible connection is with a Thomas Wilkinson
   who served the HBC for a number of years in the 1680s and may have been one of the HBC
   men whom the French, when they took over HBC posts, sent off to survive on their own in the
   Albany area (Scott Stephen, personal communication, November 2004).

advice. One of the usual sound advice from his sister is not to do anything that is dangerous for his health, and of course, he sweared to his chest [crossed himself] that he will not do anything that he's not supposed to do. But unfortunately, like any other child, he will go right on doing exactly the opposite of what he promised not to do. It was one of those days that he had done something which he had tried in the farthest extent—something that he used to do but didn't know the result. Because he was a shaman, he had accomplished to be able to travel far with his mind power, to be instantly where he wants to be by his own shaman power.

So he had been using this skill for his benefit and when he wants it—not all the time—and therefore it was one day in the evening that he wanted to go way out into a large body of water which they call the dirty water— it's the salt water—where they always found the shore birds that are very beautiful to eat. Shore birds—so it always happen in the Hudson Bay and James Bay area.[27] But he was living inland—quite a distance inland at that time, but he wanted to have the shore birds, you know, for supper. It was very late in the evening—very close to sunset. So he decide to travel there instantly with his power. So as he wished it—as he willed to do it, instantly he was standing on the shore of the big water, Ki-sti-ka-min, so they call it—big water. There he stands and sure enough there are shore birds and all that stuff; they were already flying because this was the month of August. And as he stand there on the shore and using his bow and arrow, shooting these birds, as he get a few of them, then he decide, "well, this should be OK."

Then as he was sitting there enjoying this nice sunset, very calm, there was an echo. He know that there was an echo as he was sitting there and watching the water disappear into the horizon, almost seem to blend to the sky. He heard a noise all of a sudden towards the bay, towards the water, which sounds, ho-hee, ho-hee, ho-hee, and he wonders, it's a human voice, it's not any animal voice, it's a human. So he stood there and wondered. What human can be out there? There is no land, no nothing. Could there be a land out there which I cannot see? He was very curious but it was sunset already, and time for him to get home. So he decided, maybe I should go home first, so he just traveled backwards again the way he had traveled—speed traveling! So he find himself right close where he left, not far from his home, still having this mind bugging him, want-

---

27 The Cree name for Hudson Bay is win-ni-peg, dirty (undrinkable) or salt water. See Chapter 2 in which Louis's story of the Giant Skunk and the wolverine explains how the water became dirty.

ing to know what that is. He went home with his birds and everything. And when he got to his home, he just walk right in—not really thinking about anything but enjoy to be home in the evening. He brought in his hunting bag and give it to his sister as usual, and she dig in and she found the shore birds and everything.

So, she says, "What was your day?" and he says, "Well, I had a very good day." And she says, "When did you go to the shore?" "Ah," he says, "just close to the evening." Then his sister right away understand. So she says, "So you fooled around, eh?" And he says, "Well, I just couldn't help it, I wanted to have a shore birds for supper. So I just take the time to get there." That means he uses his power to get there very quickly. Then he begin to remember what he heard, and he says, "My sister, I heard something when I was there." His sister says, "What is it like, what does it sound like?" And he says, "It sound like this: ho-hee, ho-hee, ho-hee—three times," he says, "and it's a human voice. And out there I don't see a thing, just water." Then his sister says, "Well, do you remember I told you that you had to watch yourself what you do? Sometimes when you travel with this power, sometimes you can land somewhere that you don't know what it is." So he says, "Ah, and what could that be?" The sister says, "You never know when or what—how far can you travel when you use your power that way?" And he begin to wonder, mmm. Then they sort of talked about it for a little while, and the sister says, "You could have been traveling very far in the future, or even back or something like that, and landed there in a different time than your own time." And that put more curiosity into his mind. So his sister says, "Don't you ever do that again. I told you many times, things that you do sometimes can kill you. And this one is one of most dangerous things to do."

So he promised seriously as he did all the time; he says, "Sister, you scare me, I'm not going to do that again." His sister says, "Promise me, you are not going to do that again." So he says, "Sister, I promise you, cross my heart (something in that nature); I will not do that again." Of course, none of this mean anything to him, the more he promise the more he was curious; he wanted to know how did that happen? So sure enough they went to bed very peacefully, and in the morning he got up with a good grouchy feeling like any other person, not really willing to go, but that's his job—to hunt. His sister automatically prepare his breakfast, and also hand him over his clothes and his dry socks and moccasins and whatever that he needs, and bit of everything to eat and maybe a bit of lunch, and send him off. So he went out, so he remembers—he didn't remember much, so he just took off some other direction, tried to be far away from the camp before the sunrise, which is the custom. As he was heading out there, he had promised his sister not to go towards the bay but to go the opposite direction. So he went to this opposite direction which he promise he will go, away from the bay, because he had promised not to go there for the time being—and therefore he took off.

Then, as he walks away, he remember this promise that he was not going to go there and it bothers him over this; heavy curiosity, he wants to know, he just couldn't understand. So he walks towards to the west or wherever, away from the bay, and then as his curiosity grab him, he just make a U-turn, back towards the bay. But he did not go right away, he just traveled for awhile arguing with himself and trying to remember the warning of his sister. Temporary he stop; he says, "Ok, whatever, I'm just going to hunt here. Don't have to do that." So he hunted all day, not successful very much, but at least he did his job.

It was again in the evening by the time when he remembers this curiosity that get the hold of him all of a sudden because it was beautiful evening. Then he decide, "Maybe I should go—I should go there. I wonder if I could hear that voice again." And his sister has said, "Don't you ever go there again." It was in the morning that he was told what it was because his sister has to dream first, the vision dream. He had heard the answer in the morning; his sister has said, "What you have heard is that you have traveled in a time that is going to happen in the future. And you have came upon the human being that sailed on the sea with the ship with the sailing. A big ship and that's what you hear. These people—what you hear is what they yell when they haul the sailing material up, and that's what you hear." That's what make Cha-ka-pesh so curious—that his promise had to be broken, and that's what he wanted to see. So in that time he stayed out very late just to exactly the time that he have traveled to that place, hoping that he was going to be right on time again where he left off. So he did, he just willed his power—there he was, instantly into the time of yesterday when he was there. When he turned back, when he decided to go home, there he stood again backwards to hear the voice again, and he did hear it. So he decided this I have to go and see, to see those humans wherever they are.

So what he did was, some people say he took a shot at the seagull—knock it down—and then as the seagull is stunned and there on the ground, he jumped to its body and he took off towards the sea, fly over there in that instant, you know, before sunset. Right directly where the voice came from, he went there, and there he saw this strange little island which has a cloud over it. Then he looked at it and fly towards it as a sea-gull will do and landed on top of its trees, which is actually the mast of the sailing vessel. And there he sits, and he watched those people walking the bottom and then they were busy working away somehow, and he saw what they do. Every time when they work together, when they pull some-thing heavy with the string, with the strange kind of gadget, then one of them would say, not "ho heap," but he would say, "Heave ho, heave ho, heave ho," and that's what he heard the night before. His sister has said that exactly and that's what he saw.

He stick around for a little while and he came down to the gunwale—stand there to watch, to investigate the things they were using. And it was that time one of the persons was chewing something, eating something—throw it down and it drops on the floor, and he picks it up, and he eat—of course the seagulls always pick up something. So one of the sailors just threw a little bit of piece to him, to the seagull—and he grab that piece and took off because the other person was ready to throw a stick at him, so he decided to take off. He fly towards the shore of course, and jump out of the seagull's body and became him—Cha-ka-pesh. Then he looked at what he pick up and this was an object that people eating [hard tack or ship's biscuit?]. He just put it in his bag and then again travel back to his place. So he have seen—but it's sort of a scary experience, you know; what if he was hit with a stick or whatever he was thrown at? He couldn't under-stand these people, the language they speak was different, and strange boats and strange things—many things were strange.... Better not to men-tion anything to his sister because he had promised never to go there.

That evening he went home. He hunted along the way and he did get a few rabbits, and then when he get home he gave the bag to his sister as usual, and she pick out the rabbits. Then also that object came out which was totally different, and she says, "What's this?" And he—"Oh, oh, yes that's the stuff that ..."— he couldn't name it—what it is. He tried to say, "It's—it's a mushroom"; but she say, "No way, this is not a mushroom that I know of." So she break the piece off and taste it, and it taste very—something strange. Instantly she remembers that she had warn her brother yesterday not to go back to the place where he hear something. She says, "I see that you did not listen to me. You went to investigate the place I said don't go." Of course he say, "I am sorry," and furiously trying to apologize to his sister for disobeying. But his sister was very mad, give him all the verbal punishment, saying, "If that guy had hit your head, what would happen to you then? You would die and that's what I've been trying to tell you. When you do these things, you will lose your life and I will never find you." So he just submit to his sister and said, "I am sorry, I'm sorry," and that was the end of the story for that one. So this was a long time before— we should put this story before any other story. Then we know it is a start—that life would change on the shores of Hudson Bay and James Bay.

Strangers on Akimiski Island: Helping a Grounded Ship

It so happen later in years, that the people in Hudson Bay finally actually get to contact some people who have the sailing ships. These were the Europeans and they were the ones who say "Heave ho," every time when they pull the string to hoist the sail. It has been predicted a long time ago that they will be here. When it happens then the first time, the Omushkego people on the shores of James Bay or Hudson Bay, they have seen, they have heard these noises, they have heard the thunders of the fire stick that they have on these ships when they fought each other on the Bay amongst the ice floes.[28] People used to think it is the ice that really cracks to each other and that is what they hear, but it was one time proven to be—it was the guns of those ships that they heard and saw the light ... between York Factory and the tip of the south of James Bay. Nobody knows exactly where, but some people pinpoint fully into the Cape Henrietta Maria today. Where the shore sometimes used to [be] very, very close when the high tide is there—ships can go turn there—turn around, and it was in that spot that sometimes the ship will wait on one side until the high water come. And it so happened they come upon to each other, and then of course—they blasted at each other with their cannon and this is what the First Nation heard.[29] They didn't see, but it was later in time they saw a flash when this happen.

---

28 The English and French engaged in sporadic conflict for control of Hudson Bay from the 1680s until the Treaty of Utrecht in 1713, which awarded Hudson Bay to the English. Hudson, James, and others also fired their ships' guns as signals and salutes, and the strange sounds and flashes carried long distances over the low-lying shores of the Bay.

29 In 1631, as noted earlier, Thomas James named this cape after Queen Henrietta Maria; see note 13 for the Cree name. James met rival explorer Luke Fox somewhere north of the cape on 29–31 August 1631. The two English ships would have signaled and greeted each other with guns, peacefully in this instance (Davies 2003: 224–25).

Then it begin to be known at that time later that they so happen to find some of these European wayfarers that got stuck on the north side of the Akimiski Island, which is located inside of James Bay—close to the west shore of the Hudson Bay. The island is large and the north side of it is just like any other shores of the Hudson Bay shore. It has a long, long stretch—slope of tidewater. And it was there that a person saw something that is extraordinary sight, which looks like a whole bunch of trees that washed into the bay with the roots and land floating out of the mouth of the waters, which usually happens—you could see these things stick out of the mouth of the river—a tree standing on the moss and everything, and that's all they think.[30] They said, "This is unusual, washed trees into the land." But it was so big, and they begin to investigate from the distance, and they know it was not the trees; it was something else. So they looked at it from the distance, three or four families and they been watching it; they come closer, closer—sneaking up onto the shore—from the shore, hiding. Then finally they saw it is a ship and there is people in it and the trees they thought [they saw], it was the mast. Each time when there is a tide coming, they would see those sails being hoist and when the wind is from the land, they tried to sail out—apparently that's what they were doing. They'd been watching them and studying them. Without success— these people couldn't move because the tide is not high enough. So they're stuck; they begin to know that they are stuck.

One day, they [Omushkegowak] decided to expose themselves to them. They send in a decoy—one man agreed to walk in the open towards those people. He walks onto the high point of land, expose himself there as if he doesn't see anything. Sure enough, these white people saw him, and they begin to get down to the dry land and then walk towards him and give him a sign that they are friendly. And the man just stood his ground, giving himself whatever happens, to find out whether these people are dangerous or not. So the people came up to him and he understand the sign that is a friendly sign, so he allowed them to come. Of course they could not communicate because they speak not the same language—differ- ent language, which he couldn't understand. But the sign language he can understand—yes, he could understand the sign language—so he under- stood that they were friendly, and the visitors understand him that he has no intention of doing anything. Somehow they meet.

---

30 Spring floods often carry huge hunks of riverbanks with trees still on them down to the mouths of the rivers on Hudson Bay; what was odd was to see such a thing away from the mouth of a river.

And the people speak to him in that sign language saying, "Bring your friends, and show them the boat that we are stuck," and says, "We need help." He understands that. I think they gave him some kind of an item, whether it was food or anything I don't know; it's a gift—a sign of peace which he understand. So he went back. He went back to meet his friends and tell them, these people are actually friendly, for the time being anyway, and he says, "As I understand, they need our help. I think they are stuck there, and they cannot get out." So they all agree, say, "OK, we will go and help"; but they are very careful—"Maybe it's a trick."

So the whole group—I don't know exactly how many people were, but they went to see them, and they saw exactly their problem—they've been stuck. They have been washed into the shore or came to the shore—two crews—on the highest tide of the day when it usually happen in the middle of the full moon when the water's high. They were stuck there until the next full moon—they understand that—of course they cannot speak to them, but they understand the situation. And these people are working hard during that period and trying to push their boat out into the deep, but they couldn't do it. They tried to make a slipway by the drifting logs and everything, and try to put the stones away and all that stuff towards the deep water. And they had their string that angles out into the water which helps them to pull, and also hoisted the sail so to help them to try to go into the deep water. Of course, since the water is too shallow, they couldn't make it. So when they get there, they went to work for them, those Native people. They work together, and they explain to them that you have to wait until the next high moon—high tide. Of course also the people understand that, but they want to prepare other stuff that it will come much easier, quicker. So they did prepare for that special day, and in the meantime they get friendly and then they begin to admire each other, and maybe study each other—the guns and things that they have.

It was at that time that these First Nation people begin to understand the kind of tools they have. The axe, the steel axe, and a few other things, and the small utensils they use. So there was a little exchange—very little, and of course the white people wanted to have some examples of their clothing, they say. That was the first time they ever meet the Europeans in the Hudson Bay or in the James Bay—they managed to have those people to release their boat from the shore and then able to sail out. That was the first time, they say, that they actually contact with these people but they didn't know who they are. They didn't know what kind of people they were, what nationality they were. They only understand the sign language; whatever object they get from them they didn't keep, [it] could not be traced what kind of a European were they. That is the end of the story.[31]

So begin the fur trade later, and the impact of this trade begin to change the lives of these first people who saw the European. And it was about that time too, the trade begin and the effect and the things that comes along with it. The trade goods were sometimes useful, sometimes were not much of a good thing. The most valuable items they exchange from the white man—the men was very thankful about the fire-stick, or the thunder-sticks they call it, which was the gun. And as cruel as it is, they still like to try it out. Another thing that they really enjoy was the steel axe. The steel axe was very useful—it's durable, very different from the stone knives, so they enjoy the trade. They even mention about the sound of steel when you hit the tree and singing, it must have been tempered well. They also enjoy the small items as the kettles. Women enjoyed decorating with kind of things that they can trade from these strange people.

Wa-pa-mo-win, the Mirror

There was a story about the trade that became funny. The mirror was a fascinating thing, and the story goes to say that there was this man, it was later in years, not the first time—it was well into the 1800s, I think, that the mirror came in to be traded for a shiny object. Of course they valued it very much, the first people, when they saw that and enjoyed it. One man was a good hunter and the Hudson's Bay Company [trader] want the people to compete with each other so they can bring much fur which he needs. And the trader trick this guy who was a good hunter, who was not a very good trapper, but he wanted to persuade him to go trapping to bring more fur. So the trick the Hudson Bay managers used to do is that they used to have many strange objects which they kind of left in front of those men to make them want it so much, and they would make a bargain with them.

And it was one of those things that the manager has—a small—I don't know what size of a mirror it was—so he showed it to him, he says, "I will

---

31 In 1996, an Ojibwe (Anishinaabe) elder, Charlie George Owen (Omishoosh) of Pauingassi, Manitoba, told a story about an Ojibwe first contact, possibly with French traders on James Bay in the 1680s when the French were challenging HBC claims to fur trade monopoly. Its outcome was darker, perhaps reflecting the trade dominance that the HBC was to achieve. See Brown and Roulette, in press, 2005.

give you this if you'll bring me some more fur." I don't know exactly what he did, but anyway the man must have been a very stupid man, so he look at the mirror and he saw himself there and he admire himself. Knowing what he looks like (and I guess he thought he was a very hand-some man), he thought he will keep it, and he went trapping and he brought a lot of fur to this manager and he finally got his reward. So he treasures this gift, his special prize and never allow anyone to look at it. He has his own medicine bag, shall we say, which nobody is supposed to peek in. He had this little bag in which he keeps this item.

And he had a wife, and maybe he had a kid; but anyway, his wife was now getting old and he was an old man. But every so often, he will bring out an object in their home in the early morning and he would look at it, and the wife would watch him and he would smile—many different smiles and very beautiful smile at time, and she begin to wonder, what does he look at? She begin to know that there are pictures—human pictures—like an artist who draw the faces of things. So she thought it's a picture, it must be a picture, she thought. She'd get curious—she knows it's against the custom to dig into the man's personal belongings—especially the med-icine bag. She couldn't help. She begin to get jealous, she thinks that it's a woman in there that he looks at so lovingly and, "Never do that to me," she thought. Then she promised herself, "I'm going to look into that woman and I'm going to find out what that woman is and give him [her] a blast of my mind after that."

So one day she had enough courage to look into his personal bag—medicine bag—and very eagerly or, what do they call it—the feeling of wanting something so much, and the curiosity is so strong and high that she literally shake, mad at the same time and wonder, and took the object out—take a look at it—feeling momentarily—she scream, and she said, "Ahhh, what an awful-looking lady! How come he could admire such ugly looking woman?" And she put it aside. She threw it back in there very quickly and went back to her place and satisfied. No, it was not a beautiful lady he was looking at! But the thing is—what she saw there, it was her face, and that is the joke upon her. So this has been a story that has been repeated for our fun today. That's the end of that.

6

"The Wailing Clouds"
(Pa-so-way-yan-nask chi-pe-ta-so-win)[1]

Introduction
ANNE LINDSAY[2]

The story of "The Wailing Clouds" is a vibrant part of the Omushkego oral tradition. It teaches the Omushkego worldview and the very tangible consequences of failing to listen to an elder as well as of "sinning against nature." It describes and explains the devastation created by diseases brought to the lowlands through trade with Europeans as well as what happened when the people failed to respect their value system. It also describes the cultural strategies the Omushkegowak used to combat a previously unknown disease. "The Wailing Clouds" locates traditional practices like hunting and competitive games within a cultural fabric and tells about the seasonal migrations of the people, the spring festivals, and the use of the wealth of resources in the region as seen by the Omushkegowak, though sometimes missed by Europeans.[3] The story is embedded in and enriches Omushkego

---

1 Louis translates Pa-so-way-yan-nask chi-pe-ta-so-win as "night before sound echoed to predict the doomsday for those people" (personal communication, 17 July 2003).

2 My thanks to all the people who generously contributed their expertise and resources. In particular, I thank Louis Bird, who not only contributed the story itself, but patiently explained many details and concepts, and provided valuable context. I would also like to thank Jennifer Brown, who has provided resources, given insights, asked provocative questions, and edited the final work. I thank George Fulford for his help with both language and concepts, and Paul Hackett who provided resources and comments on disease and epidemics in the "Petit Nord." My thanks also to D. Ann Herring for her comments and suggestions, and David Pentland for his help with understanding Cree concepts in language; the staff of the Provincial Archives of Manitoba; Donna Sutherland for her knowledge of fur trade history and Louis Bird's genealogy; and Brian Myhre, Robert Tymstra, and Kreg Ettenger for their input and ideas.

3 These spring festivals were not necessarily held annually but they might be held every two or three years, depending on weather and hunting conditions (Bird, personal communication, 10 July 2003). John Oldmixon stated in 1708 that "[the Native people] meet every Spring and Fall, to settle the Disposition of their Quarters for Hunting, Fowling, and Fishing" (Tyrrell 1931: 382).

places like the Ekwan River and Akimiski Island, while preserving Omushkego names in language and history. Today this rich narrative continues to resonate as it provides a sense of continuity between past and present, an understanding of foundation and change, and a source of insight into Omushkego worldview for both Omushkego and other audiences.

Cree narratives can be broken into two broad categories, a-ta-noo-ka-nak, and ti-pa-chi-moo-wi-nan. A-ta-noo-ka-nak are "legends or sacred stories." They tell about events that happened so long ago that nobody knows the people they happened to. Ti-pa-chi-moo-wi-nan recount recent historical events and involve people known to or remembered by the storyteller.[4] "The Wailing Clouds" is an example of a ti-pa-chi-moo-win. Louis Bird describes "The Wailing Clouds" as a quotation story, one that is so well known that the teller need only quote a few words for a knowledgeable audience to recall the whole piece. In this case, the quotation is ha-shyi-ki-ki-na-ki-chi-pa-na-wow-o-ma-ka-ith-ti-yek, literally translated as "you are all tickled to death," then ha-shyi-kit-ashi-it-ti-so-wow-o-ma, ka-ith-ti-yek, or "you are now on last joy before towards your death," "stop, you are overdoing it, your over enjoyment means death," or, more evocatively, "you are dancing to your death."[5]

"The Wailing Clouds" is a story about cultural values, about "blasphemy and retribution."[6] What Louis translates into English as "blasphemy" has two forms: pas-sta-ho-win, a blasphemous act, and pas-sta-moo-win, a spoken blasphemy. In "The Wailing Clouds," the blasphemy is acted, pas-sta-ho-win. The story describes what happens when people break natural law, or forget the rules of righteous living, qua-yask-pi-maa-ti-win.[7] Although Louis uses the closest English terms to describe these concepts, the Omushkego idea of a "sin against nature" cannot be equated with the sort of "natural law" discussed by philosophers like John Locke; rather, it is a set of natural laws where inappropriate acts

---

4 Richard Preston (2002: 76, 254–55) describes these categories in eastern James Bay Cree as âtiyô(h)kan and tépâciman. John Long (1988: 227) states that the Omushkegowak define "ati-nokan" as stories from "time immemorial." Louis states, "Let me explain a little bit of what, the way I understand about the use and application of legends. Legends are supposed to, supposed to be, the actual living stories of individual in time past, where no one can remember who it was, and we don't know when. So the name is applied, fictitious name as "Wi-sa-kay-chak," "Cha-ka-pesh," "We-mis-shoosh," "I-yas," "An-way," all those characters are given to that name for those people who experienced life way back. We don't even know who they are, but it happens to them (Bird, class presentation, University of Winnipeg, 1 April 2003, transcribed by Anne Lindsay).

5 Bird, personal communication, 21 June, 10 July, and 17 July 2003.

6 Bird, quoted in DePasquale, Chapter 2, this volume.

7 Linguist David Pentland describes pas-sta-ho-win as going against the mores of the group, or breaking a taboo (personal communication, 14 July 2003).

result in grave consequences.[8] Louis compares this to children's play getting out of hand. A parent might warn them, telling them to slow down or they will be sorry. If they persist and someone gets hurt, this is not a deliberate punishment but a natural consequence. In "The Wailing Clouds" the festival revelers become so engrossed in their game of tug-of-war they forget themselves, running "out of control." Pas-sta-ho-win, Louis explains, is something that happens just before something goes wrong.[9]

The story of "The Wailing Clouds" tells about spiritual practices such as the Shaking Tent and affirms traditional values such as respect for the knowledge of elders.[10] It describes the importance of following cultural mores, in keeping with traditional values such as qua-yask-pi-maa-ti-win. The terrible consequence of failing to respect qua-yask-pi-maa-ti-win was a catastrophic epidemic. Yet the story does not end with this. It goes on to teach the best way to face an overwhelming problem; the people regain self-control and confront the problem by observing it empirically. By paying attention to the elders' thoughtful study of the problem and through deliberate action, they found a cure for the disease, ending the epidemic. In keeping with Omushkego culture, the story stresses self-control as an appropriate response to a world that can be harsh and threatening.

In the story of "The Wailing Clouds," although the Omushkegowak faced a formidable epidemic disease, they were not passive victims. Their solution to the epidemic was active and practical, and incorporated spiritual and empirical views. For a Western audience, the story underscores the fact that in Omushkego culture, the spiritual and empirical were not opposites in a binary system.[11] The Omushkegowak drew on traditional medical practice—the use of bear grease as an emetic—showing both innovation and continuity of practices. Through this story, it is clear that Omushkego culture and medicine evolved to meet new challenges, including the changes brought by the fur trade.

While "The Wailing Clouds" teaches about proper conduct and cultural values, it also relates historical events that resulted in profound social and demographic changes. Louis suggests that this story happened in the late 1700s or early 1800s, basing this belief on the sequence of family members

---

8 George Fulford, personal communication, 13 June 2003.
9 Bird, class presentation, 1 April 2003: 5.
10 See Chapter 3 in this book.
11 Emetics were a part of the cultural response to a number of problems, for instance, J.S.H. Brown (1971: 20–22) discusses the use of bear grease emetic in the treatment of "Windigos." The intent of the practice appears to be to induce vomiting to expel the "heart of ice" of the wih-ti-go. On changes brought by the trade of guns, see Chapter 7 of this book.

who transmitted "The Wailing Clouds" through the generations. He heard the story from his mother, who in turn heard it from her grandfather, Grand William, or William O-ki-maw. Grand William had heard it from his grandmother. This sequence places the story back at least five generations.[12] The event decimated a once robust population. Louis recalls that "Grand William who told the story, they say that every time when he tell the story you can see his tears running down.... So that, in the years after that, in that, where they talked about [it happening], in the years later, there used to be some bones sticking out from the ground, because they didn't bury them properly. Sometimes the, the foxes would just dig out the bones, all around that ridge that was there. So the story is true, it is very true."[13]

While the overall tone of "The Wailing Clouds" is sombre, it also shows the happiness that life could hold in the James Bay-Hudson Bay Lowlands, the strength of the people, and their active strategy for dealing with a powerful unknown disease. Louis describes the seasonal migrations of the Omushkegowak and the joy of being reunited with friends and family at the spring festival. He depicts the exuberance and pride expressed in the many competitive games and the bounty of food. The spring festival had something for everyone who could attend.

While situated in the past, "The Wailing Clouds" is woven into the current lives of Omushkego listeners. It evokes a familiar landscape, the shores of James Bay, and ties it to memories of traditional foods, activities, games, and hunting practices. It provides a glimpse of a time when the fur trade had changed the lives of the Omushkegowak only a little. Before the devastation of the epidemic, the Omushkegowak of the story were numerous and enjoyed a rich life. They traveled in small family groups to take advantage of the seasonal resources of the region and looked forward to the spring gatherings when families would be reunited. Guns and some trade goods had had an impact on their lives, but not to the extent that later contact would.[14] Following the time of the story, the population was decimated, and the festival grounds abandoned.

---

12 Louis Bird's mother, Scholastique Pennishish, was the daughter of David Okimaaw, who was the son of William. The full name "is Okimaawininiiw. O-ki-maw means—boss or leader; wi, is a connecting word; ininiiw, is a person: the boss human" (Bird, personal communication, 21 June 2003; and Donna Sutherland, personal communication, 6 June 2003). Thomas Gorst (recorded by Oldmixon) stated: "the Indians ... have each an Okimah, as they call him, or Captain over them, who is an Old Man, consider'd only for his Prudence and Experience" (see Tyrrell 1931: 382; Bird, class presentation, 1 April 2003.

13 Bird, class presentation, 1 April 2003.

14 Louis (personal communication, 7 July 2003) notes that the introduction of guns brought about the competitive shooting of loons. Previously, loons were difficult to kill with bow and arrow, but a skilled marksman could kill them with a gun, although even this was a challenge.

Much like the Athapascan stories that anthropologist Julie Cruikshank (1984) writes about, "The Wailing Clouds" is set not in a time but a place. The date of the events can only be speculated upon, yet the description and names of the places are vivid and specific and remain meaningful to this day. Cruikshank has identified a number of functions that place names perform in Athapascan narratives. In much the same way as in Omushkego culture, locations in the landscape provide a mnemonic or memory trigger for stories. Just as a date, say 1867, might remind Euro-Canadians of Canada's confederation, places call events and stories to mind for the Omushkegowak. Through the vivid telling of "The Wailing Clouds," the mouth of the Ekwan River looking over to Akimiski Island evokes the memory of terrible suffering and loss. As place names encode information about a location, the places themselves are in turn given a far richer meaning through that association.[15] "The Wailing Clouds" gives a deep cultural meaning to the mouth of the Ekwan River. As late as the twentieth century, Louis states that his mother's grandfather "Grand William ... looked in that area as an old man, and he looked at it, 'Before these people died,' he says, 'this land was full with people.' And he says, 'Now it's empty.' And my mother saw him, my mother saw the old man, he just stand there with his cane, shaking-leg, and look at the area. 'The land is empty,' he says, exactly the place where it happens."[16]

As Cruikshank notes, when the use of English begins to overwhelm a group, place names recited in stories provide a way to maintain traditional languages. Louis's community is losing its language to English as southern culture encroaches in the forms of video games, radio, and television. This story incorporates Omushkego names such as "Kashechewan," rather than "Albany," and "Akimiski" instead of the numerous English names for the island.[17] Place names are not simply symbols for locations, but part of the living language. Just as Kreg Ettenger found in Eastern James Bay, Western James Bay Cree place names are descriptive, encoding rich cultural information. "Ekwan" means "the river frequently used" or "preferable way to

---

15 Cruikshank 1990: 63–64; Norman 1977: 184–87. Kreg Ettenger (2002: 1–5) has found that place names preserve information about a landscape that is changing geologically in response to ongoing glacial rebound. As water levels lower and an island becomes a point of land, place names record the older geological formations.
16 Bird, class presentation, 1 April 2003.
17 Thwaites 1901: 372. These include "Viner's Island," "White Bear," and "Bristol." It is interesting to compare the functional and descriptive names used by the Omushkegowak to the names the English applied to places. Some, like "Severn River," were reflections of places they had left behind. Others, like "Viner's Island" and "Cape Henrietta Maria," were honorific, that is, meant to honour an important person or patron; Sir Robert Viner was a governor of the HBC and Queen Henrietta Maria was the wife of King Charles I.

go."[18] This name came about because it is very hard to travel around Cape Henrietta Maria before the Bay ice has cleared the coast. To get to the western James Bay coast from areas north of the cape, people go upriver from Winisk, "then take first tributary toward south on Say-say-mat-ta-wow River, up to the lake, then take most southern outlet creek called 'It-ta-hon-na-ni-zi-pi' which means, 'way-to-go.' This creek runs close parallel with Ekwan River some distance up and that is where a portage is located to go to Ekwan River. Then on to James Bay. It work both ways."[19] "Akimiski," the name of the largest island in James Bay, means "the land across." The name describes the place, an island seen across a strait from the mainland.[20] The place names preserve geographic and geological information as well as the naming system used by the Omushkego.

The places and some of the practices described in "The Wailing Clouds" are still familiar to the Winisk people today as they strive to navigate between traditional values and modern challenges. A coherent "cosmology," the persons and places in the Omushkego universe underpin the story. The narrative builds on the foundation of this constancy but also describes change from a time when there were many Native people on the land to when there were very few. The story explains a change in land use: why a cherished, resource-rich area is no longer used for the festivals that everyone so looked forward to.

By including vivid images of the land, games and social activities, humour and fun as well as lessons and examples of appropriate and inappropriate behaviour, "The Wailing Clouds" is deeply engaging. It combines happy descriptions of an exciting festival with suspense and drama to create an enthralling tale that draws the listener in. Through its retelling and preservation by a long line of gifted storytellers, and now through Louis's efforts to collect and maintain the oral history of the Omushkego, it remains an active and important part of the present as well as a reflection of the past.

"The Wailing Clouds" fleshes out the written record of the James Bay-Hudson Bay lowlands by offering an Omushkego account of a significant event. Written European records such as those of the HBC tell only a small part of Hudson Bay history. As anthropologist Richard Preston

---

18 Bird, personal communication, 21 June 2003.
19 Bird, personal communication, 21 June 2003.
20 Bird, personal communication, 21 June 2003; and John Long, personal communication, 17 June 2003. Lytwyn (2002: 153) states: "In the vicinity of Albany Fort, the caribou hunt was focused on Akimiski Island."

states, "Whitemen's reports, whether resident or travelers, are based on what they see and hear at the post or enroute between posts. These reports do not tell us what was happening back in the bush where Cree people were trying to get on with their lives."[21] Fur traders, immersed in their own cosmology, could fail to observe or understand the meaning that events held for the Omushkegowak. In "The Wailing Clouds," the epidemic is only peripherally noted as originating in the fur trade. The story focuses on the responsibility of the people in bringing the calamity on themselves and their own responsibility and strategy for solving the problem, an Omushkego perspective.

Louis recorded this version of "The Wailing Clouds" in English on audiotape in 2003. An earlier account was published in *The Northern Review*, under the title "The Wailing in the Clouds," edited by Ann Taylor (Bird 1993: 35–43). A simplified version of the story, "The Old Blind Squaw," appeared in the *Oakville Journal Record* under the byline of Vita Rordam (Rordam 1972). The transcript presented here is a more encompassing narrative told in response to the needs and questions of an English-speaking audience. Louis verified the text and clarified many names, terms, and topics mentioned.

The Wailing Clouds

My story is, as always, about the Omushkego people who lived, and still some left, on the James Bay Lowland, as we know it today. There are many stories that has been told by our forefathers in that area, our First Nation Omushkegos. They have many stories which has happened long time ago. Many of those stories has been passed down from mouth to mouth for one generation to the other, and in that place where I am telling a story from, it is on the west coast of James Bay, and continue on to the northwest, on the southwest coast of Hudson Bay.

Once upon a time there were many people living in that area. It has been said by the Omushkego elders that at times, long time before the European came, that area was different than it is today. And apparently also it was different way of many things. There were times when people

---

21 Preston 2000: 374–84, 1. Victor Lytwyn (1999: 162) also notes: "It is difficult to measure the success or failure of Lowland Cree attempts to stem the onslaught of the smallpox epidemic [of the early 1780s] since most of the coping with the disease took place far away from the HBC traders who wrote about the epidemic."

were so many in a given few decade when the country was in plenty, when the land was plentiful with food, when the weather was favourable and animals grow very healthy and the land provide a lot of stuff. Some elders that I have listened to said, "The land itself seems to make itself one abundance because there were so many people living." Our people unfortunately, has never really have any use of counting or multiplying, or dividing or adding so much as "100," the number.

So the numbering system was not important for them, and therefore their stories cannot be numbered, cannot be measured on today's measure. So in time past, when the First Nation says, "There were many people," they say that at one time or other, in one period, in the James Bay Lowland, the people were so many that there was no place in the land that, that a person would not encounter one family to the other, they were that many. And at the same time, there were also plenty of animals who seemed to mingle with the people, at times, and then, sometimes, a natural event would decimate the animals and also the human beings. And it is part of this story that I am going to tell, briefly, if I may. I once told this story, a long time ago. And it has been called "The Wailing in the Clouds" (see above). This story was so fascinating when I used to listen as a young boy. I used to listen to many kind of elders and some of them [stories] were just summation, and sometimes they were vividly a dramatized story. So what I have done, is, I blend them, I put as many, many versions as I can, so it can be recorded.

Therefore, here is a story in the Hudson Bay, southwest coast of Hudson Bay. All around, about two hundred miles, inland from the sea, people live there as the animals move—they move with animals, they move with season. In the summertime they move on the coastal area, to get away from the flies and to stay in the open place where the flies will blow away. And sometimes many waterfowl, I mean the birds that migrate during the winter, they usually come up on the coast to the Hudson Bay or James Bay shore to moult, to change their feathers.[22] So for the moulting season they stay there, and for that reason alone the Omushkego people used to live close by, by the coast, the coastal region. So they had one reason to stay there because it is easy for them to hunt

---

22 "As many as 250,000 Lesser Snow Geese (14% of the national population) have spent short periods staging along the north shore [of Akimiski Island alone]." The Lowlands have long been a major staging area for migratory birds, ducks, and geese (Alexander *et al.* 1991: 168–69). For descriptions of many of the birds and waterfowl that migrated through the region, see Graham 1969; Bell 1879: Section C: 67c–70c; and Macoun 1881: 23–28.

these birds, who do not fly, in summertime. And [the] other reason why they are there, the fish that are been wintered inland, they would go out into the Bay. Fish like whitefish we call them, and the trout fish, brook trout. They go out into the sea during the summer and they feed there. They swim around the shore and they stay there during the summer, and then after that, in the month of August or September they come inland.

And in September or October all those whitefish and also the brook trout, they go up the river as far as two hundred miles or so, to go spawning. The whitefish, they follow the major rivers, and then they go to the tributaries and then follow the river right up to the lakes and rivers again, then they spawn there. Some whitefish, they would just stay inside the major lakes, the deep water, and they will winter there, it is believed. And some of those whitefish will go back down before the river freezes right down to the bottom. They go back out into the bay. It's also believed some brook trout do the same thing. And it is for this reason, during the summer, that these whitefish, and the brook trout, feed on the shores of Hudson Bay and James Bay. And for that reason also, the Omushkego people move to the coastal region, on the shores of the Hudson Bay and James Bay.[23]

Also the caribou usually hang around on the shores of the Hudson Bay and James Bay. For the same reason, to get away from the flies and also to have some seaweeds which they need in summer when they sweat—they sweat out the salt and then they eat the leaves that are washed into the shore, the seaweeds, and then they eat on the shore and then once in a while they go out into the tide water. They even sleep there. As the water recede, far out, they lay down there and the water comes, they move up a little bit and they lay down and they lick the water. And for that reason, the animals used the sea, the James Bay and Hudson Bay. And human follow those animals and that's the reason why those people used to live there in summertime. In the winter time most of them do the same thing, fish, animals, birds, go inland, and some birds, even the geese, like Canada Geese and Wavies,[24] they migrate down south. Ducks of all kinds and other waterfowl, they call them. That's the reason why people used to move, like migrating one place to the other, and that's still lifestyle, and

---

23 For a description of the fish in the region see Graham 1949: 167–71; Isham 1949.
24 Wavies are also known as Way-ways or Snow Geese, according to Pike 1892: 161.

these were the Omushkegos.[25] And while doing so, each spring, when the river free of ice and when the leaves begin to bud, and then they would come down the river and have a short celebration in any place, any given place where there is a main outlet of the river system. And then they would choose the spot every season to visit each other and the area became the "festival ground." And it was one of those event that a story came out, in my stories.[26]

My mother used to tell us a story, which she heard from her own grandfather. Her own grandfather, most adventurous person, and his name was William Okimaaw, and he was mixed breed. He's part white man. And he lives around 1800[s], he may have born somewhere around 1875. And he lives to be a man during the 1900[s], even before then. "Bill," I used to call him in English, William Okimaaw, have heard his grandmother, from his mother's side, who told the story of the time in the past when she was maybe young, we don't even know if she has witnessed the story, all we know is that she told the story to this person, William. And William told the story where my mother was young. So therefore, the story is about three, maybe fourth generation old, maybe more. So it seemed to indicate the time may have been about 1700 or maybe early 1700, somewhere around there, we don't know for sure. Could be early 1800, because most of the Hudson Bay outpost were in operation, like Kashechewan[27] and

---

25 Victor Lytwyn describes the seasonal availability of fish, geese and caribou and how they were procured. He notes that "[m]any Albany River Lowland Cree spent the summer on Akimiski Island, hunting caribou. In most years the hunt must have been successful, because the Indians brought venison, tongues, and fat to trade at Albany Fort. In some years the caribou did not migrate as far as Akimiski Island and the Lowland Cree were forced to return early to the vicinity of Albany Fort to wait for the arrival of the geese" (2002: 93–97).

26 Lytwyn states that "[i]n winter, the people usually lived in small groups of several closely related families.... Most remained in their winter camps until the end of winter, when they gravitated towards the coastal area. The movement toward the coastal trading post was motivated by a number of factors. They came to trade extra furs and hides procured in the winter, to renew social relationships with other coastal Cree and the European fur traders, and to give and receive gifts, thereby continuing to renew bonds of friendship and alliance." Lytwyn concludes that the seasonal migrations of the Lowland Cree represented "distinctive strategies for living in their different ecological zones." Coastal people focused on hunting migratory birds, fishing the rivers, and to some extent, hunting marine mammals, while Inland people focused on beaver and inland fishing. Both groups concentrated their efforts on the seasonal caribou hunts (2002: 16, 112–13).

27 The HBC renamed this river Albany and the post at its mouth Fort Albany (HBCA, Post History: Albany). Long (1988: 233–34) cites James Wesley, a Kashechewan Cree, who in 1988 stated that the "[r]ivers were given English names, French names, Cree names. This was a very long process of white men competing against each other to possess and gain resources from lands that were formerly occupied by Indians." According to Long (1995: 65), Moose Fort was established in 1673; Kashechewan, or Albany Fort, was in operation from 1675; and Fort Charles, which became Rupert House, began in 1668. Cree narratives, like those studied by Cruikshank (1984) in the Yukon, are situated more by location than date. See also Doxtator 2001: 33–47. Similarly, this story describes the physical location precisely and vividly while chronology is vague and unstated. It is important to note, though, that this was in fact a discrete historical event.

Moose Factory and on the east coast of James Bay. The Hudson Bay Company have already found an island within the James Bay which was known, "Charlton Island." What year that they found that island, they used that island for the harbour, I don't know, and it was at that time.[28]

So the story begin: it was in that period that the European brought the disease with them as they arrived.[29] And the Native people of that time, the Omushkego people, was so plenty, according to Mr. William's grandmother, if the people stopped some place for celebration, or spring celebration, the teepee would be within twenty feet to each other and would set up the camp somewhere outside of this famous river they used to meet with each other, it was called, in southwest coast of James Bay, it was called Ekwan River.[30] And it was the most famous place where the Omushkegos used to gather together in the spring, to have celebration, to welcome each other, to reunion with their friends, and also to have a celebration, to celebrate being, surviving during the winter. And it was a great time, and they were by themselves. There were no European then. They carried this tradition from years and way out in the back. And it was a custom for them to come and wait [for] each other outside of that, the mouth of the river.

28 "In 1674, after consultation, they [the HBC explorers] proposed removing to Monsebi, or Moose river ... accordingly the governor sailed to discover it, and from thence sailed to Schatawam, afterwards called Albany river ... and from thence also by Viner's [Akimiski] island ... going ashore at the river Equam ..." (Robson, 1752: 6). John Oldmixon stated that Bayly treated with "the King, and his Son" of the Schettawan River. From there Bayly traveled towards Cape Henrietta Maria and renamed Akimiski Island Viner's Island, undoubtedly for Sir Robert Viner, a governor of the HBC. The remark "... and wee hope before this comes to you a good large dry substanciall Warehouse will be there [at Charlton Island] erected to receive the Cargo wee send you, as it was agreed to be, before Mr, Baily left you [in 1679]," suggests that Charlton Island was in use during the earliest operations of the HBC (HBCA A.6/1, London Correspondence Outward, 29 May 1680).

29 For a description of epidemic diseases in the "Petit Nord" or area north of Lake Superior and east of Lake Winnipeg, see Hackett 2002: 50. Both Hackett and Lytwyn (2002: 126–27) describe an incident that they feel may have been one of the earliest epidemics. In 1674 Thomas Bayly arrived at Akimiski Island where he found some distressed Cree. He took them to the mouth of the Ekwan River. There he found a number of people had died. Bayly ascribed these deaths to starvation, but Hackett and Lytwyn challenge this on the basis that the area was so abundant, particularly in the summer, which is when Bayly arrived at the site. Long reports that "Among the Cree of western Hudson Bay, oral tradition attributes the Ekwan River deaths to another cause altogether. Chief George Hunter of Peawanuck blames them on intertribal warfare: the dead Indians were Iroquois who were ambushed by the Cree in retaliation for an earlier raid" (Long 1988: 234). "Grand William" indicated that the event told in "The Wailing Clouds" was not the only catastrophic epidemic his people faced, as this happened at least once before. Bayly's story seems too early to be the event commemorated in "The Wailing Clouds" but may have related to a previous epidemic.

30 Lytwyn estimates the lowland populations in the years before the smallpox epidemic of 1782–83 at between 1,500 and 2,000. Smallpox cut that number, Lytwyn estimates, by half. By the 1820s, however, "the Lowland Cree population appears to have rebounded to near the pre-smallpox numbers. For example, at Albany Fort in 1829, an enumeration counted a total population of 259" (2002: 24–25).

At the mouth of this river there was so nice, and the beach was just sand, beautiful and everything. And the land was on the shore, on the direction of the north and south. And it was a nice harbour place there, safe from the north wind or any other or even the west wind. So it was a very ideal place for them to gather and to have a celebration for the spring.[31] Our ancestors would always have a celebration every spring. The Omushkego people have the tradition in celebrating their survival every spring, and they would come together at one place to have a festivity in a very thanksgiving way.[32]

And it was at this point that the story took place because the Europeans have the rights already, our ancestors at that time, at the last time that they gathered there, they already have some guns, a gun from the whiteman, which you load from the muzzle area, you load it from the front, and they had a few of those.[33] Having that added the excitement because at that place it was the earliest place that the sea ice would melt faster in there because there is an island right across from the Ekwan River.[34] You could see the land across the bay, which is about twenty, maybe fifteen miles across. And, at that time, it always opened soon, and they would have all kinds of food there, the waterfowl that stays in the bay would be

---

31 Father Albanel, a Jesuit who traveled overland to the James Bay-Hudson Bay Lowlands in the seventeenth century, described in 1671–72 "the well-known Island of Ouabaskou [Akimiski], four leagues long by twenty wide, abounding in all kinds of animals, but especially notable for its white bears." He added, "I say nothing of the abundance of wild fowl in this region. On the Island of Ouabaskouk, if the Savages are to be believed, they are so numerous that in one place, where the birds shed their feathers at molting time, any Savages or deer coming to the spot are buried in feathers over their heads, and are ... often unable to extricate themselves. Nor do I speak of the variety and plenty of fruits growing here ..." Thwaites lists a number of names the island has been known by, including "Viner's, White Bear, Bristol, and Agoomska" (Thwaites 1901: 203).
    Akimiski continues to be an important staging area for birds. The Akimiski Island Bird Sanctuary is part of the James Bay Preserve (Alexander *et al.* 1991: 168–69).
32 Louis states, "[e]very time when the rivers, it's clear off, people used to come from Winisk River into Ekwan River, Attawapiskat River, they all get into that place, because it's beautiful. Because of good hunting ground. There is an island there in the bay, and there is this channel. It opens early, and there's always lots of seals, and lots of hunting, like the loons—common loons, and the red-throated loon, and also, what do they call those, 'scooters,' the ones that stay in the water, okay. And it's plenty to eat there. That's why people like to go there. And it's lots to eat and the fish, good fishing in there, in that season, eh? So that's why people go there, and they can stay there for a few days without running out of food, and they bring their food with them also. You know, to exchange? It's just like a feast. It's a great feast, for three days. And also, the, many thing goes also with it" (Bird, class presentation, 1 April 2003). Robert Bell (1884: 487) states "In the spring, as soon as the water opens at the mouths of the rivers, they [loons] sometimes assemble in incredible numbers, as if by a previous understanding about a common meeting place. At such time they may be much more easily shot than usual."
33 See Roland Bohr, Chapter 7 on guns.
34 Father Albanel stated, "There is said to be a small bay [at Akimiski Island] where the water never freezes, and in which vessels can pass the winter very comfortably" (Thwaites 1901: 203).

plenty, for example, the loons, all three different kinds of loons.[35] And also the, the diving ducks will be so plenty, and of course the Canada Geese and other geese will be there. It was a very good place for them to have, because they can get the food very easily. And it was that place they choose for their seasonal celebration, at the mouth of the Ekwan River.[36]

And, if one stands on the north shore of the mouth of the river, the Ekwan, you would look to the northeast, and you would see a bluff out there, or the height of land, which is come to a point. And it is usually high, in between there the beach will be just beautiful, and beside the beach, a bit inland and then there's a grassy land that is very nice and dry and plenty of driftwood. And if you go a bit more inland another thousand feet, then you have another ridge, that now have a white moss or lichen and maybe two feet of willows, the ideal place to camp. And of course also a lot of wood that's scattered around the area. That is why people choose that place to come together.[37] And when they do, seems that there were so many at the time, the village became large. People from

---

35 The loons, and especially red-throated loons were valued because they were a change of diet from the beaver and other food the people had been eating for the winter and also because they represented a greater challenge to hunters. If startled, the loons would dive instead of flying off, so the hunter had to get his shot off accurately, rather than being able to shoot into a rising cloud of them. In this way, the loons provided both food and excitement at the festival. Robert Tymstra, who travels in the area performing bird counts, reports that local Cree hunters have told him that the loons can hear the bullet and duck before it hits them (Bird, personal communication, 5 June 2003; and Robert Tymstra, personal communication, 19 June 2003). The red-throated loons (Gavia stellata) that migrate through Churchill usually arrive about the middle of June, and are plentiful for only about five days (Jehl and Smith 1970: 22). The loons fly over the water in flocks of fifteen or less, so the numbers here described suggest the birds were staging. The "splash dive" is described as a "[s]hort-duration dive, with foot kicks sufficiently forceful to make loud slapping noise and throw up large sprays of water ... Directed toward intruders, from conspecies to humans" (Barr et al. 2000: 5, 9). Andrew Graham gave the Native name of the red-throated loon as "Asse-Moqua, the Red-throated Diver." He stated that "[i]t appears about the settlements when the rivers are open, and retires about the end of September. Its note is harsh and disagreeable like squalling. They make no nest, only lining the place with a little down from the breast, and on which they deposit their eggs towards the end of June, and which are of a stone colour and two in number. The young ones wing before the end of August. They live on fish, are excellent divers and very troublesome to the nets. I have seen fourteen caught in them at one tide" (Graham 1969: 50) Fur trader George Nelson described the loon as a "humorous visitor to the shaking lodge. The Loon would call out "Nee-weah-wee-wey."" According to Nelson, this sounded like "I want to marry!" in Cree (Brown and Brightman 1988: 114). Today a few red-throated loons visit Akimiski Island, but not as many as in the past (Bird, personal communication, 5 June 2003). Robert Tymstra reports that the guides in the area call the birds "Ash Mog," and that there are a few scattered flocks in the region, the largest he has seen numbering thirty (Tymstra, personal communication, 18 June 2003). See DePasquale, Chapter 2, this volume, for more about the loon.

36 Isham (1949: 76–78) gives his own version of a Goose Feast, which is interesting in how it differs from First Nations descriptions.

37 This description of the area around the Ekwan River mouth and Akimiski Island underlines the differences in the way Europeans and First Nations have viewed the region. Older historians like Arthur S. Morton emphasized the "harsh environmental conditions," and believed that the region was uninhabited until the HBC posts drew the Cree into the region (Lytwyn 2002: 28–30).

within the land, they came from there. The people who lived in Winisk River they come there, all those people who can make it, and all the people who have lived up the river Ekwan, and they would come down and gather together there. And the people who were using the Attawapiskat River, they also came across, because it's not far. But there was no village yet, there was no white man settlement. So, we did this, even though there were European already in Kashechewan, perhaps in Moose Factory and, and in York Factory. Perhaps there were some in Fort Severn, because these were the oldest Hudson Bay settlements in the past.

But the people, settlement doesn't mean a thing to them, they just live in the bush the way they live forever, for a long time. They didn't mind that, they didn't care about making a settlement, because they satisfied [with] the way they live. That is why they come here and this time they have established this tradition, customary thing, and they come to meet with each other. And it was in that place they were camping. It has been said that, from the Ekwan River into the north, there is a little creek there, I forget what it's called, but it is about two and a half miles between, and when people arrive they put their teepees right across. Two miles long and about a mile wide into the bush. And those who didn't have no canvas, whatever, or teepee covering, they make lean-tos into the bush, into the tree line.[38] And for that reason, once they come all in, you could see all them and you cannot see through the teepees, because there is so many. That's what the Grand William said from his grand, grandmother. And it was a great celebration there. When they do that, when they have all the people who can think of, have arrived, then the organization begins. The elders begin to give out the orders, and to how to organize the camp, and that everything will be in order. Everybody that's arrived have brought their own food to last them maybe three days, and those who don't, they will share it, and everything as, who has more.

And everything was so festival mood. People meet with each other, they tell each other stories about their life in the bush during the winter. The women talk about their own gossiping ways in very enjoyable mood. The children play together, all those who have not seen each other for during the winter. And the elder women, who have come to visit again, stay down their own ways and tell each other stories and comfort each other with their company, of those who [they] haven't saw. And the elder men, who have arrived, the men folks exchange their activity during the winter, and

---

38 For illustrations of tents see Isham 1949: 89, 91.

the hunters talks about the area where they have hunted during the winter. Then the elders who are now not trapping or hunting any more, tell the stories about where they spent the winter, and everything they know, the winter, the animals, the fish, so everything was in a festival mood, at that time. By the time they organized themselves to have a well-settled village, temporary village, so they organized their activities. There were those who were assigned to look after the games, and competitive games of all kinds. Most popular they have during the afternoon hours is that young people would have a race, a foot race. They would because the distance of the village is about two and a half miles. So they have what we call a "dash." Who is going to get one end to the other faster than the other, and how far a person will go to give up. And it was the only measurement they have. So those who win usually get a little bit of reward. I don't know for sure what kind of a reward system they have. The young women did the same thing; they did all kinds of games. The men games were a bit more rougher, because they have a game called we-pa-chi-skway-ask-wa-hi-gan—it means the two balls that [are] tied together and are drawn with the stick that has a bit of a hook.[39] The stick can be about three and a half feet long, or a metre long. Just long enough for a man to hold it on his height and can touch the ground to grab across these two balls that are tightly [knotted together], and this they will have to try to throw it between the two poles that are designed as a goal. And it doesn't matter how many men, as long as equal number on each side. The scoring system is, I don't know, but they was there. And this game, it's very rough, it's only good for the young people who are fast and also in good health.

Then there was also another game that they do as well. Racing, a footracing, or something like a dash. One hundred-metre dash, whatever you call it today? That kind of stuff. And then they also have a wrestling matches, between men. A wrestling matches between young ladies, too. And also the young, teenaged, the little boys who also have different games in separate places. And at the same time, the elders will have a designated area where they could visit each other. And the old men will find themselves closer to the river, and sit by themselves and tell stories. And the rest, the whole village was in action in the afternoon. And it always begin in the afternoon, and in the evening, after the games have been

---

39 Michael Payne (1984: 80) notes "Cree games of dexterity took several forms." He describes a primarily female game called "'tishevy's' which James Isham translated as 'a pair of stones,' or testicles." Louis refers to a game that seems similar: "pim-mi-tish-soo-way-pa-hi-gan" (see Cree Glossary and also note 41).

done, exhaustive games, and then, the other games will begin, less physical, and sometimes that's where the story came from. The stories are used. Amongst the older people, they would gather together and then sit around, and then they will take turn to tell stories. Who is going to be most fascinating? And then they also have a reward system for those who do that. And of course they arrange the audience in very nice way. So everything can be enjoyed. And the ladies do the same thing. It doesn't mean they were separated. There were men and women, the elders together, and there were the middle-aged mothers and fathers, they would also get together. There was no separation between men and women. Here was a system, where the women were respected for the certain period of time. They also had their area where they can enjoy themselves.

Everything was well-organized, it's said, and everybody has a festival mood. There were those who like to hunt and they were allowed to go to hunt. There, they have a competitive game in hunting, who is going to shoot many loons and who's going to have more, and then they brought food at the same time. And there were young women who set out to catch rabbits and to catch fish and they bring in the food, the fresh food for the old people, and also to feed the young children who are, also have their own activity.[40] All this thing was well-organized and it was fun for all to have. And it was in that last time, those Omushkegos have such [fun] that the story came to us, from our ancestors.

It was in that time also, that I want to get back to the reason why they were doing that. One of the things they liked to do was that, at that period in time, they would arrange marriages—parents and fathers would talk together about their children, how they are, who is now able to get married, and their daughters and everything. So it was a very enjoyable time. It was at that mood that they had this festivity, and everybody enjoyed themselves. And this story goes on to say that sometimes in the evening there are different activities. In the evening it was in that period in time only, that we hear the story about the Omushkego organizing the drumming. They had big drums just that season, to have a group, a drumming. And also to dance. There were dancers, and they would also dress for the dance. And another section, where the elders alone exchanged their stories in spiritual nature, and there were those who went to act, who went to

---

40 Ellen Smallboy, who lived in the Moose Factory area from the mid-1800s well into the twentieth century, described some traditional women's roles: setting snares, making and setting wooden traps, sewing, cooking, and using fishnets. She said that setting a rabbit snare was something that "a girl of six can do" and that netting snowshoes could be done by a girl of fifteen (Flannery 1995: 7, 13).

participate on, spiritual renewal, I think. Sometimes it was at that time, people also exercised, or experimented, their knowledge about medicine. To show other people how they heal their diseases, awhile there's a woman part of that activity. And everything else happening.

It was in this time that some competitive games emerge in the evening amongst the young men. They had this game that is strenuous, and a lot of strength it requires. It was some sort of a soccer game. It was similar to the soccer, but it was not, it was Natively designed. They created their own ball which they carried it most of the time or kicking it with their feet. And it's made out of the grass and also the hide and whatever, they make.[41] So, that game was strenuous and it was mostly young men would play that game. And those who were watching would take side for their team, and, and then there would be a lot of screaming and yelling. And sometimes they get hurt, too. The sprain, not necessarily broke any bones. And they also have the people who control the game, who watch and direct things that they won't go so haywire. And then the women games also were the same looked after, and it was a place where also young people can meet and play together. It was totally a festival mood, it was freedom at once, one season only, when they come together. And it was that time also that people would exercise their spiritual practices—those who wanted to set up a shaking tent, they would do it in a designated area.[42] And there were those who compete with each other, with the mi-te-wi-win, and that also has a place in that place. They have a designated area where this thing is going to take place. And the camp is so arranged that the children can be mostly in one place where they can meet, and they would be in a safe place from those rough games, whatever they was.

There were many things that were talked about in those days. But it only last maybe three days, maybe a bit more. That depends on how much

---

41 Louis states, "There was a game there that the young people used to have, what they call, kwa-skwe-chi-si-we-hi-kan [laughter], they call that. It means two stone tied together and you have a stick about three feet long, and you catch it and you throw it over the goal, you know, two sticks standing together. And it have about ten or fifteen men playing together.... I don't know why they said chi-si-we-hi-kan. Do you know what that means? It is the two balls, tied together about this far, you know? So these balls, they mean something in our language. But the names fit, anyway [laughter]. And so that was the name of the game. And it was very strenuous for the young people, they compete, and they were the audience, they were screaming, and, you know, just cheering with the team. And it used to last all afternoon" (Bird, class presentation, 1 April 2003). See also footnote 39.

42 On the shaking tent, see Chapter 3, Brown and Brightman 1988, and Preston 2002, especially 81–85. Louis states, "then there's a certain given area where the elders, the mi-te-wak, exercised their skills. Mi-tew, I mean the shaman's art, skills and certain powers. So they apply that area to test each other what can do what. This is funny part. You know, where those mi-tew designated areas, it is always in the creek, in the Ekwan River" (class presentation, 1 April 2003).

people have their provisions, if they have brought enough food with them, and they could stay a week. Sometimes people used to stay more than that, because they just didn't want to leave each other. So at this moment, and it was the last time they ever did that, we don't know the year. But it's said they have totally enjoyed themselves, even said, over-reacting. And that's why the story came out.

It was this last evening that people really let go of themselves. They lost control, they said, they just simply go into the hyper, they just simply couldn't stop playing, everybody was involved. Many different games were happening, and all the length of the village. You can hear all the yells and screams and laughs and everything, they said, all through this camp. And it's two and half miles long. And it was a mile or so wide. And it was this evening for the last time that they were going to stay there before they move out that they played the most active games. They organize it. And they have dances for the young people, and the middle-aged group, many of the activities that are strenuous and fun. And it was in [that] particular place, where the story pick up, that, that a family, a middle-aged group, I think, were camping, and they had their own elders, yes. And because the village was so temporary, there were those who joined their teepees together and put the stick across, and they used to call these shaa-poo-ta-wan, it just mean, the tree, it just says, "the teepee that is open right through," that is all it says, shaa-poo-ta-wan. Because you go—one end to go in, and there's also at the other end, there's also a door. So, shaa-poo-ta-wan means "the door right through." But this was made only for the protection of the families who do not have enough covering—putting together their covering material together makes them have a big, big teepee, and also visit each other, for three day, it was long enough.

So the game go on, and it was one of those shaa-poo-ta-wan, the "long house" sort of a teepee, that the game carried on during the night. They organized what they call "tug-of-war" in those groups, I don't know how many families there were. Some people said there were about five families inside the teepee. And there were visitors. First of all it start with the kids. The kids play a tug-of-war inside there. And then they begin to expand, the teenagers jump in, and after that and then the young mothers join in and the parents jump in, and all the elders begin to jump in, expanded and expanded and, and the mood was exciting and adding the rope string as they "lost control" [of the] situation.

In the middle, there was an old lady, who was blind, and she was just sitting in the middle, where the respectable section was supposed to be. And she was there, but she was blind. And she was told to hold that string, where the knot is, to make sure she was to judge who is winning, who is not, because if she was pulled too far into the left, she would yell that these group are lost on the right. You see, if she was pulled too far into her right, then she would scream and say, "You lost! You lost to the left!" So she was sort of a score-keeper, for the first, that is, and then, finally, when the game get out of hand, those people that extended themself into the teepee and some visitors join in and their friends join in and the string was added and added and then finally, the string they use was one of those raw hides, you know they call it "babiche." That thing is very strong, and sometimes people used to have those things. So they just tie a knot at the end and then extend it, and then they break it, and that's fun. And they put it back together, and do it again. And then the string was getting longer and longer past the two teepees, and then it goes outside. And the more they do that, the more excited they became, and they laugh and scream, just like children together.

And by that time, the old lady was saying, "Okay, that's enough, you are overdoing it. Okay, stop now!" She says, because the people were kicking up a dust, the fireplace was out, the fire was out, because they'd been pulling each other over it, and all that stuff. And then she was worried, 'cause it might set the fire on the teepee. So she was saying, "Okay! That's enough. Stop now!" And they just went on, they didn't even listen to her. Finally, she gave up, and she just crawl away, into the corner of the teepee. Then she just sat there and she says to her fellow elder, "I think these kids are overdoing it."[43] And then once more she yell at them and says, "Stop now! You are"—what do they call that? kaa-paa-sta-ho-naaw it mean, "blaspheme"—"You are blaspheming. You act the blasphemy because you are overdoing it." But the young people, they're [saying], "Let us do this and let us have fun and never mind the blasphemy, we'll go with it." And they just carried on. And the game went on, it was so much fun.

This was about midnight, and the night was not very long, because in the month of June, it's the longest day. And then finally, they break the

---

43 Louis (personal communication, 5 June 2003) refers to this as pas-sta-ho-win, that is, something you do just before something goes wrong. The warnings the old woman gave were: ha-shyi-ki-ki-na-ki-chi-pa-na-wow-o-ma-ka-ith-ti-yek, or "You are all tickled to death," and ha-shyi-kit-ashi-it-ti-so-wow-o-ma, ka-ith-ti-yek, or "You are now on last joy before towards your death" (Bird, personal communication, 17 July 2003).

teepee, they knock the teepee down, you know, this wigwam. They knock it down partially, and it was dangerous for the kids and the elder lady. So they finally stop for a little while and repair it, and back to the tug-of-war again. And just simply scream. They just simply yelled at each other, and they had good fun. Nobody got mad. But it was so much fun. So, finally they were saying that, "Let us, let us," they say, "Let us paa-sta-ho." Paa-sta- means sin, some sort of. People call that "sin against nature," when it's bad, but this one was a good fun, supposed to be. But the whole village became that way. The whole village just simply went haywire that last night. Finally, after midnight or so, they begin to exhaust themselves and they went back home, they went to bed. I think they fall asleep, everybody fall asleep. But of course there were those elders who did not play, who went to bed just regularly. People who were not so well, and the mothers and parents who have small children, so they went to bed early. They were not bothered, they knew, just a fun game. And some of those men, they didn't sleep right, they didn't sleep that night because they want to go hunt early morning, before sunrise. They want to go out there into the open water, you know, to shoot loons. Because it's another game, competitive game amongst the men, so all the young men were out there who has canoes and those who do not, they stand at the shore of the bay and each morning the loons would come into the shore and then they would fly up and up and down the coast. When the water moves, that's when the fish come, and that's why loons do that.

So, then, that's the time when the people shoot the loon, because the loons will fish right there, and as the water move fast into the south direction, and when they get to the end of the open ice and then they fly up again, up into the north section, within five miles and that's when those hunters were shooting. And it was said, "When a man begin to shoot, you can hear this fire"—I mean firing shot—"goes from one south section to the other north in two mile distance." And they say, "If there was a war, it would have sound like that, in that time." With the black powder, the smoke. And it was another addition or activity. And that's what the men like, and they wanted to compete also, who is going to get the more loons.

Anyway, the loons were very delicious, according to them. It was one of the luxury food, for that period in time. So that is why everything seems to be so festival. It was at that time that these hunters, who were out there, it so happened that morning that the wind was so calm, and the cloud formation was beautiful, it was just like a sand beach up there, and as the sun came to shine on it, it looks like a sand beach and it's parallel with the shore of the James Bay. And the wind was so calm, and the echo carries a long distance. And those people who shoot the loon, they didn't like it very much, because the loons didn't want to fly, because there's no wind, and there were only a few shots. So anyway, at this morning it was very quiet when they went there. In the camp the elders would get up early before sunrise, they would enjoy the quietness, regardless of the fun and all the screaming that happened last night. Everything was in a good mood. But somehow, this morning, it was different. Something was as if a calmness, the quiet, as if, listening itself, something to happen. Just like a silence before the storm. Much more, impending doom was felt that morning.

When the elders got up, they couldn't sleep, and they find that something was wrong. But they couldn't touch. And it was in that time, just before the sunrise that they begin to hear some noise, out in the sky. This noise that sounded like, because there were loons, eh, there were some loons that were flying. Because the loons would come from inland, and they would come into the open water, into the sea, to fish. When they arrive, you could hear these loons, and they cry, they have like the laughing sound, and mourning sound, they would carry the echo back and forth into the ground and up in the sky. For the time being, that's what the people hear. Very soon the sound begin to change like the way it sounded, a night before. At this morning, and those who have so much fun during the night were now fall fast asleep. They didn't get up, they didn't hear anything. But those who hunt in the early morning, and those elders who get up early morning, and the parents who did not join the activity got up early, because the children get up early. So they were up and around, and making their fire, picking up the firewood and driftwood and everything. And they also hear this strange noise that echoes into the sky, into the cloud. And they look up there and they saw this peculiar formation of the cloud, which looks just like a sand beach up there. And it was shining, it was getting to reflect the sunlight before the sunrise. It's when they begin to hear a particular noise, which sound like a human's laughing. But they knew the loons were making that noise, little bit, too.

The human voices, the human voices were echoing up there, and they just couldn't understand, at the beginning. Because they hear these noises that sounds to come, that seems to come from the cloud. And the more they listen to it, the more they were so sure they were human voices. They begin to hear, exactly the way it sound last night, when the whole village was enjoying and laughing and screaming and yelling. So they begin to say, "Listen to this," to each other. All around. And those who were hunting out in the bay, they also hear. So they yell at each other: "Do you hear that?" And they said, "Yes, I hear it." And then (on camp) they begin to wake up other people and finally, many people came out from their teepee, and they begin to listen, and they look up into the cloud. Sure enough, it was exactly the same noise that they have heard the night before, during the night, when people were screaming and yelling and laughing last night, having so much fun and so much joy, but this morning, as they mystified by this echo sound from last night, they begin to hear the change of noise, they begin to hear these people, these voices that they hear up in the sky, they begin to sound different, they begin to sound as if they are in pain. Wailing, crying, screaming with anger, screaming with despair, and all this blend into the cloud.

And the cloud that hangs there, there were like a sand, stone shore, like stones that are on the shores. And then these stone-shape cloud begin to have faces with what seems to them, faces are crying and in pain. And in painful sorrow or something like that. So these people finally said, "Look at this, look at this." And they all wake each other too, so who could get up. Then they get up there and that's what they saw, that's what they hear. So they stood there with awe, awesome, with mystic and terrified. They said, "Truly, we have blasphemed, last night. Truly it's the sign that we have overdone." So they remembered the old lady, who warned them not to overdo their enjoyment. So, after that it's faded, the sun seemed to fade away, and back to the normal noise of the loons flying over and making that sound. Whatever happens that moment, something had happened. They know it, they all know it. It's a prediction of something that's going to happen. The elders know for sure. They said, "Whatever come to us, whatever happen to us, it's a revelation."

So, as the sun rises, they begin to move. Those who were ready to go, they dismantle their teepees and put things down and they move. But many of those people didn't have no canoes.[44] They begin to walk. They carried their own belongings. And those who have canoes, they move, they put their stuff in the canoes and they start to paddle. Many of them were just walking. And then finally, there was no more village. And those who didn't hear the voice in the morning were mystified by the stories

---

44 Lytwyn (2002: 113) notes that "Coaster Lowland Cree depended more upon pedestrian travel along the coastal beach ridges," while the "Inlander Lowland Cree ... made greater use of canoes than did the Coasters."

they were told. But everybody knows that something has shown to them that something will happen. But they didn't know.

So they went back to their own activities. Nobody know for sure exactly where they go. But we know, as William told us that, at that time, people when they come from their hunting areas, they usually carry a lot of fur, that they usually trade at the post. And it was usually in Kashechewan that the main post was located at that time. So they moved there, many of them. To do their trade with their fur with the Hudson's Bay Company. Whatever happens after that, they may have turned back into their hunting areas to survive, during the summer, because it is said that they were out there in their own way, when the Hudson Bay freight came into the Charlton Island, you know, the small island that the Hudson Bay used for their unloading?

And so it was in the month of August that the goods arrive into Kashechewan, this Hudson Bay post. And also the Hudson Bay, and also on the east coast. And also, way out there in York Factory, it was taken, same thing. But most of those people were now going in to Kashechewan, those who were trapping in Winisk area, and all who were trapping in Ekwan, and all that James Bay Lowland. So they all gathered together to go help out unload the goods that are coming. And they were unloaded at Charlton Island, and then the goods were shipped from there to Kashechewan and all the shore settlements that belongs to the Hudson's Bay. It was that time, in the month of August, or at the end of August, that people come to the village to do the trade, to buy the goods, and everything. And it was that time that disease have arrived with sailors who came from across the sea, and they brought a disease with them which decimate most of the First Nation. It was in that time that people died, so many of them died.

The Hudson's Bay factor, they called him, chief factor, trying to discourage people to come to the community, hoping that they won't get sick, because he know for sure they gonna get sick and die. I don't know myself, or even Grand William, who tells the story [if he] knew what kind of a disease it was. But he said that it kills people very, very quickly. And even though these people were told not to come to the community, they just simply didn't understand. Some people resented this, and [said], "They just don't want us." So they just come anyway. So, what they saw sort of mystifies them, because they see people who are sick just for the few days, and just simply passed away. So they begin to believe. So they try to leave, after they do their business with the Hudson's Bay Company. By that time they already got sick, they already catch the disease that was spreading very fast, because the disease was so contagious at that time, and being the first of its kind for them, the First Nation, they just simply couldn't resist the disease. The Europeans were much better off, because perhaps they may have immune system with them. But the First Nations, they just simply didn't have no immune to this disease. So they died just like flies. So the Grand William say.

He says they die in three days, as soon as they contact the disease. And those who died, after they die, they would vomit or the black stuff will come out from their mouth and their noses.[45] And those who survived, they said, they have vomit the stuff, and they survived. It was that knowledge that the First Nation elders begin to understand disease may be able to avoid. At that time, then they begin to try to stay away from the village, and those who came from up north, who have came together at the Ekwan River, they used to go back to the gathering ground in the fall to say goodbye and to have a few moments over there. In the past, what they did before this, they used to gather together there again maybe for a day or two, to say good-bye and to rearrange everything where they gonna hunt or sometimes have a marriage take place in there, amongst themselves. And so the people knew that they have to get away from the settlement, try to get away back into their hunting area. Because this was already the end of August and soon the winter's gonna come.

So they went back as much as they can, those who were not yet sick, and those who are now sick, all together they move towards to this area. Ekwan River, where they usually stay, and those Attawapiskat people, they usually come to stay there for temporary visit. They manage to do that, but again, they came to this place, Ekwan, where they had the last celebration of them together, with the good health. They came here, now, arriving, sick and dying. And by the time they get together here, they were only maybe half of them surviving. And it was in that place that the elders begin to think about fighting the disease, and they find out that they could make people vomit as soon as they feel sick, by giving them a mixture of water and black bear oil, or any other kind of oil, just to clean the stomach. At least the stomach. So those who were treated this way survived.

---

45 The violence with which this illness struck is consistent with, but not limited to, hemorrhagic smallpox, which Jody Decker (1988: 17) identifies as the illness that swept across the plains in the early 1780s. D. Ann Herring (personal communication, 22 May 2003), an expert in epidemiology, points out that it would be risky to make a positive statement of what particular disease this is since the symptoms are not unique to one illness.

But it was too late by that time, because half of them, the Grand William say, half of them, die. Even in that place where they have festivity in the early spring, there were many who died in that spot.

And it was that time that it was said—it is not the Grand William who witnessed this event—it was his grandmother who told the story, and she says, "All the camp, when people arrive, they were many who were sick, and those who were well, they could not even catch up with the dying people to bury them properly. Every teepee that has family of five, sometimes, three would die, in one night." That's how fast they die. And then, it was in that time that people begin to recognize, what they have heard before. It was in that temporary village that people were crying of grief, of sorrow, of despair, and in pain, that they cry, and they scream with the despair, because another loved one has died. The children died, and the men, and the men and women died, and this shock carried the echoes of the voice of suffering human.

It was that what they have heard at springtime, when they hear the noise in the cloud. Which give the story title, "The Wailing in the Cloud." The Grand William's grandmother have heard the story. Whether she was alive at the time or she passed it on from her own parents, that is unfortunate thing that we cannot know exactly when. But it was said that those people who died in that particular place were just mass buried on the shore. Because they could not bury them all, those who survived, they were so weak, they cannot do much, but just barely bury the dead bodies.

And then those who were left over went inland to try to survive in their own hunting areas. With so sad stories, so poor, so moving, even the Grand William, who was powerful man, had tears in his eyes, my mother used to say, even Grand William, who was a powerful man, in his days, have tears rolling down his cheeks, as he told the story. So the last time, the Omushkego population was decimated, merely a quarter what it was before. So Grand William state. And as he went, as he told the story, in 1920, he looked over to the area, and he said, "This land is empty. At once this place was full with people; since then, it has been like empty land."

And that was the story of the Grand William. It has been passed down to my mother, and I have listened to my mother telling us, and repeating the stories. So that is the story about "The Wailing in the Cloud." I am doing my best to retell the story as much as it were. There are many, many things that I have not mentioned, because I wanted to tell the story in the way they, the people, felt the grief they feel when they tell the story. And myself today, to think, I have passed that place. Twice I have seen that area. To look at it today, it seems like nothing has ever happened at that place. If one goes there today, at the mouth of Ekwan River, the shores that those people camped at that time are now in the tree line. There are trees there now. Because the Bay is receding continuously ever since. The new shores are there now. They are not as good as they were. It's more like flat and muddy. It's not at all the way it has been described in the story. The Ekwan River is still there. The creek two miles north of, from the Ekwan River, it's still there. So that's the story about "The Wailing Cloud."

7

Arrows and Thunder Sticks
Technologies Old and New

Introduction
ROLAND BOHR

Big-game hunting has been a major means of food procurement for the Omushkegowak of the Hudson and James Bay Lowlands since earliest times. Through practical experience and observation, they acquired a vast body of knowledge about their environment and the interaction and inter-dependence of its plants, animals, topography, climate, and weather patterns. Based on this knowledge, they fine-tuned their equipment to meet their needs in an environment that, with its harsh climate and few available wood species, placed severe restrictions on their options for making tools and weapons, given the harsh climate and the few available wood species. The technology and methods of big-game hunting and combat developed and used by the Omushkegowak underwent tremendous changes from pre-contact times to the end of the nineteenth century.

Relatively rich information is available on Native trapping methods in the subarctic (Cooper 1938; Williams 1969; Isham 1949). However, little information has been collected on Native hunting weapons such as lances, spears, and bows and arrows, especially for the regions west and south of Hudson Bay. Louis Bird has deep knowledge of this technology. In this chapter, he provides a close examination of some traditional Omushkego hunting and combat weapons. He also discusses how and why Omushkego people adapted European tools, weapons, and materials to their own specific needs and purposes, while maintaining much of their traditional technology. His insights contribute fresh perspectives, for example, on a scholarly controversy about the changing importance of goose hunting to the Omushkego people. The anthropologist John J.

Honigmann stated that by 1771, the HBC "looked for a special line of guns for the Indian trade," and that "firearms altered and eased subsistence hunting; especially they allowed the Indians to rely on waterfowl as a seasonal staple food" (Honigmann 1978: 218, 223) On the contrary, archaeologist Jean-Luc Pilon noted that, in pre-contact times, "although guns were not available, evidence from the Brant River suggests that waterfowl could be taken in significant numbers, especially during the molt, with technologically simpler means" (Pilon 1987: 35; quoted in Lytwyn 2002: 92).

When Louis described this process, he noted that because the birds could not fly during the moult, the Omushkegowak would walk into the nesting areas and simply pick up the number of birds that they wanted.[1] However, taking temporarily flightless waterfowl during the moult was limited to a brief time, while bows and arrows, as well as firearms, allowed the Omushkegowak to take waterfowl while they were airborne. Louis mentioned that it was possible to kill up to three birds with one arrow at a time, an observation corroborated by explorer and fur trader Pierre Radisson who asserted that he saw Native people do just that during his claimed travels through the James Bay area in 1660.[2] However, a fowling piece and shot enabled a proficient hunter to kill more than three times as many birds with one shot.[3] Furthermore, Louis noted that the introduction of guns brought about the competitive shooting of loons. Previously, loons had been difficult to kill with a bow and arrow, but a skilled marksman could easily kill them with a gun.[4]

The Omushkegowak accepted technological change on their own terms, as determined by their specific needs and purposes, and adopted a succession of European firearms. Historian John Long quotes James Wesley, a Cree from Kashechewan, as saying, "When the Company first came, it brought with it a gun ... [that] had an external firing primer called flint. This was the first gun. It was a good hunting weapon" (Long 1988: 231). Although modern scholars have maligned these early firearms for their lack of accuracy, by the mid-1700s HBC trader James Isham observed of the Swampy Cree, "these Natives are good Mark's men" (Isham 1949: 117).

---

1 Bird, personal communication to Anne Lindsay, 10 July 2003.
2 Lytwyn 2002: 92–93. It has not been demonstrated that Radisson actually reached James Bay.
3 Bird, personal communication to Roland Bohr, October 2001.
4 Bird, personal communication to Anne Lindsay, 7 July 2003.

Contemporary black-powder enthusiasts are able to hit plate-sized targets accurately at distances from forty to sixty metres with their modern-day replicas of eighteenth- and nineteenth-century flintlock guns. Accuracy with any distance weapon is much more dependent on the user's ability and training than on the quality or sophistication of the equipment. Rather than trying to improve their archery gear beyond its basic functionality, Native archers would simply practise more if they found their marksmanship deficient. This approach to marksmanship was probably also applied to the newly introduced firearms. Ethnohistorian Patrick Malone has argued that Native men in seventeenth-century New England were more skilled as marksmen than their European contemporaries because they were already accustomed to being hunters and warriors and appreciated the weaponry skills this demanded. In contrast, most European colonists were primarily agriculturalists. They lacked familiarity with firearms and other weapons because they came from a class-based society that severely restricted the use and ownership of weaponry to a privileged few (Malone 1991: 62–66).

The most striking features of early firearms to the Omushkegowak, and probably to most other Native people, were the extreme damage that a musket ball could cause and its instant killing power, especially at close range. While arrow hits on vital organs could be deadly, they did not necessarily instantly disable a human opponent or a large animal. A hit in the torso with a musket ball, however, especially when the firearm was loaded properly and fired at point-blank range, was usually lethal and would instantly have disabled the person being hit.[5]

This deadly power was paramount in increasing the psychological impact of firearms on the Omushkegowak and probably on other Native peoples as well. Because of their force, spiritual connotations were attributed to these weapons. The religious beliefs of many peoples of the Algonquian and Siouan language families contain concepts of the "Thunderbird." According to Louis, this spiritual entity represented a powerful force inherent in many aspects of the natural world and manifest

---

5 In order to illustrate this point, the German historian Marcus Junkelmann presented data obtained from a comparative study on early firearms undertaken by the provincial armory of Graz, Austria. According to this study a lead ball of a weight of 30.93g, fired from a musket of the 1686 Montecuccoli type, pierced a sheet of steel of 4 mm thickness at a distance of 30 m. The initial energy of the musket ball was 377.4 Joule. These data were contrasted with those obtained from shooting a replica of an Asiatic composite bow made from horn, wood, and sinew. The bow had a draw weight of 28 kg (ca. 56 lbs) at a draw length of 87 cm. The initial energy of the arrow was 62 Joule. The arrow pierced a piece of sheet steel of a thickness of 0.75 mm (Junkelmann 1992: 171, 172).

in such phenomena as thunderstorms and lightning strikes. Thunderbirds were thought to have great powers for healing as well as for destruction. The explosive discharge of a firearm—not only the muzzle flash, noise, and smoke, but mostly the tremendous destructive impact of the projectile on the target—were interpreted as manifestations of their power. Therefore, whoever operated a firearm partook in an activity that was permeated by religious and spiritual importance, harnessing the power of the Thunderbird. If those attacked with firearms held similar beliefs, they therefore deemed themselves under attack by powerful enemies who could marshal immense spiritual powers against them. Firearms instilled fear and panic in those attacked while greatly reinforcing the self-confidence of the attackers.

Oral traditions indicate that the firearms that the Omushkegowak obtained in trade from the HBC led to their eventual military ascendancy over their Inuit foes. At least for the mid- to late-eighteenth century, HBC records support this view (Williams 1969: 214, 236).[6]

For the Omushkegowak the positive aspects of these early firearms far outweighed the negative ones. For instance, even though their reloading took time, an experienced user could overcome this problem by using various, though sometimes unsafe, shortcuts in loading and priming a muzzle loading weapon, especially if it was a flintlock. However, improper handling of these weapons, especially by inexperienced users, could lead to serious injury. In 1776, Thomas Hutchins, the post manager at Fort Albany, noted in his journal:

> Oct, 11 [1776] Sent Mr. Jarvis the Surgeon to see an Indian 6 miles off who Unfortunately shattered his hand & wrist by the Gun going off in Loading it.
> Oct. 12, Mr. Jarvis returned, the Indian very ill.
> Oct. 25, Mr Watlington has the Misfortune to Wound his hand by the Accidental discharge of his Gun, Assisted Mr. Jarvis to amputate the middle Finger & also two of those of the Indians mentioned the 11th Instant.[7]

In 1777, George Sutherland, while traveling in the Albany River country as a guest of an Omushkego family, wrote:

---

6 HBCA E. 2/7 [1771]: fo. 18-18d.
7 HBCA, B. 3/a/71, Fort Albany Journal, 11, 12, 25 October 1776.

23th Saturday [August], the Indian with whom I Tent met with an axcedent afiring at Ducks a bit Broke out of the flint of his Gun Cut his Eye greatly so that already he is in danger of loosing his sight stayed at the Tent.[8]

Similarly, James Sutherland wrote in 1782:

28th Saturday [Sept] Late in the Evening 2 of Lieu^{t}. Newauchishickwabs young Men arrived here for Medicins and advice he having broken his Collar bone with the gun, which renders him unable to hunt, for his family. 10th [Oct] Thursday ... Late at Night Lieut Newauckisheckwab Came in with Geese &c. I am sorry to observe the badness of our guns becomes a General Complaint among all the Indians.[9]

It is true that early firearms were sometimes problematic, especially in very cold weather, because of frozen locks and weak springs. But wooden bows without sinew backing were also unreliable under such conditions and had their own problems. The subarctic is not an environment that favours archery. Prime raw materials for bow-making, such as eastern hardwoods like ash (*fraxinus Americana*), black locust (*robinia pseudoacacia*), hickory (*caraya cordiformis*), and osage orange (*maclura pomifera*) are not available in the region. Therefore, the Omushkegowak mainly relied on tamarack (*larix laricina*) and birch (*betula*). Although they have certain favourable qualities, neither of these woods is ideal for bow making, due to their lack of tensile and compressive strength.

When a bow is being drawn, the side that faces the target (the back) undergoes tension strain, while the side facing the archer (the belly) undergoes compression. For a bow to work properly, these basic forces have to be accommodated and utilized. The Omushkegowak made bows that distributed tension and compression forces most evenly. These bows were fairly long. Their limbs or "arms" had a flat cross-section. The bows were widest at the center of each limb where the most stress would occur. The bows were narrowest at the handle and at the tips.

---

8 HBCA, B.3/a/73, Journal of George Sutherland, 27 June 1777 to 27 June 1778, 23th [sic] Saturday [August, 1777], fo.11d.
9 HBCA, B.78/a/8 Gloucester House Journal 1782–1783, fo. 6–7.

a-cha-pe-ow,
General term for bow
ᐊᒐᐱᐤ
(lit. "moving string")

Oh-ta-ta-se-ke-ow
ᐅᐦᑕᑕᓯᑭᐤ
Strong bow for big game
(lit. "to flatten out together)

1. ka-ta-pa-ka-pet or
ᑲᑕᐸᑲᐱᐟ
ka-o-che-ta-pa-ka-pet
ᑲᐅᐦᒋ ᑕᐸᑲᐱᐟ
Nock for bowstring

2, ka-es-ake-pa-nek
ᑲᐃᐢᐊᑭᐸᓂᐠ
Limb or arm of bow (lit. "spring")

3. ka-es-ta-te-net
ᑲᐃᐢ ᑕᑎᓂᐟ
Grip section

4. ah-cha-pe-ya-pe-ow
ᐊᐦᒐᐱᔭᐱᐤ
Bowstring (general term)

a-ske-ma-ne-ya-pe–ow
ᐊᐢᑭᒪᓂᔭᐱᐤ
Raw hide string.

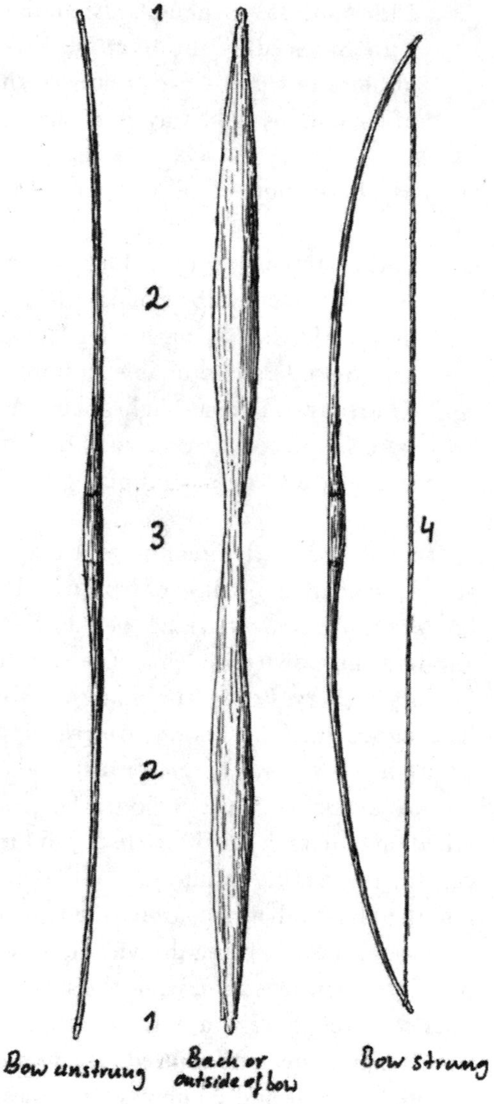

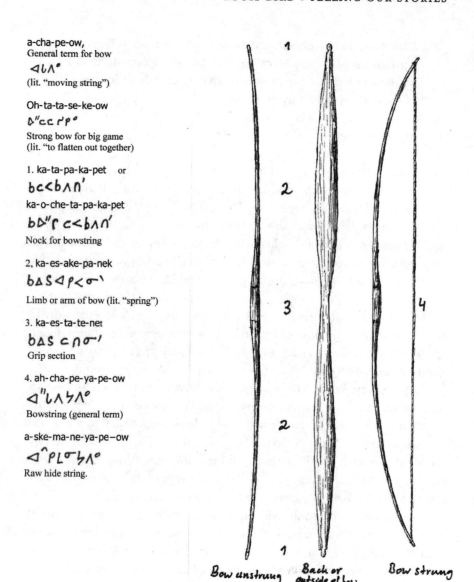

FIGURE 6: *Omushkego Cree self bow. Drawn by Roland Bohr with guidance from Louis Bird.*[10]

10 In this drawing, the Cree words for the parts of the bow appear in syllabics as well as in roman orthography; each symbol stands for a syllable. This writing system, developed by Methodist missionary James Evans at Norway House (MB) in the early 1840s to teach scriptures and hymns in Cree, spread rapidly across the Hudson Bay Lowlands as it was so easy for Cree-speakers to learn (see Brown 2004). Louis Bird and many other Omushkegowak prefer to use the syllabics when writing in Cree. For an example of a syllabic text, please visit <http://www.ourvoices.ca> and click on "Cree"; the Faries *Dictionary of the Cree Language* cited at the end of the Glossary of Cree Terms (this volume) also contains a "Key to the Cree syllabic system" (1938: x).

One way of increasing the tensile strength in a wooden bow at any time of the year was to apply a sinew backing. Fibers of sinew from large animals, such as deer, caribou, or moose, taken from the leg tendons or from the back straps running along either side of the spine, have far greater tensile strength than wood. Therefore, Native people who were forced to use wood of marginal quality and length strengthened the backs of their bows by either gluing sinew fibers lengthwise along the backs of their bows from tip to tip, as was done on the Great Plains, or by twisting and braiding the fibers into a long string, which was made into a strong, multi-string cable attached to the back of the bow, as was done by Inuit people in northern Manitoba. In both cases, the sinew rather than the wood absorbed the tension strain when the bow was drawn.

However, when Louis viewed a variety of sinew-cable-backed Inuit bows from northern Manitoba at the Manitoba Museum, he stated that he was not familiar with this kind of backing. His father had used only a wooden bow with a groove cut into the back along the longitudinal axis. This groove had held a cable or string, made from a material that Louis called "sturgeon spine" or "sturgeon sinew." Louis had never seen such a bow, since his father has used it in his youth before Louis was born, when these weapons were already very rare. The lack of compressive rather than tensile strength in the woods available for making bows may have been the main reason why the Omushkegowak and other Native peoples of the subarctic did not generally adopt sinew backing. Even if the tensile stress had been accommodated by some form of sinew backing, bows would still break in the extreme cold, because the wood cells on the belly would collapse when the bow was drawn far enough to launch the fairly long arrows common throughout the region.

The Omushkegowak made a wide variety of arrows adapted to specific game animals and hunting situations, or for practice. These arrows were mainly differentiated by their arrowheads. To catch small game or geese and to shoot fish, the wooden shaft of an arrow was sharpened to a point. Louis also mentioned an arrowhead, or an entire fishing spear, made from copper wire or similar materials. In order to disable or kill birds and small game, arrows with a bulbous, club shaped arrowhead could be used. For large game, hunters used arrows with bladed arrowheads made from bone, stone, or metal.

Subarctic arrows were sometimes made from saplings and shoots, but more commonly from split coniferous woods such as spruce. Once a shaft was trimmed close to its basic dimensions in diameter and length, it could be straightened by bending out the crooks with heat. Applying the fletching feathers was delicate work that needed to be executed with precision to make the projectile fly true. Furthermore, if the front and rear parts of the fletching were held in place with sinew, these wrappings had to be very smooth to avoid injury because in discharge the arrow would pass over the bare back of the archer's bow hand.

In the following section, Louis provides insights into little known but significant details of Omushkego material culture in regard to hunting technology and combat weaponry. This knowledge helps to illuminate some of the reasons why the Omushkegowak adopted and adapted European technology, and the impact this had on their methods of hunting, modes of violent conflict, and spiritual concepts.[11]

On Firearms and Archery

Well, one thing the firearm does, it kills instantly, and then it is more accurate in the distance than the bow and arrow. It has a greater range and is also more accurate, if you know how to use it. The bow and arrow, it's straight at a certain distance and it can kill, but usually the power, the strength of it, is sometimes not very strong and the animal will just run quite a ways before it dies. But the gun, you hit it in the right spot, takes only a few minutes before it drops and dies, or is unable to run. And then in birds, because there is the pellets in it, you can kill more than one at one shot. And also the gun can kill the large animals like moose, caribou, black bear, polar bear, much easier than bow and arrow. Bow and arrows are just as good, but they are not as quickly as the gun. So that's one good thing about it. And also one thing that I have remembered people say, when you have a gun and the sound makes you feel you're so confident, brings confidence in you. You know you're discharging something to kill and the noise also gives you power, gives you confidence. That's the positive side of this thing.

We didn't have any well-planned wars. We didn't have that kind of thing in our area. Not up here anyway. May happen down south. One way for the person who is using it, who has acquired it, the gun gives him addi-

---

11 The following section was compiled from Bird 0014, Bird 0116, and Bird 0117, all recorded by Louis Bird in 2001.

tional power because it added the fear in enemy because you have gun—
gives you confidence as an attacker or if you are defending. So the gun
gives you that additional confidence and also the powder gun, the sound
also brings more power to your side, because it's a loud noise and also it
has the mystic fire-smoke. They call it a fire stick. Also this gun, because of
its noise and because of its fire, it's similar to what the dream quest visualized, the thunder, the lightning and everything. So this gun brings that kind
of a being into a person who uses it. As it gives them confidence. And the
enemy that comes also has the same idea, so he is fearful of this thing.
When our Omushkego finally got the gun from the European, in the beginning of the fur trade, it helps them to hunt better and all those things that
has been hard to do, the gun gives an easier way to hunt. And also many
other things. The Omushkego, when they were at war with the Inuit, on the
James Bay, so they're fighting over their rights to hunt, they are fighting for
the hunting area, seals and all that. So the Omushkego have the gun first
and the Inuit didn't have it. So they had the advantage and the most startling thing was, they have a gun, the sound of fire, so the Inuit, they haven't
seen this. So they called it a fire stick at that time.

So it improved the Omushkegos' life, bringing in food easier and it
also provide clothing. And also those who move around, they have a
dwelling, covering, like a covering material for the teepee, and durable
because of the hides. And also it gives them the assurance to be able to kill
dangerous animals, like a polar bear, a black bear. And at mating season,
the bull moose is very dangerous and charge you, if you are there. So,
usually when that happens, if then somebody got the gun, has a chance to
load and he'll be able to knock down the moose, instead of hightailing it.
Instead of running away. So, many of those things have been benefiting
our Omushkego people.

And one other thing at the beginning is that the first gun the Native
people have, it needs a primary fire to fire the main chamber. And sometimes that makes people accidentally shoot themselves when they think,
"Well, it doesn't go," and then they put it down and pchuck! [Louis indicates a person looking down the barrel of a musket while the weapon is
going off by accident.][12]

And then sometimes they would just bust their eardrums, or even sometimes shoot themselves partially, because it didn't shoot, and at first people

---

12 There often was a slight time gap between the ignition of the powder in the priming pan and
the main charge in the barrel. This time gap might have been unexpected by some Native gun
users and may have led them to believe there was a problem with their gun.

who load the guns, they usually load the guns with a fire powder [loose black powder] already, but they just dropped the slug or pellets when they see the animals. And sometimes, when you have this matter of fire, it touches on a stick, it creates the sparks. After they have the spark, they had the flint and it touches the spark. It doesn't kill them, as long as there is no pellets or bullets, but it burns them. They had to be very careful. So that's the negative side of the firearm for them.[13]

But in caribou hunting, with a gun you can kill more than one caribou at once; that is in the wintertime, also in the summer time. They [the hunters] can follow the caribou and then they're gonna shoot it, first by sneaking up on it and once they shot the first shot, they can take the guts out of the first one they killed and put it away and then follow the other group that's still there. And then in an hour, an hour and a half, because the way they follow it, they would sort of bypass the path of them, go ahead and then wait for them, and they'd kill another one. And then they'd do the same thing, they'd take the guts out of the animal, then put it away nicely and follow one more. So in a day they can kill three caribous if there is only shot. In winter this can't be done with a bow because it's cold. It breaks. But in the summertime they can do it with the bow. That's the only thing about the bow; it's not so reliable that way. So that's the good thing about the gun.

The first gun they have, it was not so good. They know it was not reliable, so they used to keep their bow and arrow, just in case. In case the gun doesn't work and in summer time, especially. And also, during the wintertime, they know the bow and arrow cannot be used during the coldest weather, at least part of December, January, February. That time it's really

---

13 Maurice Doll, curator of firearms at the Provincial Museum of Alberta in Edmonton, demonstrated several short cuts in loading a muzzle-loading flintlock weapon. Keeping a powder charge in the gun, long before the shot, and then only adding the bullet when needed, was one way to cut back loading time. With muzzle-loading weapons, it is of outmost importance that the bullet or pellets be seated firmly against the powder charge in the barrel; otherwise, the breech of the gun might explode when the main charge is ignited. This firm contact was usually accomplished by placing a wad between the powder charge and the bullet and by ramming the bullet down the barrel with a ramrod which allows the bullet to be pressed firmly against the powder charge. For smooth-bore weapons this time-consuming process could be cut short by omitting the wad and by banging the gunstock on the ground sharply to make the bullet slide down the barrel and to make it rest directly against the previously inserted powder charge. Instead of using fine powder from a special dispenser for priming the pan, the weapon could be tilted on its side, so that the canal between priming pan and main chamber pointed slightly downwards. A sharp rap against the side of the breech would then cause some powder from the main chamber to spill onto the pan. Thus, the weapon could be primed in an instant. Using such quick, albeit unsafe loading methods, a flintlock smoothbore musket could be fired up to six times a minute (Maurice Doll, personal communication and demonstration to Roland Bohr, Provincial Museum of Alberta, Edmonton, August 2002).

hard to use bow and arrow, just to bring it out and shoot, because it's frozen stiff. The only time they can use bow and arrow in those days was if they were funneling caribou.[14] So they can create a fire behind a snow bank, so the caribou doesn't see that, so they can hold their bow there to warm it up so it doesn't break. As soon as they [the caribou] are coming here, that's when they shoot quickly. So that's the problem with the bow and arrow only in that three-months period; it's not reliable, really. But it can be. There was a way to hunt, even the moose hunting. They had a special way to do that, so the shooter would sit some place where this moose is gonna be chased. He already has that fire, where he can just wait for it. And this way, when the moose appears, then he can shoot. So it's a bit harder, not like in summer. In summer they can shoot it any time.

Also the gun, when you shoot an animal, you don't have to try to retrieve anything, the bullets; you just don't have to find them. But the bow, you have to find the arrow, if you don't know how to make an arrow.[15]

To make the arrow shaft you would use willow. Willow is the easiest thing to make, because you don't have to shape it. You just cut the very straight stuff. Sometimes it doesn't have to be good, it could be a bit curved. But you make that into a place where it could be straightened. And you take the raw stuff. And when it's dry, it's very, very strong, durable. It's flexible. It can bend; it doesn't break. But they can be very straight. That's what they liked. Another one you still find is cedar, tamarack, and also the other kind of spruce tree.

Women would sometimes help in putting the feathers on arrows. That was while they were still using bow and arrows. Yes, the women, they're very good, making those feathers for the end of the arrow. The women were good at that, because they can make string with the sinew from the animals, sometimes just the beavers and the otters make a fine sinew. And

---

14 The Omushkegowak occasionally hunted caribou just as Plains Indians hunted bison on foot by driving them into enclosures where they could be killed. Two long lines of obstacles extended from such an enclosure, forming a large V: the two lines almost converging at the entrance to the enclosure while they were farthest apart at the points farthest from it. Selected hunters would lure and drive a herd of caribou into the opening of this "funnel." Once the animals began to run in panic, other hunters would jump up from behind the obstacles in the funnel to drive the passing animals farther towards the enclosure. When all the animals were inside the enclosure, it would be closed and the animals could then be killed at close range with lances, spears, or arrows. In this situation traditional weapons were safer to use than firearms, because their projectiles would not carry as far as musket balls and were thus less likely to injure hunters on the opposite side of the enclosure.

15 Another problem encountered in archery, but not in using firearms, was the search for lost projectiles. Arrow-making is a time-consuming and laborious task; a well-made arrow requires more than a full day's work. Therefore, in case of a miss, or if an arrow passed through its target, archers, past and present, have been keen to find their lost projectile.

that's what they used to wrap these feathers on, so they won't hurt on the hand and the finger of the man. They were good at that. So the women usually used to make that. The men would put on the arrowhead, if there is a big game animal. And if it's a goose they had just put a little sharp thing. Very easy to go on through. And sometimes we got the big head, like a club, just to knock it down.

A bow would be about five feet long. That's average, but if you're a tall man, could be a bit more. My father was six foot, two inches. The bow was about as high as him, six feet two. Usually the bow would be as tall as the man, but not necessarily. If you have a good stick, it don't need to be very long. Or good material, whatever you use. This is something that I have asked my uncle. One time I asked him: What did they use to make a bow? Mostly in our area it's tamarack; that's the best for them. And it has to be that red wood. Many have the stem out there, on the southeast side of the tree, there's always that red wood. They think that's the most springy. It's very hard to pull and it goes back fast. And later on it gets stronger, so you don't necessarily have to pull so far. You could just pull so much and it is very stiff, too. It doesn't break. After a year it's better. The first year is not so good. After a year it begin to condition in some way. The springy stuff, it's really flexible and very powerful. And the older it gets, maybe after four years, it remains the same, and after that it begins to rot and then it's no more strength. And that's when sometimes you don't keep it that long. Four years at the most. If you can keep it that long. Sometimes you can't even keep it that long. An accident happen, or maybe it's just broken by something.

So it can be when they used to have a bow and arrow, they used to look, try every kind of tree. I know some people say birch makes a good bow.[16] In certain condition. You don't use it right away, gotta let it stay light, dry it long, condition into something. I don't know if they put it in anything. That way if the board is smeared with something, I don't know. But at least they conditioning it. And then it last longer, but not necessarily strong. It's very flexible, but not actually much faster as the other one.

My father was saying you can have any stick, whether it's tamarack, or any other kind tree, there's a tamarack, there's a black spruce and then there is, I don't know the name of this tree kind. Black spruce [*picea maricina*], it's not recommended. It breaks easy. And the other one, we call

---

16 Isham 1949: 118. The Hudson's Bay Company factor James Isham provided an illustration of a simple "D" bow, made of "berch" [sic], by Cree near York Factory.

minahik.[17] This is the tree that usually grow on the riverbank, on the small creeks. And usually have lots of that red wood, springy wood. And then at the back [of the bow], they cut a groove in there. They're going up the back, from the centre to the ends and that's where you put this string, the sturgeon spine, I think it is. [Louis indicates that a groove with somewhat of a half-round cross section is cut into the back of the bow, from tip to tip, parallel to the bow's longitudinal axis.] You also use a whale spine, for instance. So they take that and they stretch it and then they put that on the back. And that makes the bow springier, faster. They put it right in the middle there, right on the back here. It would be right there and hooked on there, and it goes behind in there and be hooked right in here. [Louis indicates that some sort of cable is attached to the bow's back by hooking it over the tips of the bow and by binding it to the limbs as well.][18] And the bowstring is on the other side. But this kind of bow would also break in very cold weather. I mean, any stick will do, any kind of stick will do. But it's brittle when it's cold. It cracks [to] pieces. Almost any kind of wood will do that. Tamarack may be a little bit more flexible. A little bit, but if it's too cold, it's too cold.

The thing that is mostly notable about the firearm is the noise. Noise will prevent you to hunt quietly, as with the bow and arrow. When you have bow and arrow and you are hunting in the fall, in the day, it doesn't matter what time of the day, there is a chance that you could kill an animal here, quietly, and be able to go on and not far away encounter another animal who has not yet heard anything. It gives you a chance to hunt a variety of animals close by. And when you shoot, it's different. As soon as the firearm is heard, this animal is ready to run, and also the other ones around him. But bow and arrows doesn't do that. So the sound sometimes can carry quite a distance under different conditions of atmosphere. Sometimes it'll roll a long, long ways and you are now disturbing the animals so far distant. You only got one chance to have a good shot in the morning, if you can kill them. That's bad thing about it.

And also, the animals know that. When they hear the gun, they get used to it. When they hear the gun, they know there is a human here, so the caribous can be ready to just go, get away, when they hear which direction there is a gun. And for migrating geese, sometimes they come in

17 This is white spruce (picea glauca), according to Marles et al. 2000: 92–94.
18 This is very similar to an Inuit-style bow with a sinew cable backing. When I showed Louis a drawing of an Inuit bow with a simple single cable backing, he agreed that this was how the bows he described must have looked.

during the fall, they settle into a field, and when they settle into the field, there is a feeding ground, and then there is a sleeping area. That's where they go, every day. Every morning they go into the feeding area. And in the evening they go down to sleep by the water. But if you shoot a gun late after sunset, this gun will throw the flame out, the fire. And the geese see that and they don't like that. They know it's dangerous thing and they leave the area and go some other place. That's why the Native people say, "Don't fire a gun after sunset, because the geese will see that." When you hunt the geese when they are flying and if you have black powder, you know how a muzzleloader can make a fire, the geese begin to see that. They see from distance. There is a smoke and they know that's where the man is and they don't go there, they go around. So that's a negative side of the gun. And if you fire the gun in the dark, this black powder will give lots of flash. And that's what makes the geese afraid of it. And that's why we, the Native people, begin to have a new teaching after the European came. It sort of added to their rule how to behave, how to respect animals. So they firmly say, do not fire the gun after sunset. And don't fire the gun also before sunrise. You know, it scared the animals. But recently, after the gunpowder is improved, after the black powder, this thing doesn't affect too much [meaning after the introduction of cartridge ammunition]. At least there is no light when you fire so much. Just a few sparks, but still the noise bothers the birds and they know not to go anywhere they hear shot, in the evening especially. They don't want that. They don't like that sound. So that's about the negative side of this gun for the people.

But the gun gives more success in hunting big game animals. And a greater number of geese to shoot in the fall. They can shoot two at a time, maybe more. And they're all in one shot, which they couldn't do with the bow and arrow. And also they can have more things to store for their winter food. They'll have more food to preserve in the fall. So firearm did bring much improved life to First Nations in North America. But it did sort of deny the other people who used the bow and arrow, when there is a gun around. It sort of limit their capability with the bow and arrow. Otherwise, the other one is getting more.[19] But that didn't stop them from

---

19 Even though the noise gave confidence to warriors using firearms in combat, hunters found that it was a great disadvantage compared to traditional equipment. The noise made animals more wary and alert, such that even hunters with quiet traditional weapons found it more difficult to approach them within range of their weapons. This is reflected to some extent in modern hunting regulations, which allow an archery season for several weeks before firearms can be used. Thus, hunters who adopted firearms may have forced other hunters to do the same, in order to catch enough animals to feed their people.

having bow and arrow. They still have bow and arrow. Those people, they didn't stay always close with each other, they always have their own area. So those who don't have a gun, they will hunt with the bow and arrow only. They won't even see the gun; the guy who has a gun is a long way out there some other place. So it doesn't affect them. And later on, when they able to acquire the gun, then they slowly change. Once they get the mastery of this gun, they still keep the bow. And then slowly they started putting it away. But they keep practice anyhow, because it requires a skill. It also requires the proper wood for you to make a bow. But in time, about a hundred years that maybe, then the bow hunting is getting to be discarded. But it's still there. One other thing about the gun is that the first ones only shot once, and then they improved and a new design was a double barrel and that's improved more. And after that it was the repeating rifle that was very good for the big game animals. And that further improved their hunting technique and also improved their lifestyle.

But it diminished the animal population. Very fast. For example, the geese. The geese began to dwindle when there was a heavy hunting, heavy harvesting of geese. And also the time when the Hudson's Bay Company began to establish goose camps, the geese began to diminish slowly, because it's easier to kill a lot of them. When this Hudson's Bay goose hunting operation came to exist, that was a long time ago, probably around 1700 or 1750. And there were lots of geese. And then, when the people began to hunt, then there were few. And also they began to avoid where the people hunt. The geese began to know that's where the people are, so they would bypass that area and they would go to another place. Because the Hudson's Bay Company wanted to have more wild meat than anything for their food, they gave what they called one ounce of black powder. One ounce of black powder can create about eleven shells [shots?]. And the Native people are getting accustomed how to do. So they have their little black powder and just a minimum amount of pellets and then they hunt in a special way, they can shoot many geese. They [the geese] don't have to be on the ground, the ground is preferable, but they can shoot them as they land. Then there's so many heads put together and they're in line, sideways. And that's what they shoot, right in the heads, all of those. And they can knock eleven geese at once.[20] Eleven geese! One shot! They're only required to bring in five geese for one ounce

---

20 Isham 1949: 117–19. Hudson's Bay Company factor James Isham described a very similar method for multiple killings of geese by Cree hunters at York Factory.

of black powder, the rest of it, they have. That's it. So they shoot first. Whenever it's possible, they shoot. If they could shoot at least five at once, they already have their limit for exchange. The rest of it is their geese. So that's what makes hunting so fast, they kill five, ten geese at one shot. That's what makes a difference. So after a while the geese began to avoid the area wherever there is hunting.

There was a rule, maybe we didn't have any game laws, not like today. We didn't have those. Of course, not written ones. But we did learn when we were young; when we are young, we are told: When you hunt the geese, they say, shoot only the male, don't shoot the female. Shoot the male and don't shoot all the young ones. Sometimes if you want to shoot the young ones, it says, leave some, maybe two. That's the teaching, that's to keep the population stay the same. And we were told to do that with the geese, with the ducks and any game birds that we eat.

And same thing with the beavers. When you go [to a] beaver house we know there'll be two adults, two parents, and maybe four from last year and then there'll be four maybe a year before. You know, there will be about ten beavers all together in there. So for the parents, say, leave the female, if you can. Just kill one, whether it's a female or not. But only take one. And then take two of the other half size and then, if you need to take two of the little ones. So that way you have them for the next spring, they will be mating some other place. And it's same thing with the family of otters. Sometimes the otters, you see by the trail there are five of them. You know there is two, there is one mother and four young ones. So they teach us, that's why we have to know the trail to be able to read, which one is an elder, when you see the trail. Okay, this is the biggest one, and you see that these are the young ones, so you try to catch one, only when you see them. Or if you have to trap them, when you see if it's a mother, then let the two of them stay alive, if you can. It's for, maybe you could call that in English "conservation"? A conservation practice. We did that all the time before the European came. And only then as the European came, these things were not observed any more. They changed. Because of the fur trade. So people just kill off everything and then they depleted the animals very quickly. We did. My grandparents did. They know they were doing something wrong, but trading for the goods with the other person was stronger.

So we have those rules. But we learned them when we were small, when we were young. Parents tell you, the elders tell you. You know, you don't wanna kill them all off. And if we shoot, if we hunted the ducks, they say leave the mother alone. So we have to do that. Same thing with the caribous. Leave the females and if you see them, especially in the month of March, when you see that they carry the young ones, you don't kill them. But kill a buck, if you have to, or two years old one. So they always teach us that, and people know exactly which one is this, even the moose. They know if it's a female, they know it's last year's young one, they know it's a bull out there; they know that. But if this is the month of March, or thereafter, you have to leave them a mother, because she's gonna have a calf, so if you kill that one, you kill two. So you kill only the bull.

Very long ago caribou were hunted in big drives. In those times there were plenty of caribous. They were coming in and they know that they're not gonna kill them all off. So that's the time they do that. These are migrating caribous. They migrate from some place and they travel here, they will travel only in a certain month. So that's when you kill as much as you can, but don't kill them all off.

So these were the ones who did that. Sometimes you see maybe twenty-five, maybe fifteen, you can do that. Sometimes, if you have fifteen, then there's no problem with that. But when they're in declining period, the caribous come and go, every twenty-five years or so, so there are plenty and then after that, not because you killed them off, because they move to other place. They would be hunted in drives. It was done. But it was done in such a way because sometimes people knew this is the only month that they can do that, March and April; May it's a bit too late to do that. Only March and April that they can do that very easily. And in May they're not gonna be able to hunt big game animals because of slush. So they have to have extra. Something that they can cache at their camp, during that time. That's the only reason they do that. They have a reason when to kill many animals. Other than that you just don't shoot them for anything. There's no sport hunting. There's no such thing.

When the gun came, that's when really our people just killed as many as they can. They forget about the old practice. But long time ago they only killed so many at a certain time. I can say in the springtime. Or sometimes they kill the caribous just about November, when it starts to freeze, because they're gonna migrate away, they're gonna go a long ways away. And then you never know where they're gonna be. And this is the only time you gonna have and that's when you kill as much as you can, as long as it's not too many. Then you would kill, you would kill only the female and the last year ones. That time you don't have to shoot the buck, because he's totally depleted himself on mating. [Laughs] He's not much good to eat. So that's the practice. That was a conservation practice.

I know my ancestors used spears a little bit, not as much, but they used it when sometimes they don't happen to have bow and arrow for some reason. I'm just thinking. I never asked. You do not always carry the bow when you move with your family. You just don't walk there and carry just bow and arrow. You help. You carry everything. And sometimes the bow and arrow were used sometimes as a cane, or supporting stick. And sometimes you can't even carry that, because you have to carry so much. So the bow sometimes, it's kind of awkward to carry around. Sometimes they leave it where they had camped. Leave it there for some other. So they move without it, until they find a place where they can stay. Then they make another bow. So maybe, sometimes, in between that they used to make something to throw. That's why I think throwing a spear is something that is an emergency sort of thing. That's not exactly the way they hunt, it's just temporary thing. And of course, they also have a sling, just like a bolo tie [pe-mi-ti-shway-hi-gan—bola, a cord with two weights attached, to throw around the legs of caribou]. They have that. Some people were good at it too. Hunting. I'm not so sure if they kill caribou with that, at least they knock it down. I know they used two stones to trip the caribous down. Sometimes they find a good shape, maybe two pounds each. And the other one, same way. And they tie their string and moose hide, or caribou hide, and then this would be about a foot, two feet altogether. And in the middle they have a little handle. And then they throw it into the legs of the animal, so the caribou would just fall down with the legs tangled up with this thing. And so they run up to it and spear it. Or maybe hit it with the tomahawk.

There was something that I forgot to mention about the results of the firearm. In the Mushkego country some of our ancestors, when they have seen the gun, it has given them the idea how to use it in their own shaman power. And there is a story; it's about some mi-tew personal practice [where shamans] were able to use the firearm, or a gun without reloading. They were able, supposedly, to keep aiming and cause it to fire as if it has been reloaded. This they have done during the time when other tribes used to come and attack them unexpectedly. And those who had shaman power, sometimes they would defend their families by using this, just the gun itself, but without any gunpowder and the slugs. And were able to defend their family. So for that reason the gun, the firearm have given a strength to the First Nation and it has given some additional ideas because of the firearm. And there's a story about also the greater shaman will have an idea how to harness his dream quest, having the thunder being his helper, and was able to use a similar object as a gun barrel to guide the lightning bolt to kill his enemies. So the gun had brought an extra idea amongst the First Nation in Omushkego land. There is a story about this. The story is very fascinating and it's very powerful. They called it "The Omushkego Who Fought With Thunderbolt." So, there goes. Shows us how powerful influence this firearm can be. And there were some who have tried the similar situation. Those who pretend to be a shaman, trying to use only the barrel to fire the gun, which, sometimes it was not actually work, they were just tricked to use.

There's a man who have lived in Winisk about 1955 up to 1965, ten years. And this man, his grandfather has been a mi-tew, one of the Omushkego most admired mi-tew, in the James Bay area. This guy I have seen living, has tried to imitate his grandfather by pretending to be able to fire gun without any stock, but just the barrel, even double barrel. Everybody believes that the first time that he was able to do that. Even the other person did the same thing. But the thing is, he was not doing that. He was not actually doing that. All he did was, he put the shells into the barrel and hit them with the axe or a hammer, hit the primer and causes to discharge, to fire the shell. This was a dangerous thing to do. He could have killed himself by doing that. And he did it only to impress his own people, to impress for something that he was trying to impress. And the guy was not a mi-tew. He got sick and then he got what we called in our life, he committed a blaspheme act, which means sin against nature, in our tribe, in our tribal beliefs.[21] And this man, later in his life, he became crazy. Lost his mind. And people said, that is the reason. Because he have done such a thing. He used to scare people because of that, because he pretended to be a shaman and scare people with this object and with this action.

So therefore, in our culture, there is stories that tells us something that we want to know. So that's one of the things that has influenced our First Nation people by the firearm, which actually was not really true. It's just the nature of some Omushkegowak that have [are] so proud of themselves, they want to be something which they are not, trying to be a mys-

---

21 For discussion of blasphemous acts (pa-sta-ho-win) and Omushkego ideas about "sin against nature," see Lindsay's introduction to Chapter 6.

tical person which they not truly are. It's just shameful to say that, but it is. It has happened. So, one of the things that influenced people about the firearm. So there you have it. I gave you the extra story.

8

Mi-Te-Wi-Win Versus Christianity
Grand Sophia's Story

Introduction
DONNA G. SUTHERLAND

I met Louis Bird in 1998 at a storytelling event at the University of Winnipeg. We quickly discovered we shared kinship ties among some of our ancestors who resided on Hudson and James Bays during the eighteenth century. One ancestor in particular was a Scottish-born fur trader, James Sutherland, who worked for the HBC. Louis also descends from a man named James Sutherland, although we have not yet found the critical link to tell us if we descend from the same man.

In my never-ending quest to uncover stories about Swampy Cree women who formed marital unions with fur traders such as James Sutherland, I asked Louis if he knew any stories about them. Louis said he did not know much about the early Sutherland women but he did know a few stories about the women of his mother's family.

I asked him if he would share one of those stories with me. He said, "Sure, I'll tell you a woman's story." True to his word, he sent me two ninety-minute cassette tapes about his maternal ancestors. The first story was a tragic tale about his great-great grandmother. The second story, a fascinating narrative about the conflict between Swampy Cree and Christian religion, appears here. It tells of a traumatic event that happened to his maternal great-grandmother or, as Louis calls her, his Kokum, the Swampy Cree word for grandmother. Louis also calls her Kii-she-swa-fii, or in English, Grand Sophia.[1]

---

1 Louis was born in 1934. His mother was Scholastique Okimaawininiiw (1906–74). She married Michen Pennishish/Bird (1900–56) in 1919. His grandmother Christine (ca.1880–1907)

Grand Sophia's earthwalk began around 1860 in her family's tent near their much-favoured gathering place called Kas-ska-ta-ma-gan. The name means "something to eat or catch, or a place where you can eat from."[2] Famous for its trout fishing, Kas-ska-ta-ma-gan is situated about fifty miles inland from the shores of Hudson Bay. It lies between the Hudson's Bay Company settlements of York Factory and Fort Severn on an old elevated beach ridge that, in places, ascends 800 feet above sea level.[3]

Louis does not remember the names of Grand Sophia's parents but he believes their surname is Thomas—a name that has been connected to the HBC since the mid-eighteenth century.[4] Grand Sophia may have been raised for the most part by her grandparents, given that her mother died as a result of being accused of becoming a wih-ti-go or a being with cannibalistic tendencies when Grand Sophia was a little girl.[5] She had at least two older brothers and a younger sister who died in infancy; their names are not known.

---

married David Okimaawininiiw. His great-grandmother Grand Sophia or Kii-she-swa-fii (ca.1860–1913) married twice; her first husband is unknown, her second husband was John Anishinaabe. His great-great grandmother, name unknown but referred to as Kokum (ca. 1840–65), married a man with the surname Thomas. Possibly his great-great grandmother was Cahkokap (b. ca. 1820) married to Mîsîwikitik (Robert Beardy).

2 Bird, personal conversation, April 2003.

3 York Factory has also been known as York Fort, Fort Bourbon, and Port Nelson. Established in 1684, the first York Factory post stood on the northwest bank of the Hayes River, about half a mile below its present location. The company built a new fort in 1742 that lasted for forty years. However, when three French warships under the command of Jean-François de Galaup, Comte de la Pérouse, sailed into Hudson Bay in 1782 in the aftermath of the American War of Independence, they burned the post. The HBC rebuilt in 1783 on the north bank of the Hayes River, about four miles above the old post. In 1821 a final fort was built on the west side of Hayes River on the point formed by the Hayes and Nelson River (HBC Archives, York Factory Post History). See maps, this volume.

   Fort Severn also held the names of: Severn House, Severn Fort, Fort James or James Fort (1759), Churchill Fort (1685–90), and New Severn (1685–90). The initial post identified as Severn in HBC records dates to 1685. The post was built and destroyed several times in the 1700s and 1800s (HBC Archives, Severn Post History).

4 John Thomas (ca. 1751–1822) joined the HBC in 1769 as a writer at Moose Factory. The HBC dismissed Thomas from their service in 1813. His Swampy Cree wife, Margaret, a woman with whom he fathered nine children, died that same year. After Margaret's death, Thomas married another Cree woman named Meenish. Thomas died in Vaudreuil (Lower Canada) in 1822.

   Thomas Thomas Sr. joined the HBC as a surgeon in 1789 at York Factory. He was master at Fort Severn from 1796 to 1810 and then became superintendent of Moose Factory, Eastmain, and Albany, with headquarters at Albany. In 1813, he became governor of the Northern Department. He retired to Red River Settlement in 1820. He formally married his Cree wife, Sarah, on 30 March 1821 at Red River Settlement. Their family consisted of eight children: William, Catharine, Frances, Jane, Thomas, Sophia, Elizabeth, and Anne. Another Thomas Thomas also served as a surgeon at York Factory for three years in the 1790s, but is not known to have had a family in Hudson Bay (research files belonging to Jennifer S.H. Brown and Donna G. Sutherland).

5 In Bird 0006, recorded in 2001, Louis tells the daunting story of how Grand Sophia's mother was thought to be a wih-ti-go. See Sutherland 2004: 337–47.

As a young girl Grand Sophia spent much of her time near the small settlement of Attawapiskat on the north side of the Attawapiskat River. Attawapiskat is about five kilometres from the James Bay coastline and approximately 160 kilometres north of Moosonee. During Grand Sophia's childhood, several traveling missionaries who did not yet have permanent missions introduced strict religious teachings to the community. Some of the missionaries were Roman Catholic; others were Anglican. By 1893 the Roman Catholics established a permanent mission at Attawapiskat.[6] Louis says Grand Sophia accepted Catholicism completely, rejecting the age-old spiritual practices of her ancestors.

Grand Sophia married a man whose name Louis cannot remember. Two daughters were born to the union, Christine and Sophia. After the birth of Sophia, the words "Grand" and "Little" were added to distinguish mother from daughter—Grand meant "The Older One." Christine married David Okimaawininiiw (a.k.a. Okimaaw) around 1899. She became Louis Bird's grandmother. Unfortunately she never lived long enough to know her offspring; she died around 1906 shortly after the birth of her daughter—Louis Bird's mother, Scholastique, who was then raised by Grand Sophia. Grand Sophia and her family stayed in Attawapiskat until after the death of her first husband.

Grand Sophia later married an exceptionally skilful caribou hunter named John Anishinaabe, an Oji-Cree man who spoke both Ojibwa and Swampy Cree. Anishinaabe came to the Attawapiskat area from the region of Big Trout Lake. Louis believes that a Roman Catholic missionary married them. After the marriage, Grand Sophia and her young children, Christine and Sophia, accompanied John Anishinaabe in his seasonal excursions to track woodland caribou.

While she had faith in her husband's ability to carry out successful hunts, Grand Sophia tried to ensure his victories by reciting scripture from her Bible and praying to the Roman Catholic God. A consequence

---

6 HBC Archives Search File: Attawapiskat. For a brief period in the 1680s Father Antoine Silvy, a Jesuit missionary resided in the James Bay area (Long 1986a: 314). Rev. George Barnley established a Methodist mission at Moose Factory in 1840 (Brown 2004: 106; Hutchinson 1985: 30). Barnley abandoned his mission in 1847, but in the summer of that same year two Oblate priests from Timiskaming visited Moose Factory. The (Anglican) Church Missionary Society established a mission at Moose Factory on 4 September 1851 under the direction of Rev. John Horden (1828–93) (HBC Archives/AM Church Missionary Society Records [CMS]—Reel A88). Four years later in 1855, the CMS established a mission a little farther north at Fort Albany with the Oblates erecting a mission there as well in 1892 (Long 1986a: 314–16). Beginning in the late nineteenth century, Roman Catholic and Anglican missionaries played a significant role in the lives of the James Bay people.

FIGURE 7: *My mother, Scholastique Bird, in her teepee home in Winisk in the 1950s. Scholastique was brought up by her grandmother, Grand Sophia, and told me many stories. Credit: Copyright Canadian Museum of Civilization, photo Vita Rordam, 1955, no. S93-9988.*

of her private actions on one particular hunting trip was a frightening threat of a retaliatory attack by a powerful mi-tew (shaman). This is the story of Grand Sophia's horrifying experience as told by Louis in the summer of 1998.

Grand Sophia's Near-Death Experience

So I want to tell a story about Grand Sophia. According to her story— you know, passed down to us—she tells a story to her granddaughter which is my mother [Scholastique]. It is my mother who told me those stories. So my stories are second-third-hand sort of stories but they are very vivid. My mother tells me this story. According to her grandmother's story it is like this.

You're not going to find the name of this person because she is a woman.[7] I want to prepare first why am I telling this story. There is three things involved—three, I think. The first one is the lady herself. It involves the Christianity versus the First Nations spiritual beliefs and practices— that's the important thing. And the other thing is to show the will of a woman who wants to stay with her husband. And the danger of having two religions or two spiritual beliefs and practices encountered. The clash between the two ideas, that's the important thing.

So I place this story in 1885 or 95, the story that took place at that time. I know that the Anglican Church arrived in Churchill and in York Factory at the early years of the fur trade.[8] The Anglican priests came with the Company of Adventurers.[9] But the French people did not come here to settle until later so the Catholic Church did not come until about 1840. They begin to intensify converting the Cree people in that period in time and it went on for so very, very—what should I say—it was driving very hard.

And the first priest came around in the James Bay and Hudson Bay because the Anglican Church was already here or I forget the other name—there was another name. And then this Native person pretend to be the teacher, you know, just because of Christianity.[10] There are a lot of people who do that today even. So anyway, he did that and he came to convert people to Christianity by himself, and have his own Christian version and his own way. And it's quite a story, but anyway.

---

7 Louis has shared several stories about men such as his paternal grandfather John Pennishish, great-grandfather Joseph Pennishish, and possibly great-great-great grandfather Pennishish, also known as Snowbird. These men were all connected in various ways to the HBC, and I found their names in archival records. But as he noted, women are rarely mentioned.

8 For the Omushkego peoples, exposure to Roman Catholicism began in the 1680s when Jesuit missionaries traveled from New France to fur trade posts on the Moose, Albany, and Nelson Rivers. Father Antoine Silvy made a brief visit to the area in the 1680s (Long 1986a: 314). Throughout the eighteenth and nineteenth centuries, HBC postmasters performed "Divine Service" at most HBC posts. The first Protestant missionary and chaplain for the HBC, John West, arrived at York Factory in the fall of 1820. He stayed in North America for three years, residing in Red River Settlement (present-day Winnipeg); he also made several journeys to York Factory and Norway House where he performed baptisms and marriages (West 1966). After Methodist missionary George Barnley left Moose Factory in 1847, Anglican CMS missions began work there in 1851 and in Fort Albany in 1855 (Long 1986a: 314–16). In the mid-1800s, Roman Catholic Oblate priests began regular summer visits to the James Bay area (HBC Archives "Search file" for Weenusk/Winisk Post; Fulford and Bird 2003: 294–96).

9 "The Governor and Company of Adventurers" is the original name of the HBC. On 2 May 1670, at Whitehall Palace in London, England, King Charles II declared eighteen men (including his cousin Prince Rupert) as "the true and absolute Lordes and Proprietors" of Rupert's Land through his Royal Charter. Rupert's Land was the HBC term for the Hudson Bay watershed—about 40 per cent of modern Canada (Moore 2000: 7).

10 Louis is referring to the prophet Abishabis ("Small Eyes") and Wasitek or Wasitay ("The Light") who became active in 1842–43, drawing upon the Cree syllabics introduced by Methodist missionary James Evans at Norway House, Manitoba (Brown 2004).

So it is in that period when Grand Sophia was beginning to emerge. The French had already converted most of the people but there was a resistance—quite a bit of resistance by the Omushkegowak. They didn't want to take the Christianity because they still strongly relied upon their own beliefs and practices because it is geared for them in the wilderness. So the men didn't want to join the Christianity because they would lose their power of skills, of hunting, and all that is associated with their beliefs and practices. And then besides that, there is still other tribes who was still so powerful with their former practice. Because this word mi-te-wi-win, it's not a very perfect thing—mi-te-wi-win—it's not love thy neighbour— it's not turn the other cheek sort of thing—no. It's something like an eye for an eye. If your neighbour comes and be friendly with you, you be friendly with him, but if your neighbour comes and stab you from behind or even uses his magic power or mi-tew, if he bothers you, you fight back—it's him or you.

So the Christianity when it comes, it teaches turn the other cheek, and love thy neighbour. But that was contrary to what people were surviving from. People know that there is no such thing as turn the other cheek because you would just die. So the men who will fight for life and the harshness of the wilderness, you know, they just simply—this Christianity doesn't work here. So they resisted, but the priests are very smart. They approached the wife or even the kids, so they sort of persuaded the men that way. So for long time the men just didn't join the Christianity but the women did, and that's the story about this Grand Sophia.

Grand Sophia understands and believes because she has seen the work- ings of the old—the Omushkego mi-te-wi-win. She feared it because she saw many things and she believed it worked. She wanted to join the Christianity because it has a softer teaching in it—love thy neighbour. It sounds very attractive to her because she saw many scary situations in her lifetime and that's why she wanted to try something else that was much more easier in mind and in body. So, she tried the Christianity. The story then begins at that period and time and the reason why it hap- pened—is the effect of Christianity.

And then also it will show us the story about how the Omushkego lived with nature. They followed things, our ancestors, the Omushkego; they were not settling type of people. They move with the nature—move with the environment—they lived with the environment. They didn't change it. So they move with the whole thing. They move with animals—

fish—wherever they can find the fish—when the season changes they will go there. And for that reason they did not settle in any one place.

And the Church they didn't know, that's far from it—they couldn't have the unity of the church because they have to be alive, they have to move, they have to be mobile. They can't build anything that holds them back in order to survive. They have a very mobile unit and also they have a system to build a home in the season of time only, and never stay in one place very much. That is why they don't leave any trace at all wherever they lived in this part of the country, especially in the James Bay lowland area.

In the James Bay lowland the conditions are so different—it is so harsh. The weather is so severe, it can change the land; within ten or fifteen years you can see the changes. Fifteen years' time, it's quite a change.

So, we will leave it at that—these things we will have in our mind. These are the controlling factors—not a person. The harshness of the land, and no church can change that. So our people long time ago—they resisted Christianity for that reason—because their beliefs and practices was suitable to the way they lived. If you stop that—you kill them—that's exactly what happened. When they joined the Christianity they fell down—they had no more power on their own, the way they used to have it on their own from the wilderness. They just simply lose it.

Grand Sophia is my great-grandmother—me, Louis Bird. My mother's maiden name was Okimaawininiiw. The first part—O-ki-maw—means "boss or leader"; wi—is a connecting word, to connect to the next one—ininiiw—is a person or human. This "ininiiw" is sometimes applied to man, but if you see a person in a distance—it's an ininiiw, it's not an animal—it's a human. But this centre word "wi"—it's a connecting word when you put two names together. So O-ki-maw means "the boss" or "the boss human," so that's what my mother's maiden name was. My mother's father was David Okimaawininiiw. He married Christine, my mother's mother and Christine is a daughter of Grand Sophia.

Grand Sophia married twice. She married her [first] husband some place around Fort Severn. But her husband is one of those people who during the fur trade used to trade in York Factory and Kashechewan.[11] Fort Severn was an outpost from York Factory, so people either had to

---

11 Kashechewan is an Omushkego (Swampy Cree) name meaning "strong current." For centuries, the Omushkego people used this river to travel inland which in 1679 prompted the Hudson's Bay Company to establish a trading post at this location. They called it Fort Albany. The community is on the coast of James Bay between Cape Henrietta Maria and Moose Factory. Grand Sophia received a Christian baptism at Kashechewan/Fort Albany—date unknown.

trade at Kashechewan or Fort Severn. Some of those who traded in Fort Severn—the men—usually associated to the Hudson's Bay activity, they go to York Factory to load and unload the ship that comes from Europe.

So Grand Sophia moved with her husband across the land from York Factory to Attawapiskat, which is between the distances of four hundred to seven hundred miles. So not every season her husband would work in York Factory—but once in awhile—the first husband. I don't remember his name. I don't know if he had a last name, he may have only one name. The first husband, she had at least two children with him; one was Christine, my mother's mother, and the other younger daughter's name was also Sophia. So they call her Sophia Jr. But the Grand was known as Grand Sophia (great: the older, the senior) whatever word you want to use. In Cree the word is Kii-she-swa-fii.

Anyway, when she married the second husband, this man was already Christianized—his name was John Anishinaabe. He was an Oji-Cree kind of person. He spoke both languages; they use a dialect in the middle, which they call themselves Oji-Cree. I really don't know exactly where he came from. Sometimes my mother used to think he came from Big Trout area. I am not too sure if it was Big Trout Lake but I think it was. Almost any people who were raised and came from Big Trout area were associated with York Factory. They had routes there that go back and forth. Big Trout Lake is about two hundred miles from the Hudson Bay coast. It's on a plateau, the first plateau of the land where all the lakes exist, all the major rivers, they are the first lake, the first plateau. Some of the headwaters, the lakes, they have their outlet into the lake and those following creeks, they sort of twist around and head up somewhere in that area.

The York Factory area has two river systems—two major rivers that empty into the same area. One of them is the Hayes River and the other is the Nelson River. The Hayes River is a large river and it goes to one hundred and fifty or two hundred miles up towards the south and it branch off almost in the middle. One goes to the southeast and the other goes to the west. The one that turns southeast eventually begins the lake; some of the tributaries are called Shamattawa, ki-she-ma-ta-wa—The Great Spirit Lake. In this area, the land is rugged; it's hilly about eight hundred or nine hundred feet above sea level. So it's a mountain for our people, the Omushkego people.

So what happened here in the Bay area where the Omushkego were living? They are caribou hunters, some of them—yes. Some of them within land, like Big Trout Lake area, they prefer to eat moose. But the coastal people they prefer—they usually have caribou, that's the reason. The old migrating caribou from the northwest used to come as far as Fort Severn. They swing into the west, hit the great lakes of Winnipeg, and then turn back into the north; that's what the old people used to say. So it was those migrating caribou from the north who used to come and travel and benefit the Omushkego people for the material, teepee coverings and clothes.

This man, the second husband of Grand Sophia, was a very good hunter, he was an expert hunter of the caribou and he loves to eat them. And that was his most favourite food, and he can also get everything from it—and he was a well-off man. He was admired for his good hunting—his skilful hunting for the caribou. I guess that's the reason Grand Sophia married him.

So anyway, the story goes. There were some years that there were no caribou, some years after she married her husband, maybe two or five years after. I think they were living between Fort Severn and York Factory. There is a famous place there—it is called Kas-ska-ta-ma-gan, and on the south side of this area there are hills that are high—about eighteen hundred feet from the sea level, and usually when there is no caribou they usually stick around there—in that hilly side. And that is where this man [John Anishinaabe] went to look for the caribou. He was there but he didn't find them. He was with this group of people; there were lots of people living in that area—lots of Omushkegos from York Factory and also Fort Severn.

Anyway, somehow he happened to get stuck there in the fall and he lived with those people—this man, Grand Sophia's husband and her, the family, and they have their friends. Their friend was nicknamed (I don't know, maybe that was his real name), they call him Ka-pa-ki-soot; it means *He-who-explodes*. A long time ago when people used to buy gunpowder from the Hudson's Bay Company, it used to be a black powder and that black powder could explode in your face. Usually at that time, those guns, you load them from the front, and if they misfire, or if they backfire, that black smoke will just shoot into your face and you turn into black face.

So that guy didn't happen that way but he just have a very dark skin in his face, so they name him for the appearance of being black. So they call him Ka-pa-ki-soot—*He-who-explodes-in-the-face*. Blackened—whatever the English name suited. So that's why they call him that. But he was a great man. He was just as good as Grand Sophia's husband and they were like friends, sort of buddies in hunting, Ka-pa-ki-soot and Grand Sophia's husband.

So anyway, they went to this area first to look for the caribou—that within fifty miles of the Bay. And then they saw the caribou have left in the fall. Usually the good hunter can see that, they say the next stop will be within the next fifty miles—they know the area, so he went to look for those caribou. It was around March when he does that. He knows they are going to stay wherever they are; they are not going to move. He did find some but he didn't kill any and he move on, way inland into the headwaters of the Hayes Rivers junctions. Then he encounters different tribes, like Oji-Cree tribes. In one of those areas (which is very heavy wooded), he runs into a large family; an elder who was about sixty-five and he had three married sons. He encountered them, this Grand Sophia, her husband, and his friend Ka-pa-ki-soot, and his wife—four of them and with the small children. Ka-pa-ki-soot didn't have no children, but Grand Sophia had two.

So they stick with these people for a little while because they have to rest. This was just the beginning of March; they were about two hundred miles inland from the Bay. These people, they encounter—there are people who live by the rabbits, so they have extraordinary clothing. They have rabbit skin coat, rabbit skin legging, rabbit skin blanket, rabbit skin every-thing, almost—except the covering of the teepee—it is moose. They were not very good hunters. They usually lived in the wooden teepee in the summer time, also in the bark from the trees that they used for that cov-ering. So they were sort of different kind of tribes. But they still speak the language, you know partially Cree and all that stuff, they understand each other because Grand Sophia's husband was an Oji-Cree speaker. And so is Ka-pa-ki-soot, so they have no problem with communication.

So they were staying there because the lake had a lot of fish—a lot of suckers. That's what these guys are living on, the rabbits and the suckers. They were well off, but the thing is, there was no moose and what this old man need was clothes—hides. But he couldn't have it—the old man. When the old man found out that Grand Sophia's husband is an expert caribou hunter, he welcomes him and says, "I know exactly where the caribou are." Because he, this old man doesn't care much about the caribou meat—it's not the kind that he likes, but occasionally he would hunt the caribou for the moccasins and teepee covering. So he wanted the fresh teepee covering, so he takes advantage of this man and he says, "I will take you to the caribou in time but first I want you to stay and relax."

He went trapping with him; he went beaver trapping and other stuff with this man—an elder—and his two sons. And he has two young daughters that are not married yet. They were marriage age, and he wanted to get rid of them.

A few days after they arrived, Grand Sophia's husband was getting tired of sitting around, he was anxious to go hunting. So he waited for the old man, this great hunter, he wanted the old man to say, "Let's go." So he persuaded him, he said, "Let's go hunting." So the old man says, "OK, I'll take you." So they left and they actually found the caribou—the herds of caribou that usually winterize in one place. So they kill about fifteen. The man [John Anishinaabe] killed them all in which he gives about half to this old man; so fifteen caribou—they each get seven hides.

But he, the older man, made a deal with the young hunter. He says, "You give me some more of your hides, you don't need them because you have lots anyway, your teepee covering is good." He says, "I would like to have enough for me to have a new teepee." So the great hunter says "OK, you can have all the hides, I don't care, we have all our covering." The old man was so impressed he says, "This is the man that I would like to have as a son-in-law if he was not married."

So after the great hunt they have a celebration, then the old man begins to celebrate by setting up a shaking tent with his practice. So they set up the teepee and invite everyone to come and sit around outside. This is in the month of March and it's getting warm, a bit, so they can do that. But Grand Sophia was a big devoted Catholic. She had books, and she had everything, and she sing and pray every evening. Then one evening she was about to pray her evening prayers when this old man—the mi-tew— started setting up his teepee—the shaking tent. When he goes in to get it started, it won't work. He can hear Grand Sophia singing the Christian songs and he begin to blame her. He says, "That's the reason why I can't get this thing started." So he give it up for a little while; he says, "We will wait for another time," because he didn't want to be ashamed.

So another time he was trying it out and the same thing happened. He came out and he says, "There is something wrong." So he listens, and he can hear Grand Sophia singing in the tree—some of the echoes—she was singing a Christian song. Then he got mad and he says, "I know what's wrong."

So he went into Grand Sophia's tent because Grand Sophia's husband was sitting with the old man because he was invited. So she was just staying home because she don't believe in that stuff, and she wants to pray by herself and with the two kids. The old man found out that's the reason why his shaking tent wouldn't work, so he went to see Grand Sophia. Grand Sophia was sitting there reading her pray book and he walks in, straight to her, and grabbed the book and throw them into the fire. And he says, "If you sing again, I will kill you, because you are disturbing my activity, because you don't join me."

Grand Sophia was so startled and scared and everything because she thought she was going to get killed. But nothing flashes in her mind yet because it is just so sudden. After the man went out, she begin to think, "Why is he mad at me?" Because she didn't know that he was trying to run his shaking tent. And then, she begins to pray just the same, after the old man left; she prays by herself slowly. But she still has this cross—crucifix I mean. She had it between her breasts and was attached with a strip of rawhide, but it was very strong.

Between that time, getting back to the normal day, let's leave that time being, and then they went hunting again. This old man knows another place where there is wintering caribou, so he says to Grand Sophia's husband, "I'll take you there."

Ka-pa-ki-soot sometimes goes with them, and sometimes not, because he liked tending to his family needs at home. So they went and they brought the caribou again. So by this time, this old man has made up his mind. He wants to have this man [John Anishinaabe], so he offers him his daughter. The old man says, "Don't go away, stay with us," when they were hunting out there: "Stay here and I will give you my daughter to marry." "You can have my daughter"; but he did not say, "Get rid of your wife." But apparently he has decided that he will kill Grand Sophia because she is disturbing him, and he has the right to kill her because his shaking tent did not work; because she does something else—she is not joining. He decided himself to take action, so he says, "I will kill the lady and give the man another wife."

So he decided it and he tells his son about the idea. Then he also said to this great hunter, "I will give you my daughter if you stay with me." That's it; he didn't say, "I'm going to kill your wife," no—he didn't. Apparently before the last hunt at this time, it was the middle of April, the season is short, and Grand Sophia was eager to go. She'd been asking her husband, she says, "Let's go now"—because she didn't want to stay there because the old man didn't like her. He hated her because of her prayers. And there was a friction between the old traditional belief and practices and the Christianity. Something was not working, so she was blamed for it, and she deserved to be punished or killed according to the custom.

So anyway, it so happened at that time that the old man was very articulate—he knows exactly how to manoeuvre things. So he entices this man [John Anishinaabe] who loved to hunt caribou. He says "Let's go again, we'll go together—leave your friend Ka-pa-ki-soot here to take care of the family, then we will go." He says, "We will go for a week." So the man [John Anishinaabe] says, "Of course," because he enjoys hunting.

But before this old guy left he had whispered to his wife, he had said, "I want this man to stay with us and I am going to offer him my daughter but I will kill his wife." That is what he told his wife. But the old lady was a very kind-hearted person and she didn't care much about this mi-te-wi-win. Killing was something she didn't think was going to happen. She begin to love these two families, and when she found out about the killing she was mad.

So when the hunting party left, those five men—as soon as they left—she went to Grand Sophia's home and she says, "You and your friend Ka-pa-ki-soot and his wife, leave now—leave." Grand Sophia says, "What's wrong?" The elder woman says, "I can't tell you." Then she begins to cry—this old lady. Grand Sophia tells us the story—she is one that tells everything. And then she says, "the old lady was just shaking and crying and mad at the same time, mad at her husband, and crying for my sake and for our sake." And the beauty of friendship has been broken. And, she [the old lady] says;

> As long as I live and over my dead body that he will kill you and give my daughter to your husband. This is not going to happen. This is not my nature but I will do my best to fight him. I will even be dead, you know, but I want you to live. For this reason, that's the reason, I give you this warning. I should not have told you, my husband says not to let you know when he returns, a few days from now—you will be killed because you are—your religion is kind of conflicting with his practice. He believes that and that's one of the reason he wants to kill you and besides that he wants to hold your husband and the only way he can hold him is to offer him his daughter. And I don't want that.

"So for this reason," says the old lady, "Take everything that you need but not everything to hold you down, but what you need and leave, this minute. Never mind everything else, just save your life and go." Grand Sophia wanted to go home but her husband could not. Ka-pa-ki-soot's wife was crying, the women were crying to leave—they didn't like what was happening. They didn't like this shaking tent operating because they were already Christianized, these two ladies. So they can't pray because they are scared of this man, so they say, "Let's go, now." So Grand Sophia begins to get everything organized and within a few minutes they were on their way. They say good-bye to the grand old lady—the lovely old lady— also the two daughters come to say good-bye.

Off they go, and then the old lady says, "Make sure you hide your tracks and travel only at night if you can. Make sure you are prepared— so you don't get caught unexpectedly and try to cover as much distance as you can today." So off they go. She hold them and kiss the babies and all that stuff and she was crying, broken-hearted. So they left, says the story from the Grand Sophia. She says, "I can feel her body shaking in grief as we left."

Off they go to the direction of the Hudson Bay, to the coastal area where they came from. Ka-pa-ki-soot (He-who-explodes), he knew where to go. But by this time the snow is crushed and the lakes were something of a snowmelt and every day there is a bit of slush. So the going was very easy because they could actually run any place almost because the snow is actually crushed and the trail doesn't show at all. Ka-pa-ki-soot knows exactly where to walk so it doesn't show any trail, just in case the old man decides to chase them.

So anyway, after the first day they stopped just to feed the babies and then at night they didn't stop. And then the following day they were traveling again, it was on the following day—they didn't carry anything— very little. They only carry the dried meat and a few other things. Light things. They scooped the water on the slush and warmed that up. They don't show no fire or anything. So they were able to travel that way—they were able to cover a long distance because in those days they were fast. Most of the time they were running, but the second night they were so tired that Ka-pa-ki-soot decided they were going to spend the night in one place so the ladies can have a rest.

So he makes a trick trail—a method used to conceal one's track. He travels way out and makes a sign, and then he turns away back—maybe quite a distance and then makes a camp right there beside his trail. He makes sure he can see the trail very clearly. He had made sure that the trail would show, that the man could follow it there, and go on into the big open space and it will take him half hour at least for someone to go find him. And actually he did, so it was that night—I think Grand Sophia took the first watch—to have a gun and shoot the person whoever come after them. They were ready to fight and the next watch was He-who-explodes' wife. She was much younger. And then He-who-explodes took the next turn after midnight. They were sort of relaxing by then, they said, "Nobody will follow us now." And it was that period in time that Grand Sophia's husband catches up to them—that night. According to Grand Sophia's story, she says "I was sleeping—barely able to sleep. I'm scared and then all of a sudden I dream and I saw my husband and I hear him talking and laughing."

And what I hear first, this Ka-pa-ki-soot, or He-who-explodes was saying "Oh my brother-in-law,[12] you could have been dead by now, I was aiming right at your head. I could have just knocked you down." And they were just laughing at that and they were just so happy. He [John Anishinaabe] was sent away—the old lady had kept her word. So they begin to talk to each other and enjoy themselves, and they ask him, "Are you sure there's nobody behind you?" He says, "I'm very sure there's nobody behind me." So he tells the story about what happened. He says:

> When we got back to the camp—to his camp—the old man—
> you guys were gone. The old lady came out with an axe, ready
> to hit the old man if he ever says anything. So she just came
> to say, "Don't look for those people. I sent them away because
> I don't want you to do anything that you had planned to do.
> And you, the great caribou hunter—you too will have to pick
> up your stuff right now and go. Go to your wife and your
> friends. Go back home before anything goes wrong because I
> am not going to allow this to happen. My husband to kill a
> person and also to force you to take my daughter is not right,
> so the best thing for you to do is to follow your wife and your
> family and leave everything behind."

---

12 Neeth-tha-wes is the word Ka-pa-ki-soot would have used. This is the Omushkego term for a brotherly friendship. This term does not mean a brother-in-law relationship through marriage, but rather it shows a close relationship through friendship. The Omushkego word for brother-in-law by marriage is niis-staw (Bird, personal conversation, March 2003).

And that is exactly what the man did. He just took his bag, and his gun, and his snowshoes, and that's how he caught up to them. But he says, "My problem was that I just can't find your trail." He says to his friend, "How could you do that?" They were very good friends, they relax and after they went to bed and then after they have full relaxation, they travel towards their home ground. So they have survived. They made it back to their homeland and to the Bay area between Fort Severn and York Factory and Grand Sophia's life seems to be just fine at that time. So the first big adventure of the Grand Sophia has come to an end. Grand Sophia's husband [John Anishinaabe] died shortly after this event. Grand Sophia died around 1913. She was buried in Attawapiskat.

So Grand Sophia was an extraordinary adventurous lady. She was a well-known person as well. Apparently she was a great comforter too, she was usually involved with people who were in sorrow and tragic events. She was always called on to soothe the people, and she knew how to survive the harshness of life. I guess for an adventurous type of being, she was called on many times.

The real story is the effect of Christianity—the clash of two different cultures. Listening to Grand Sophia about her nearly being killed for the Christianity. The main concern is that there is a near incident—she could have been killed for being Catholic. She could have been holy Sophia—I mean Saint Sophia. And if the church were to actually practise what they preach—what they told us—if you resist being punished, you should give your life for your church belief. Then you become a saint by doing that and are guaranteed to go to heaven in the name of your belief.

I understand the cause of Grand Sophia's near-death experience—crucified for her church. But it's totally opposite from the Christianity—yes. But the old man—that's his church—his culture's church. It's not a church really—it's individual stuff but it acts as a church for his family. He has a right to think that way according to our culture. Grand Sophia was the one to intrude in his domain according to him—he has a right to kill her because it interfered with his spiritual practice and belief. Grand Sophia could have also been crucified for her Christianity, it almost happened. So this is the way the story is, the way I tell the story.

Conclusion
Problems and Hopes

In Chapter 1, I talked about the Omushkego life before contact and about the impact of what comes after contact—the fur trade, Christianization, and the education, residential school. Now I want to continue up to the present and to talk about some problems, but also my hopes.

So far, I have mentioned very little about the treaty making. The treaty is something that concerns me because our young generation do not care much about it. The older generation who did not understand still have a question. But I am lucky to understand a few things. I know the treaty was not fair; it was one-sided. I know what was done, and I know how it come to be, from my grandfather John Bird (Pineshiish), who signed it, and from others.[1] The thing that I am concerned about is to try to make our young people aware of what it was. That's why these stories are collected, just in case they ever ask about the history if they want to know. What I think about all the stories that I have collected is this. I talked about hunting and the lifestyle that was there before contact, and then about the second part, after contact. That ends somewhere around 1980. The modern age begins for us somewhere around 1980. This is the last part, and it's open, there is no end yet. The contact period ends about 1980, because by that time our culture was already abandoned.

For example, we, the most isolated communities like Winisk and Fort Severn on Hudson Bay, have accepted the housing which is high standard in Canada, the national housing. So we live by that housing, in those houses, and it controls us; we have settled into community for the first

---

1 David Sutherland (Louis Bird's grandmother's brother, d. 1963) was the second of three signatories of the adhesion to Treaty 9 for Winisk, and he later recalled how its meaning was not made clear or comprehended (Bird, interview quoted in DePasquale, forthcoming 2006).

FIGURE 8: *The signing of the Treaty No. 9 adhesion at Winisk, Ontario, 28 July 1930. Standing: Father L. Ph. Martel, OMI; Omushkego signatories John Bird (Louis Bird's grandfather), Xavier Patrick, and David Sutherland (Louis's great-uncle); Dr. John Thomas O'Gorman; and John Harris (HBC post manager). Seated: Commissioners Walter C. Cain and Herbert Nathaniel Awrey. Martel, O'Gorman, and Harris signed as witnesses, along with Ray T. Wheeler who may have been the photographer. Credit: Library and Archives Canada, PA-094963.*

time, and the result is that we have lost the traditional culture. We don't practise it any more. That is why I call it the end period. The new beginning for us was in 1986 after the big flood washed away our old village of Winisk, when we move into a new community, Peawanuck, with all this new infrastructure.[2] We have the homes, the running water and electricity and many other stuff. And we have been set up to run our own community, which supposedly means determining our own life, or the way we want to be. But that's not the end. That's just the beginning.

Before I go into the future, I want to linger a bit on the subject of treaty. As I understand it today, it seems that we have settled into community in the best housing. Our young people have willingly accepted this responsibility. But they never wanted to hear much about the history of our people. They were too young to understand. They never felt it. They never experienced that kind of life. They were born in a community where everything

---

2 After the old community not far from Hudson Bay was flooded in May 1986, Peawanuck, a new planned community, was built in a safer place about forty kilometres upstream. For descriptions and photographs of life and people in Winisk in the 1950s, see Rordam 1998.

was plentiful, and there was no migrating life any more. It was in 1970 that the government started giving the funding to our chiefs, and that causes the traditional values to change. The isolated communities like Winisk and Attawapiskat are still surrounded by wilderness, but their traditional lands are not valued the way our ancestors valued them. The elders are not leaders any more. Due to funding by government, the young people take over leadership as chief and council where they have skills or education to run European-style of communities. Greed developed in communities because of the mighty dollar. That's the beginning of the end of our culture.

I think the federal government did that; and by trying to do away with the Indian "problem," they wanted, long time ago, to blend the First Nations into main society so our people don't have to have special treatment and separate status and the rest. So, slowly for the last thirty years, the federal government has been handing over the bucks to the Ontario government so we can become a provincial citizen instead of having special status. So the treaties were geared for that aim, they were geared to last only maybe a hundred years—the hidden meaning—Indians call it "fork tongue."

So the first treaty, Treaty Nine, with the Omushkego people, was done in the James Bay area in 1905 and 1906, and then an adhesion took place farther north, 1929 and 1930. And that doesn't count, but the first treaty with the Treaty Nine will come to an end next year, 2005. So, that's what is happening. That's what exactly what the treaties are. The British people are expert in making treaties that say this kind of stuff, which lasts only maybe a hundred years. There are some that last longer. The First Nation people have been fooled and instructed and told that the treaty would last a long time yet to come. But in the present day [2003], the Minister of Indian Affairs is actually working skillfully with schemes and tricks to make it end very quickly. The Minister of Indian Affairs under Jean Chrétien, Robert Nault, was actually pushing for the end, and approached the young people to do that. He ignored the old people, ignored the chiefs that had been instructed and informed about the meaning of the treaty, and also ignored the acts to benefit the Native people, to have them be looked after separately because they gave up the land. That's not the way the government look at it. The government just takes possession of the land and then all its resources and everything and include the Native people as citizens of Canada, not separate people. And all this talk about self-governing and having control of your own life in these communities, each nation, there's no such thing.[3]

Those high-level government people who understand the mechanism to run the country, they know that; the big wheels, the bureaucrats, they know that. But the representative government, the elected government people, they don't know much about that. They don't care, as long as they get there [elected] for four years, and that's all that matters to them. Any legislation they can make, you know, just to make them look nice. The treaties doesn't mean anything to them, it's just another extra problem to their administration. So the treaties are quickly done away with, and that's what makes me think. Because there are so many young people who do not care about those things. Because they got everything for free, they never work, they never sweat, and they're fed well, they never even try to make their own living. Our First Nation people, our young people, do that. And they don't care to hunt. They think hunting is a foolish thing to do. And that is the sign of the end. I have witnessed this process for the last thirty-five years. That's why I'm concerned.

So the treaties are the only thing that still have some hope for the First Nations to have some say; otherwise, they would just blend [assimilate]. I have dealt with the treaties and the Indian Act and reservations. But what if these things come to an end within ten years? After that, it's a new beginning. It's what I have been forced to consider. What do I think about that?

This brings me to the third part of this project, of this work that I am doing. The last part is the toughest one, and it is in this last part that this project will make a last link, for the last time, with the First Nation, Omushkego culture. It has to be written, because now it's not practised. The language is dying off very fast, because of the modern technology, the modern communication, and television and all those things. They killed the language; they killed the culture. And that's what concerns me. Those of us people who live in isolated communities like Peawanuck and Fort Severn and Attawapiskat in Northern Ontario. We are the most blessed,

---

3 In 1969, the government of Pierre Trudeau (with Jean Chrétien as Minister of Indian Affairs) proposed a White Paper that would end legal distinctions between "Indians" and other citizens (and by extension, treaty rights) and that would phase out the Department of Indian Affairs. Aboriginal opposition defeated this move, but left many Aboriginal people with the skepticism and suspicion expressed in this paragraph. When Robert Nault, Minister of Indian Affairs under Prime Minister Jean Chrétien, proposed a First Nations Governance Act intended to supplement the Indian Act by increasing both the governing powers and accountability of First Nations chiefs and councils, his top-down approach again stirred great concern about the government's agenda. The strongly contested proposal died with the end of the Chrétien government in 2003. For discussion and context, see Dickason 2002: 377–79, 424–25.

cultured people, because we still live in a very free land. There is no lines yet. There is no township lines, no lot lines or anything, which, when they come to be, we will be covered by the rules, policies, regulations.

But today, we are under the provincial rules in other ways. If the provincial government wants to apply the rules in the reserves, or on any Native people, they can stop us from hunting at any time. They can stop us hunting out of season. They can stop us shooting the polar bear permanently, and also from shooting any other animals that we don't use. They can do that. The conservation officers in that Ministry of Natural Resources have that authority. Regardless if they have said in the treaty that we can still live upon the surface of the land, regardless of the Polar Bear Provincial Park that has been created in the James Bay-Hudson Bay district—that can be erased with one stroke of the pen. And that will be the end.

And the rules that apply to the Ontario citizen will apply even to the First Nations. It happens already. It happens in Timmins, it happens wherever there is a township. These rules apply to anyone, doesn't matter who you are. These things will happen. For now, those of us who live outside the boundary of those township lines, we are still okay, but how long these things will last? It probably will change within twenty years. We see that a few years ago, Premier [Mike] Harris of Ontario opened the territory north of the fifty-fifth parallel. That means the mining activities will take place up into the Hudson Bay-James Bay area. They are starting right now, and the country's going to be open, and in no time, the road will come. And when the road comes, the towns will open, and the organized territory will come to exist. Townships will be created, and the survey lines will be all over the place, which will do away with freedom of movement of the First Nations; there will be no such thing after that. No more freedom.

We are already now on the way, even though it's not yet happening. We are now already being conditioned to be that way. And that's what concerns me. Because we have moved into the high standard of living, I mean housing, we are not practising anything traditional at all. We are not going into the bush to hunt for a living; we are not training our children to hunt for a living or for food, but for sport shooting. We, the elders, are the only ones who have the skill to prepare the food and to process the food that they kill. The young people don't do that. And we elders are the only ones who still baby-sit for their babies, and this actually is the end of the Omushkego culture.

These young people that were trained and taught in school by books, by textbooks—that's how they learn. They don't see the use of that training, these teachings and traditional culture. Yet, they also don't see all the things that children in the city see—jet planes, ocean liners, or big modern highways. And big, heavy transport trucks and all kinds of machines that are used to develop the land, they don't see those, our young people. They don't know half of what the provincial citizens know; we are too isolated for that. The young people are blindly led into the different culture which they do not fit, to live in. The education system is not geared for them. And for us to say that we want to keep our language, we want to keep our culture, we are speaking with "forked tongue." That's what the old Indian means when he says, "You are speaking with forked tongue." Because we are saying some things we do not practise. We have a name that we are given; we are supposed to be considered the wilderness experts. But we, the First Nations people, we are not like that any more. There are many things I could explain about that.

The modern age is coming to the most isolated communities at this time. Not by highways, not by a fleet of jet planes, or shiny cars to run over us. It comes right into our living room. It comes by television. We can see the Queen every evening, we can see the Prime Minister of Canada every evening; we can see the President Bush smashing another country's property and everything. We see every day killing and other negative pictures. Instant communication come into our life, and destroys the peaceful co-existence in the wilderness, that's what concerns me. And in time it will come that our future generation will come to awaken, and they will say, "What are we? Where were we? What are we today?"

There are many of those First Nations people in the big cities that ask that question. I have seen them. I have seen those who are totally lost in the city. They are beggars, they ask for a quarter. They go into the garbage cans to find something to sell or to eat. I have watched them. I have walked with them. I have seen cities like that, the First Nations in Canada. These First Nations young people, they could have lived in the wilderness. They could have learned to make a living by hunting and trapping, they could have provided meat for food, and helped the environment, if they had learned the cultural teaching. That is not there any more. The language is very quickly dying off. We now speak with the English word with the Native accent. It's a very shameful thing to see, to hear.

We now, in an isolated community, band office people sit in front of their office with a computer, trying to use it. And pretend to work with it. And in their homes, people who just stare at this computer, and young people use the computer to play disk games and what they call "burning disk." They got games that they can sit there for hours when it's a beautiful day outside for physical exercise and nature watch, and the nature experience and camping, right outside their doorstep. No, they don't do that. They just sit inside and watch those games they play. Many Native rules are not used. They are not applicable any more to our community. The wilderness living is gone. Let alone trying to live the cultural life that was there before contact. So, what do I think about the future? That's what I am thinking about. These are the things that make me concerned.

So the only thing that I can do, that I wish could happen, is to create the story in three parts. To write the story that was there before the European came. The benefit they have in freedom, the harshness they experience but enjoyed, the goods they enjoy, the life they enjoy, the life that make them sad and cry, and everything. Nothing to be missed, nothing to hide. The good things they do, the bad things they do, the same as any other place. These are the things that I like to write. And the skills they learned by themselves. The education system they provided their children to continuously survive. Our ancestors. The land they knew so much, and they lived by it. The rules they find from the wilderness. The way they recognize the Creator, their Great Spirit. The way they pray. That was admirable in their time. Today, there is so many different denominations of spiritual exercises that is called, in the modern world, "freedom of choice." But the freedom of choice sometimes is not that free.

The religion has divided the families in five different ways at times. There are many divisions within the communities now, because of these things. Just like the way it was long time before the European came. Except then, every family was on its own. Every family was independent. Didn't have to make anybody mad; didn't have anybody to force their way. They make their own living; they lived in freedom. They paid the price sometimes, when the land was in harsh condition and periods of being poor. But what is it today? It's the same thing—being poor, but without the culture and the freedom.

So anyway, this is my thought for the future of generations in my area. I don't see any pleasure; I don't see any benefit. I see only a very unfortunate loss and suffering. The good things come. Mining activities are

FIGURE 9: *Louis and snowshoes. "Yes! I made them." Photo provided by Louis Bird.*

coming upon us. There will be mining all over, of all kinds. Some development will take place. But would the Native people benefit from it? Not much, because they don't have the education which they require for them to be involved, to be accepted. Just like the way I am. I am not accepted in the white men intellectual field, because I don't have no written degree that I have acquired such knowledge; I don't have that. But I do have the First Nation culture certificate in my mind. Because the elders approve of me, I have acquired it. That's the only thing that I have. But I don't have to carry the paper to do that. It's all in my knowledge and my capability as long as I'm healthy. Today, because I am old, I cannot practise hunting and fishing any more. So my last effort is this, is to write our culture down so those First Nation generation that come to exist today, at least they will find a written book about their culture, the Omushkego culture. That is all I want to do. And once I create any writing out of those stories, the beneficiary should be the First Nation community, first. Whatever happen after that, it's all right. I am not concerned, as long as I can give back the written material to each community what I have got by visiting the elders, those who were kind enough to speak to me. That was my wish, to write their stories. This is the way I am going to finish this work.

I do have concern for the future of my children, my grandchildren. The way it is today, our young people only want to go as far as high school. They think that's it, that's all they need. But I keep telling them that you need more than the high school, that you should go as much as you can. I said, "You should aim higher. Get a job in your mind, the kind of job that you like to do, that you would love to do. You could get it," I said. "You could get it because, if I can do the things that you see me do, you could do better. So your life will be much easier than mine, or you'll find much happiness in what you do, rather than going astray, and become alcoholic, and become a useless individual, and go to the destruction of the human body." This is what's happening with so many young people in Canada. We have it recorded that the First Nation jails are much more populated than white. And other correction institutions, they are there. Many First Nation people occupy those positions. But there are not so many working in the good paying jobs; there are very few.

The Omushkego language itself will be gone soon. And to try to teach the young people their language without living it, it's a waste of time. We might as well teach them with the language they're going to live with, rather than waste their time in the language which is not used. "Culture's

FIGURE 10: *Louis and one of his twenty-five grandchildren. "That's me, holding my grandchild [Jessica Hunter] at home." Photo taken by Michelline Hunter, 1997, and provided by Louis Bird.*

not used any more. Why do you have to learn that language?" That's what the young people think. I do agree. I hope I didn't have to say that, but that's the truth. But I still hope and wish that some young people will make themselves useful and have a good education, and have a full life, like the rest of the people who can make it.

Now, something came up into my mind that I should add to this comment. I have said the Omushkego language is fast dying out; if it maintains the rate it goes at today, we will lose it totally by ten years. In twenty years, there will be very few people who speak it. By fifty years, it will be gone. That is why this project is very important. The stories collected by me, in the original language used by our ancestors that are over sixty-five, will be the only true Omushkego dialect that will be recorded. My group of people, those who are over sixty and seventy, we will be the last ones to speak the true Omushkego dialect. But most of us will blend with the English language, where necessary, just as I do. I can speak yet, almost perfectly well with the Omushkego language. But there are times when the Omushkego language does not have a word to express the situation which came from other cultures such as the European culture. That is why we, the Omushkego or First Nation people, have been forced to use the English language. We must understand this.

The First Nations of North America, especially in northern part of Canada, these people who migrate, who move one season to the other, were different tribes. These tribes did not settle; they did not need to establish the community, and therefore did not experience society. Society, I mean living together, establishing public services, regardless of size. If there's five or ten families, they need a service, and the more they live together, the service is required to be well organized, and when there is more than a thousand or three thousand or a million, these services has to be well established, as we understand, in the western society.

But the First Nations who lived the migrating life before the European contact, they were satisfied the way they lived. Their language was sufficient in their culture. Because they did not live in the city life or permanent community. They did not require the additional language to express the services and institutions that may have developed for that situation. Since they did not live together, they did not have to manufacture anything for more than what they need. They did not process food, for example, to be sold in a marketplace. They did not create the material for the shelter because they migrate; therefore, they didn't have to do that. They did not have to dig up the stones, the ground, to extract the minerals that they would have needed if they had. Because they lived on the surface of the land and practised the migrating life. This is the cultural history that I talk about in the first chapter and in the old stories.

Then after contact, when the European westernized people came in to live in this country, we have to stress the difference there. That's when the language begin to change. It begin to add the words which were not created by the First Nations. For example, sugar. Up north in Ontario, northern Canada, there was no sugarcane. They didn't manufacture sugar. And there was no equipment to process that kind of refinery. Also, other items that we have now—there was no wheat to grow on the land, and therefore they didn't need to know how to mill the grain. And others like that, the processed food. Also, in moving on the land and living on the land, they did not need to manufacture the shelter material, like lumber and also the other types of processed shelter materials. All they needed was the hides. Before these things came to be, for example, steel, steel tools, they did not mine, they did not smelt, they did not make steel, just a very crude copper. These materials were not necessary in their culture; that's what has to be stressed. But when other cultures come, that's when the language begins to deteriorate or sort of blend with the other language, because of the different culture. The manufacturing goods had to be named as different kind of thing, with new descriptive names by the First Nation, because they didn't manufacture them.

That is why it is important for this project to be written in the Cree language as it was before the European came. And the only place we can find these words is in the legends, or in three different kinds of stories: legends, quotations, and oral history. The oral history means that in that time period before contact, maybe two hundred years before that, things that happened before European came are still remembered. They were still remembered which family they happened to, maybe a hundred years before Europeans came. So they are oral histories. The quotations, they can blend any place between that special time and later period. In pre-contact, quotation stories were there, about the same age as legends. And they exist today, even after the contact, and they are very important, too. After contact, where do you end after contact? Where is the defining point? Where is the definition of the end of one period of history?

We understand when we say "colonialism," that practice still carries on in a different way. The colonialism did not die. It still remains today. It remains amongst the European and it remains also in the minds of the First Nation. You can hear it because the First Nation always talks about it, because they resent it very much. Even though they resent it much, it doesn't go away. So, we are talking about the time after contact, and where does it end? It doesn't end. Only a few practices are ending. For example, the fur trade is not ended, but it ends in the way it used to be. The Christianization, it has served its purpose. The residential school, it has accomplished its purpose to the First Nation, for the European. The treaties have accomplished its purpose, blending with three-pronged impacts, as I like to say. One is the fur trade, the loss of First Nation conservation rules. Then Christianization, to prepare for treaty; and the treaty to take the land; and then the residential school to detach the young people from the love of land. That has been accomplished. Then, when the residential school was shut down, we could say it ended there. But the effect of the residential school, the residential school legacy, remains. Amongst our people, my age group, even our children's group, because of the way we have been treated, its effect on us, and it carries on to our children without knowing it.

And the legacy of the Hudson's Bay Company. The missionaries, all these come to the First Nation. What our people have seen, they have believed, this is the way the Europeans live. This is exactly that each individual European is as powerful as a priest and as a Hudson Bay manager. No, that's not true. The people that came here first time, they were the enterprise venturers, and the missionaries came also to control some minds, to colonize, to bring their faith, to change persons, to amalgamate. These things they did already; it has been done.

All these remain the same, the legacy is still there. The Christianizers' legacy is here, because all the Natives are submitting to everything the European brought them, because the church has told them, "If you don't listen to the leaders of the land you are disobeying God, because they are the commissioners of God." These are very strong words in our language. But did the missionaries know they were using these words? No, they did not. So, after saying these priests' words with very harsh tone, they do not stop there, at one hundred years ago; those words remain with us. Especially in isolated communities like ours, in James Bay lowland, the people are still the same; we believe those words.

Let me go into the particular subject; let me explain something. When the First Nation begin to awaken about their capabilities to speak their mind, when they begin to acquire the education similar to the white man or the rest of the major society, when our people begin to become lawyers and doctors and teachers, they begin to have the same manufactured brain as the Europeans, because their training system is in there. And those who take the law, they study the law, they begin to understand the past, and also the present, and the main aim is applying this particular education. And then also the people who study the accounting and economy, they begin to blend in their mind with the sign of a dollar. Whenever they speak, whenever they see things, there's a dollar sign in their mind, and in their eyes. And those who went to higher education, it was the major theme for them, for their education. In religion, they become evangelists. They're also very negative. All these things are very negative. The legacy's there. It remains; it doesn't get erased. Attempts of reconciliation by church leaders did not erase those marks, even if the major society, even the leaders of the churches and even the Pope says, "I am sorry that we have mistreated you with our ideas and religion." It's too late. It's already done its purpose. One can say the damage is done already. The education system that's been instilled into the minds of the young First Nation people, it's there. And that is what happens today. Not a long time ago, back in the 1970s, when the First Nations begin to speak their mind and demand that they should be given a chance to exercise self-determination, which eventually led to the words, what they call "self-government." Why is the word always important to name something? Then the First Nations speak about self-determination. Because the government of Canada had always decided what's best for them. So they finally stood up to say, "We want to determine what is best for us."

Then finally, when they have awakened to this idea, the government itself doesn't give in that easy. They underhandedly designed some other things to take place. That's when in 1983, there was the federal parliamentary commission on Indian self-government led by Keith Penner, and it had hearings across Canada. At the same time, Indian Affairs had its own hearings to insist on using its departmental determining act for the benefit of the Native people. So a two-pronged action took place, one to satisfy the public, and the other one to satisfy the Department of Indian Affairs. And that's what happened that time. And in doing so, what did the think tank find out in Ottawa, in the government? They found how to distract the Native people from actually speaking their mind and accomplishing what they want; they have the scheme of throwing the money into them. They know what's going to happen.

So when they give the money to the band councils, the result was much more negative than it was before. Because for the first time the First Nations were actually handling the money, the core funding, they call it; they were given freedom. They [the government] say, "Use it the way you see fit. Self-determine." That's the word they use. Then after that, even though they were given those dollars, the Minister of Indian Affairs had a scheme how to distract and how to kill the idea of self-determination. The idea was to distract people from using the treaty rights and everything in order to obtain the self-determination. Things happen in that period. It was that time [1982] Mr. Trudeau created what they call the Canadian Charter of Rights and Freedoms. The man was very smart, and he knows this was happening. He created this law which withheld exercise of somebody's total freedom, especially the Native people. And also not to change anything, not to add anything. Much more like, to be able to erase what was there. Because originally that's exactly what the treaties are made for. To be erased in a period of time, because the main intention for the treaty making was to de-Indianize people, as I said.

Then, after some period, say, after ten years, it was considered that these things would be ended, there would be no special status, no reserve.

The Minister skillfully maneuvered the chiefs and funding agencies, not to give so much to the leaders of the First Nations, so they won't accomplish anything which they seek. It's called the self-determination. Then another act come in with this Minister of Indian Affairs, Mr. Nault, who insisted to design the governance system that will fit to the federal government, and also give it a chance to erase the responsibilities of the federal government to the First Nation people. These are the things that happen. It doesn't stop there. And First Nations have still encountered many difficulties that are much more, even if they are educated in the white society. But those people who are isolated in places like Peawanuck and all those little isolated communities, we are way far behind. A very few First Nation people who went to high school, to university, are able to understand this, but they are not understood by the elders, or by the band members that never went to school or high school.

Then the most negative results which the Department of Indian Affairs have foreseen is this, if you throw the money to First Nations, if you throw, for example, a piece of meat to a bunch of dogs, they will grab that one piece and they will really fight each other; only the strongest can have it. That's exactly what happened in each community. Each member of the family is fighting for that piece of meat. So it distorted the coordination, it distorted the unity and community. The community began to divide because of this. Division, it happened before that, it happens with the religion. After we have the Canadian Charter of Rights and Freedoms, it says that anybody who wants to believe in any kind of religion will have it. So at that time, every denomination of Christianity came into each community. But before that, it was the two main denominations that were controlling the minds of First Nations: Catholics and Anglicans and maybe one extra, the United Church. But then five different ones came into each community, so it's divided members spiritually into about five different ways. And plus the money that goes there, it all have to do with all of them that remain divided. These are the things that I am talking about.

I cannot say anything about what is the future for these people. The government acts the way they do. They throw the money to the band councils. And the religions are coming to the communities; even if it's only three hundred members, there are five different denominations. Plus the First Nation traditional belief and practice which, long time ago, had been condemned and rejected by the First Nations. The young people, they don't know anything about it. But because there is money, the money comes with that, and then they just form any kind of a canvas and a bit of hot stones for a sweat lodge and throw water in it and they go in there stark naked, and they say, "I am practising a tradition." No, my friend, that's not the way it is. Everything is distorted; power is money. And it divides families, it divides community, and that is a question itself. Will it ever stop?

These were the things that confused each First Nation community. The worst of all, I think it is the money. Because the way it has turned out to be, partially allowing people to practise the freedom of choice, I mean to use a government-designed leadership election, what they call "band council election." There are guidelines there, but it was not insisted they should be used. They were just guidelines. It so happened the First Nation wants to use either their well-designed leadership election or else their own choosing or selection. It was allowed to happen. But neither of those worked. Selection system did not work because in the past, before the European, only the strongest family with large membership used to have a controlling system. So the selection system was not, it is not, a democratic practice.

Then the other way was election, because the country is supposed to be a democratic country; that has been the guideline in the Indian Act. But it never was explained exactly how it works, and our First Nations did not have that legal mind to understand. So they never actually practised it, but they used that ritual. The ritual is different than actually believing or understanding. Rituals can be done; for example, you could dance a special kind of dance, if you have trained yourself and body to move with it, but you don't have to understand what it means, you just move with it, and that's the ritual. The same thing applies in practising spirituality. When you, as a Christian, when you follow the Christian rules, you follow these. You go to church, you take the Eucharist, or as a Catholic, you confess; and then there are laws, you know the church laws, you follow them. And you watch the performance in the church, and that performance became ritual, people just go there and sit, just to be there, just to be like the others. The mind can be a thousand miles away; a mind can be many things, and many different minds in that time. That's what I mean; rituals can be done without thinking, and that's what happened with this situation.

We know that families always like to see each other getting what they want. Friends that are being friends together, they usually try to unite and take what's available. That is what's happening in communities because of this band council system. It was designed by the white people on paper, but it was not ever understood what the First Nation election or leadership election is. It was never understood. But I did get the information from the elders, how was the leadership elected long time ago. They did not have to practise democratic system, no. Do you know why? Because they never lived together. The Omushkegos always moved with four seasons, and always in the individual family. So democratic system wasn't required in that time. The only thing that requires that kind of thing is whenever they get together in the short time in season, maybe a few days in some place where they meet, that's where sometimes a leader is looked at. But the leader usually is an elder who knows about life, knows about the procedures about getting together, how to do things together, and temporary; people have someone to look at, someone to listen to what should be done. And they don't have to vote, they don't have to do anything at all, it just happened automatically, it is there by cultural practice that an elder or someone who is fully skilled in doing things become a leader. So that's what it was; it was almost like in the wildlife. For example, for the herds of caribous in the mating season, there are females, there are males, so the strongest of the bulls happen to be lucky and serves the harem, the females; he service them. Because he is supposed to be naturally selected the strongest, and so the offspring can be healthy. And that is understood. And that was exactly what happened to the Native people. People automatically know who is strong and who is healthy and who is wise; when something requires somebody to lead, it is always that person. You don't have to vote, you don't have to pull sticks or anything. It just happens automatically.

Sometimes only one person will mention that and then everybody would agree. That was a traditional system in selecting a leader. But the band council system which has been created by the Department of Indian Affairs, that did not apply. It never was in force to any members of the First Nations, those who still exercise their culture, living by the land. In Winisk area, the Winisk River system people, they move with the season, they only begin to settle in community by 1955. So they'd been using that old system, long time ago, until late 1970. That's when they began to use voting. And I unfortunately am the one who introduced that, to vote, to put your papers in there, to mark the one who you think should be a leader. At that time, it was not understood what that is, but people do it anyway. Then, when they seen the result, they were mad, because that's not the person they wanted to see to be their chief, because at that time, the money was involved. That was the first time, 1970, that the federal government put money into the communities, what they call "core fund-ing." It's the process to establish the band administration.

So they just threw the money in there as I said, like meat, raw meat. And then the band didn't know what to do with it; they know that it has to be spent, but who has the skill to do that? No one. At that time, I was elected the chief. Me, I didn't know how to administer this money. It's only a small amount, it was only five thousand dollars. That was the beginning. After two years, after people see this, each member of the families begin to say, "Oh, he done it, and we can do it, too." So they begin to fight. Begin to separate, friendship begin to break down. Then more years come; there's more money coming in. The more money was poured into the community, the more division and hatred begin. Impossible to find some unity. That's what happened. The power of money can be destructive if you don't know how to use it, if you don't have the skill to handle the administration funding. To administer a community requires a skill, but that is not the First Nation skill because, especially the Omushkego people, they never live in a community. How could they get the skill? That's the problem still today.

Then for the last ten years, another new technology emerges which blends in administration, which is used as a tool in administration. And it is to be learned and to be mastered first. This machine, the bureaucratic system required to run the country; we don't have that machine, that wheel, we don't have a skill. No First Nation has that in an isolated com-munity like Peawanuck. So there's just a pretension. A bunch of families get together to outnumber the other and they get to be elected; their member is to be elected as the chief. That doesn't mean they have the knowledge. It doesn't mean they know how to run a community. This is what's happening today. That is the main problem. And it is experienced all across Canada.

At the same time, there is a teeter-totter situation. Some people get to use some traditional stuff in order to gain popularity. Popularity begins to be applied. It's not applied any more about the strong skills that a First Nation have; no, they ignore that, the band members; they just use num-bers. The more numbers a family can acquire together before election, they can win. They don't use the democratic system, even though it was supposed to be there. It's not the democratic system that is applied. These are the things that exist in our community.

All these procedures that come into the community, they all came from the white man's world. They all came in with the language of English. And therefore the Omushkego language is very fast dying off. The language doesn't fit to today's living process. The language blends very easily. For example, what do you call the computer? The First Nations never had that; they never created it. Television, the radio, they know a little bit about that. But the computer is the world-accepted tool for business. The First Nations who did not go to school or who did not understand the importance of it, they are forced to try to use it. The First Nations in isolated communities never have a chance to catch up to the modern world, but they are forced to use it. They are forced to use the language, too. That is the important thing.

It is only ten more years, we're going to die, my age group in our seventies. We are the last ones who actually speak the Cree language, the Omushkego language, which is still intact. If we don't collect the stories in that language, we will not be able to fulfill the idea of this project as history in language, as original language. If we were to do that, if we were to be able to get every Omushkego-speaking elder to speak freely his mind and to speak in the way the language was used, we would have captured the original language. Then after we would have recorded a voice, we would also write it down in its syllabic form; that would be the authenticity of it. Then it could have been translated after, into whatever language, be it French, German, or anything.

After translation of the original, it's not finished yet. You still have to interpret every word, on almost every subject. Why does it say like that? A person who never experienced the First Nation culture would never understand the words applied there. They'll need the interpretation required for all the translation, and then finally that thing will be useful; but if you don't get that, no. Also, if you get the translated material from the Aboriginal language, the First Nation language and culture, and just translate it into English right away, you are not going to catch everything. You will not be able to experience the emotional part of the culture. And if you have not lived in the country, in a style in that time where it come from, you would never actually get it. That is the problem. You have to transcribe, exactly as it was said by the speaker, then translate word for word, and then interpret, explain the meanings of the words or sentences.

So here is my final statement about this project. The reason it is so important is because we collect the stories from the only elders that speak their language, the Omushkego language. They don't have to speak a word in English. They don't have to think like a European. They have to think about the past and speak it. That would be the original stuff. To voice it, their voice, their word and the way they carry the emotion. That is the first thing I have tried to do. I collect those stories from the elders just for that reason. To keep their voice, the mentality of the language and the culture, that is what I try to capture in interviewing the elders.

After that, because the voice in any medium, tape recording or any other, is very easy to lose or to be deteriorating, the next best thing is to write it down. But write it exactly the way it has been spoken by the elder. Then you get the originality. Then this written language should be translated word for word, in order to keep the sound written, but also have another copy to be written down with interpretation of the words, their meaning and definition. It has to be produced through two steps that are required. The original material has to be written and translated, word-forword. Finally at the end, comes the final edition for the language. And it requires the final editing to be acceptable to the general public.

But the original stuff, the Cree speaking and writing, will have to go back to each community. That is the purpose of this project. The idea is to have the language in the community in written form and also translated form. So it can be the key, it can be the stones of the original language that has been, culture that has been marked in paper. It can be kept in each community. That was my idea. And that is the most important thing, for this project to be finished. But what we have now, we have only transcribed the English language, which is not at all the whole thing. It's not whole, it's still in parts; it's not original. We have not yet written down the Cree language in syllabics. We collected a few words, a few elders that speak in the old recordings. Yes, that part we want, but to write it down is not what has happened yet.

My question, will I live to be able to see that? Or can it be done by some other people? Can we persuade the young people to try to do that themselves, the First Nation young people? No, at this moment it's not possible. There's too many distractions today. There is the television and high-tech gadgets that come into play for every home. The young people use our electronic tools and even speak to them. It's all in the English language. There's no Cree language. These are the distractions. And that is why I predict within ten or twenty years this Cree language will have disappeared. By the next fifty years it will be extinguished. Now is the time to do this. We should try to write every word that is uttered by the elders, especially those who actually know how to speak it. That's my hope, and this is my personal feeling.

references

Primary Sources

Bird, Louis. Audiotapes and transcripts. Centre for Rupert's Land Studies, University of Winnipeg

NOTE: The key CRLS reference numbers are at the left. Those with an asterisk* may be found in audio and transcribed form on the website <http://www.ourvoices.ca>. All recordings are copyright 2003 by Louis Bird.

0004 The Story of Grand Sophia. Recorded 2000. Transcribed by Donna Sutherland.

*0006 Kokum's Story. Recorded 2000. Transcribed by Donna Sutherland.

0011 A-moe and She-wee-phan. Recorded February 4, 1999. Transcribed by Doug Hamm.

0012 Mitewiwin. Recorded April 12, 1999. Transcribed by Doug Hamm.

*0014 Guns and Bows. Recorded April 2001. Transcribed by Roland Bohr.

*0015 Spirituality. Recorded 2000. Transcribed by Donna Sutherland.

*0022 Wemishoosh. Date recorded unknown. Transcribed by Brian Myhre.

*0024 Ehep Legend. Date recorded unknown. Transcribed by Brian Myhre.

*0028   Legends and Prehistory. Recorded September 28, 1986. Transcribed by Brian Myhre.

*0035   Shamanism and Catechism. Date recorded unknown. Transcribed by George Fulford.

0036   Teachers and Mentors. Date recorded unknown. Transcribed by Justin Dyck.

0055   Wemishoosh. Recorded September 29, 2002. Transcribed by Brian Myhre.

*0057   Wemishoosh. Recorded December 9, 1998. Transcribed by Brian Myhre.

0065   Cree Women Stories. Recorded September 11, 1999. Transcribed by Alison Daily.

0077   Inuit Expedition. Recorded April 15, 2003. Transcribed by Roland Bohr.

0083   Stories. Recorded December 8, 1999. Transcribed by Amelia LaTouche.

0095   Storytelling. Date recorded unknown. Transcribed by Jennifer Orr.

*0104   Shamanism. Recorded February 8, 2001. Transcribed by Mark F. Ruml.

*0107   Shamanism (Cultural Story). Recorded December 8, 1999. Transcribed by Mark F. Ruml.

*0114   Early Contact (Omens and Stories). Recorded February 27, 2002. Transcribed by Donna Sutherland.

0116   Guns and Bows II. Recorded October 2001. Transcribed by Roland Bohr.

0117   Hunts Game. Recorded 2001. Transcribed by Roland Bohr.

*0123   Indian Sickness. Recorded February 15, 2003. Transcribed by Amelia LaTouche.

0125   Report for Canada Council #1. Recorded May 31, 2001. Transcribed by George Fulford.

*0130   Mystery Stories I. Recorded January 31, 2002. Transcribed by Youngok Kang-Bohr.

0132   Catechism 1. Recorded July 25, 2002. Transcribed by George Fulford.

0133 Catechism 2. Recorded July 28, 2002. Transcribed by George Fulford.

0134 Catechism 3. Recorded July 29, 2002. Transcribed by George Fulford.

0135 Catechism 4. Recorded March 1, 2002. Transcribed by George Fulford.

*0136 Legend of the Giant Skunk. Date recorded unknown. Transcribed by Kathy Mallett.

Bird, Louis. Interviews

2003. Interview with Paul DePasquale. Audiotape recorded February 22. Transcribed by Kelly Burns.

2004. Interview with Paul DePasquale. Audiotape recorded March 20.

Bird, Louis. Other Sources

"Legend of Sinkepish." CRLS #2-Bird #401. Audiotape. Date recorded unknown. Transcribed by George Fulford.

"Legend of Wiisakeechak (Landmarks)." 2002. English 1 class visit, University of Winnipeg. Audiotape recorded February 28, 2002. Transcribed by Kelly Burns.

"Louis Bird on Cree Creation Stories." Audiotape recorded April 20, 2001. Transcribed by George Fulford.

"Questioning the Elders." Videotape recorded at the University of Winnipeg, February 8, 2001. Transcribed by Kelly Burns.

"Winter Territories." 1999. Audiotape recorded April 24, 1999.

Hudson's Bay Company Archives, Archives of Manitoba (Winnipeg)

Church Missionary Society Records, Journal of Rev. John Horden (1851–69) at Moose Factory (Microfilm: A88).

Edmonton House Post Journal, B 60/a/1-42.

Fort Severn Post History #198.

York Factory Post History #239.

Manchester House Post Journal, B121/a/1.

Search Files: *Attawapiskat* and *Weenusk/Winisk*.

Secondary Sources

Alexander, S.A., Robert S. Ferguson, Kevin J. McCormick. 1991. *Key Migratory Bird Terrestrial Habitat Sites in the Northwest Territories*. Canadian Wildlife Service, Occasional Paper 7. Yellowknife, NWT: Canadian Wildlife Service.

Angel, Michael. 2002. *Preserving the Sacred: Historical Perspectives on the Ojibwa Midewiwin*. Winnipeg, MB: University of Manitoba Press.

Barr, J., C. Eberl, and J. McIntyre. 2000. "Red-Throated Loon." *Birds of North America*. Ed. A. Poole and F. Gill. Philadelphia, PA: The Birds of North America.

Bauman, Richard. 1986. Introduction. *Story, Performance, and Event: Contextual Studies of Oral Narrative*. 1–10. Cambridge: Cambridge University Press.

Bell, Robert. 1879."A List of Birds from the Region Between Norway House and the Forts Churchill and York." *The Annual Report of the Geological Survey of Canada 1879*. Montreal, QC: Geological Survey of Canada.

Bell, Robert. 1884. *Report of the Department of Agriculture, Statistics and Health of the Province of Manitoba, for the Year 1883*. Winnipeg, MB: Government of Manitoba.

Biggar, H.P. (ed.). 1922–36. *The Works of Samuel de Champlain*. Vol. 2. Toronto, ON: Champlain Society.

Bird, Louis. 1993. "The Wailing in the Clouds." Ed. Ann Taylor. *The Northern Review* (Summer): 35–43.

Brown, Jennifer S.H. 1971. "The Cure and Feeding of Windigos: A Critique." *American Anthropologist* 73: 20–22.

——. 2004. "The Wasitay Religion: Prophecy, Oral Literacy, and Belief on Hudson Bay." In *Reassessing Revitalization Movements: Perspectives from North America and the Pacific Islands*. Ed. Michael Harkin. 104–23. Lincoln, NB: University of Nebraska Press.

Brown, Jennifer S.H., and Robert Brightman. 1988. *The Orders of the Dreamed: George Nelson on Cree and Northern Ojibwa Religion and Myth, 1823*. Winnipeg, MB: University of Manitoba Press.

Brown, Jennifer S.H., and Roger Roulette. 2005, forthcoming. "Waabitigweyaa, the One Who Found the Anishinaabeg First." *Algonquian Spirit: Contemporary Translations of the Algonquian*

Literatures of North America. Ed. Brian Swann. Lincoln, NE: University of Nebraska Press.

Christy, Miller (ed.) 1894. *The Voyages of Captain Luke Foxe of Hull, and Captain Thomas James of Bristol, in Search of a North-West Passage in 1631–32.* Vols. 88, 89. London: Hakluyt Society.

Clayton, Daniel. 2003. "Captain Cook and the Spaces of Contact at 'Nootka Sound.'" *Reading beyond Words: Contexts for Native History.* Eds. Jennifer S.H. Brown and Elizabeth Vibert. Rev. ed. 133-62. Peterborough, ON: Broadview Press.

Cooke, Alan. 1979 [1966]. "Thomas James." *Dictionary of Canadian Biography.* Vol. 1: 1000–1700. 384–85. Toronto, ON: University of Toronto Press.

Cooper, John M. 1938. *Snares, Deadfalls and Other Traps of the Northern Algonquians and Athapaskans.* Washington, DC: Catholic University of America.

Cruikshank, Julie. 1984. "Tagish and Tlingit Place Names in the Southern Lakes Region, Yukon Territory." *Canoma* 10: 30–35.

——. 1990. "Getting the Words Right: Perspectives on Naming and Places in Athapaskan Oral History." *Arctic Anthropology* 27: 52–65.

——. 2003. "Discovery of Gold on the Klondike: Perspectives from Oral Tradition." *Reading beyond Words: Contexts for Native History.* Eds. Jennifer S.H. Brown and Elizabeth Vibert. Rev. ed. 435–58. Peterborough, ON: Broadview Press.

Davies, Wayne K.D. 2003. *Writing Geographical Exploration: James and the Northwest Passage 1631–33.* Calgary, AB: University of Calgary Press.

Decker, Jody. 1988. "Tracing Historical Diffusion Patterns: The Case of the 1780–82 Smallpox Epidemic among the Indians of Western Canada." *Native Studies Review* 4: 1–24.

DePasquale, Paul W. 2006, forthcoming. *Natives and Settlers Now and Then: Historical Contexts, Current Perspectives.* Introduction. University of Alberta Press.

DePasquale, Paul W., and Louis Bird. 2005, forthcoming. "Omushkego ('Swampy Cree') Traditional Literatures: 'Wissaakechaahk and the Foolish Women' and 'The Cannibal Exterminators.'" *Algonquian Spirit: Contemporary Translations of the Algonquian Literatures of North America.* Ed. Brian Swann. Lincoln, NE: University of Nebraska Press.

Dickason, Olive P. 2002. *Canada's First Nations: A History of Founding Peoples from Earliest Times*. Don Mills, ON: Oxford University Press.

Doxtator, Deborah. 2001. "Inclusive and Exclusive Perceptions of Difference: Native and Euro-Based Concepts of Time, History, and Change." *Decentring the Renaissance: Canada and Europe in Multidisciplinary Perspective, 1500–1700*. Ed. Germaine Warkentin and Carolyn Podruchny. 33–47. Toronto, ON: University of Toronto Press.

Eliade, Mircea. 1964. *Shamanism: Archaic Techniques of Ecstasy*. New York, NY: Bollingen Foundation.

Eliade, Mircea. 1987. "Shamanism: An Overview." *The Encyclopedia of Religion*. Vol. 13. Ed. Mircea Eliade. 202–08. New York, NY: Macmillan.

Ettenger, Kreg. 2002. "Cree Place Names and Myths as Evidence of Past Use and Occupancy: The Offshore Islands of Eastern James Bay." Paper presented at the Annual Meeting of the American Society for Ethnohistory, Quebec City, QC.

Fafard, François-Xavier. 1924. *Catéchisme de Persévérence*. Quebec, QC: Action Sociale. Originally published in 1899 in Montreal by Beauchemin.

Flannery, Regina, 1995. *Ellen Smallboy: Glimpses of a Cree Woman's Life*. Montreal and Kingston: McGill-Queen's University Press.

Flores, Dan. 1991. "Bison Ecology and Bison Diplomacy: The Southern Plains from 1800 to 1850." *Journal of American History* (September): 465–85.

Fogelson, Raymond D. 1989. "The Ethnohistory of Events and Nonevents." *Ethnohistory* 36(2): 133–74.

Francis, Daniel, and Toby Morantz. 1983. *Partners in Furs: A History of the Fur Trade in Eastern James Bay 1600–1870*. Montreal and Kingston: McGill-Queen's University Press.

Fulford, George, and Louis Bird. 2003. "'Who is Breaking the First Commandment?': Oblate Teachings and Cree Responses in the Hudson Bay Lowlands." *Reading Beyond Words*. Eds. J.S.H. Brown and Elizabeth Vibert. Rev. ed. 293–321. Peterborough, ON: Broadview Press.

Gill, Sam. 1987. "Native American Shamanism." *The Encyclopedia of Religion*. Vol. 13. Ed. Mircea Eliade. 216–19. New York, NY: Macmillan.

Goddard, Ives. 1978. "Synonymy [for Iroquois]." *Handbook of North American Indians*. Vol. 15: *Northeast*. Ed. William Sturtevant. 319–21. Washington, DC: Smithsonian Institution.

Goetzmann, William H., and Glyndwr Williams. 1998 [1992]. *The Atlas of North American Exploration from the Norse Voyages to the Race for the Pole*. Norman, OK: University of Oklahoma Press.

Graham, Andrew. 1969. *Andrew Graham's Observations on Hudson's Bay, 1767–91*. Ed. Glyndwr Williams. London: Hudson's Bay Record Society.

Granzberg, Gary, and Nathaniel Queskekapow. 1999. *Nathaniel Queskekapow: Cree Shaman and Storyteller*. Winnipeg, MB: University of Winnipeg.

Hackett, Paul. 2002. *A Very Remarkable Sickness: Epidemics in the Petit Nord, 1670 to 1846*. Winnipeg, MB: University of Manitoba Press.

Hallowell, A. Irving. 1942. *The Role of Conjuring in Saulteaux Society*. Publications of the Philadelphia Anthropological Society. Vol 2. Philadelphia, PA.

Hamilton, T.M. 1982. *Native American Bows*. Columbia, MO: Missouri Archaeological Society.

Hamilton, Virginia. 1988. *In the Beginning: Creation Stories from Around the World*. Illus. Barry Moser. New York, NY: Harcourt Brace.

Hamm, Doug, and Louis Bird. 2000. "Amoe: Legends of the Omushkegowak." *Papers of the Thirty-First Algonquian Conference*. Ed. John D. Nichols. 144–60. Winnipeg, MB: University of Manitoba.

Hoffman, Walter J. 1885–86. "The Mide'wiwin or 'Grand Medicine Society' of the Ojibwa." *Seventh Annual Report*. 143–300. Washington, DC: Bureau of Ethnology.

Honigmann, John J. 1978. "West Main Cree." *Handbook of North American Indians*. Vol. 6: *Subarctic*. Ed. William C. Sturtevant. 217–30. Washington, DC: Smithsonian Institution.

Hutchinson, Gerald. 1985. "British Methodists and the Hudson's Bay Company, 1840–1854." *Prairie Spirit; Perspectives on the Heritage of the United Church of Canada in the West*. Ed. Dennis L. Butcher, Catherine Macdonald, Margaret E. McPherson, Raymond T. Smith, and A. McKibbin Watts. Winnipeg, MB: University of Manitoba Press.

Isham, James. 1949. *James Isham's Observations of Hudsons Bay, 1743 and Notes and Observations on a Book Entitled A Voyage to Hudsons Bay in the Dobbs Galley, 1749.* Ed. E.E. Rich. Toronto, ON: Champlain Society.

Jehl, Joseph R., and Blanche A. Smith. 1970. *Birds of the Churchill Region, Manitoba.* Winnipeg, MB: Manitoba Museum of Man and Nature.

Junkelmann, Marcus. 1992. *Die Reiter Roms, Teil III: Zubehör, Reitweise, Bewaffnung.* Mainz: Philip von Zabern.

Kehoe, Alice B. 2000. *Shamans and Religion: An Anthropological Exploration in Critical Thinking.* Prospect Heights, IL: Waveland Press.

Lancaster, Richard. 1966. *Piegan: A Look from Within at the Life, Times and Legacy of an American Indian Tribe.* Garden City, NY: Doubleday.

Lewis, Henry T. 1982. *A Time for Burning.* Occasional Publication 17. Edmonton, AB: Boreal Institute for Northern Studies, University of Alberta.

Long, John S. 1985. "Treaty No. 9 and Fur Trade Company Families: Northeastern Ontario's Halfbreeds, Indians, Petitioners and Metis." *The New Peoples: Being and Becoming Metis in North America.* Eds. Jacqueline Peterson and Jennifer S.H. Brown. 137–62. Winnipeg, MB: University of Manitoba Press.

——. 1986a. "The Reverend George Barnley and the James Bay Cree." *Canadian Journal of Native Studies* 6(2): 313–31.

——. 1986b. *"Shaganash": Early Protestant Missionaries and the Adoption of Christianity by the Western James Bay Cree, 1840–1893.* Ph.D. Thesis. University of Toronto.

——. 1988. "Narratives of Early Encounters between Europeans and the Cree of Western James Bay." *Ontario History* 80(3).

——. 1995. "Historical Context." In Regina Flannery, *Ellen Smallboy: Glimpses of a Cree Woman's Life.* Montreal and Kingston: McGill-Queen's University Press.

Lytwyn, Victor Petro. 1993. "The Hudson Bay Lowland Cree in the Fur Trade to 1821: A Study in Historical Geography." Ph.D. Thesis. University of Manitoba, Winnipeg.

——. 1999. "'God was Angry with Their Country:' The Smallpox Epidemic of 1782–83 among the Hudson Bay Lowland Cree."

Papers of the 30th Algonquian Conference, ed. by David H. Pentland, 142–164. Winnipeg: University of Manitoba.

——. 2002. *Muskekowuck Athinuwick: Original People of the Great Swampy Land*. Winnipeg, MB: University of Manitoba Press.

Macoun, John. 1881. "Ornithological Notes." *Annual Report of the Department of the Interior for the year ending December 31, 1880*. Ottawa, ON: Queen's Printer, 1881.

Malone, Patrick M. 1991. *The Skulking Way of War: Technology and Tactics among the New England Indians*. Baltimore, MD: John Hopkins University Press.

Marles, Robin J., Christina Clavelle, Leslie Monteleone, Natalie Tays, and Donna Burns. 2000. *Aboriginal Plant Use in Canada's Northwest Boreal Forest*. Vancouver, BC: University of British Columbia Press.

Mason, Otis Tufton. 1995. *North American Bows, Arrows and Quivers*. Mattituck, NY: Amereon House. Reprint Smithsonian Report 1893.

Matthews, Maureen. 1995. "Thunderbirds." *Ideas*. Toronto, ON: CBC Radio. 15 and 16 May.

Mattina, Anthony. 1987. "Native American Indian Mythography: Editing Texts for the Printed Page." *Recovering the Word: Essays on Native American Literature*. Ed. Brian Swann and Arnold Krupat. 129–48. Los Angeles, CA: University of California Press.

Moore, Christopher. 2000. *Adventurers: Hudson's Bay Company—The Epic Story*. Toronto, ON: Madison Press Books for the Quantum Book Group.

Morantz, Toby. 1984. "Oral and Recorded History in James Bay." *Papers of the Fifteenth Algonquian Conference*. Ed. William Cowan. 171–92. Ottawa, ON: Carleton University.

——. 1992. "Old Texts, Old Questions: Another Look at the Issue of Continuity and the Early Fur Trade Period." *Canadian Historical Review* 73(2): 166–68.

——. 2001. "Plunder or Harmony? On Merging European and Native Views of Early Contact." *Decentring the Renaissance: Canada and Europe in Multidisciplinary Perspective 1500–1700*. Eds. Germaine Warkentin and Carolyn Podruchny. 48–67. Toronto, ON: University of Toronto Press.

Murray, L., and K. Rice (eds.). 1999. *Talking on the Page: Editing Aboriginal Oral Texts*. Toronto, ON: University of Toronto Press.

Neatby, L.H. 1976. "Henry Hudson." *Dictionary of Canadian Biography*. Vol. 1: 374–79. Toronto, ON: University of Toronto Press.

Norman, Howard Allan. 1977. "The Cree Personal Name," M.A. thesis. Indiana University.

Payne, Michael. 1984. *A Social History of York Factory, 1788–1870*. Ottawa, ON: Parks Canada.

Pike, Warburton. 1892. *The Barren Ground of Northern Canada*. New York, NY: Macmillan.

Pilon, Jean-Luc. 1987. *Washahoe Inninou Dahtsuounoaou: Ecological and Cultural Adaptation along the Severn River in the Hudson Bay Lowlands of Ontario*. Report No. 10: Conservation Archaeology Report, Northwestern Region. Kenora, ON: Ministry of Citizenship and Culture.

Powers, William. 1982. *Yuwipi: Vision and Experience in Lakota Ritual*. Lincoln, NE: University of Nebraska Press.

Powys, Llewelyn. 1927. *Henry Hudson*. London: John Lane, the Bodley Head.

Preston, Richard. 2000. "James Bay Cree Culture, Malnutrition, Infectious and Degenerative Diseases." *Actes du Trente-deuxième Congrès des Algonquinistes*. Ed. John D. Nichols. 374–84. Winnipeg, MB: University of Manitoba.

——. 2002. *Cree Narrative: Expressing the Personal Meaning of Events*. 2nd ed. Montreal and Kingston: McGill-Queen's University Press.

Purchas, Samuel. 1906. *Hakluytus Posthumus or Purchas His Pilgrimes Contayning a History of the World in Sea Voyages and Lande Travells by Englishmen and Others*. Vol. 13. Glasgow: James MacLehose and Sons.

Richter, Daniel K. 1992. *The Ordeal of the Longhouse: The Peoples of the Iroquois League in the Era of European Colonization*. Chapel Hill, NC: University of North Carolina Press.

Robson, Joseph. 1752. *An Account of Six Years Residence in Hudson's Bay from 1733 to 1736 and 1744 to 1747*. London: J. Payne and J. Bouquet.

Rordam, Vita. 1972. "The Old Blind Squaw." *Oakville Journal Record* (April).

——. 1998. *Winisk: A Cree Indian Settlement on Hudson Bay*. Nepean, ON: Borealis Press.

Schorcht, Blanca. 2003. *Storied Voices in Native American Texts: Harry Robinson, Thomas King, James Welch and Leslie Marmon Silko*. New York, NY: Routledge.

Scott, Simeon. 1995. "The Legend of Weesakechahk and the Flood." *Cree Legends and Narratives from the West Coast of James Bay*. Ed. and trans. C. Douglas Ellis. 34–39. Winnipeg, MB: University of Manitoba Press.

Shandel, Tom. 1975. *Potlatch: A Strict Law Bids Us Dance*. Vancouver, BC: PacificCinematique.

Seed, Patricia. 1995. *Ceremonies of Possession: Europe's Conquest of the New World 1492-1640*. Cambridge: Cambridge University Press.

Sutherland, Donna G. 2004. "Kokum's Story; Wiihtiko or Victim of Circumstance?" *Aboriginal Cultural Landscapes*. Ed. J. Oakes, R. Riewe, Y. Belanger, S. Blady, K. Legge, and P. Wiebe. 337–47. Winnipeg, MB: University of Manitoba, Aboriginal Issues Press.

Taillon, Ron. 1998. "Understanding Old Bows." *Primitive Archer* 6(2): 31–40.

Thwaites, Reuben. 1901. *The Jesuit Relations and Allied Documents: Travels and Explorations of the Jesuit Missionaries in New France, 1610–1790: The Original French, Latin, and Italian texts, with English Translations and Notes*. Vol. 72: CIHM: 07606. Cleveland, OH: Burrows, 1901.

Townsend, Joan B. 1983. "Firearms Against Native Arms: A Study in Comparative Efficiencies with an Alaskan Example." *Arctic Anthropology* 20(2): 1–32.

Treat, James (ed.) 1996. *Native and Christian: Indigenous Voices on Religious Identity in the United States and Canada*. New York, NY: Routledge.

Trigger, Bruce G. 1976. *The Children of Aataentsic: A History of the Huron People to 1660*. 2 vols. Montreal and Kingston: McGill-Queen's University Press.

Trudel, Marcel. 1966. "Nicolas de Vignau." *Dictionary of Canadian Biography*. Vol. 1: 662–63. Toronto, ON: University of Toronto Press.

Tyrrell, Joseph Burr. 1931. *Documents Relating to the Early History of Hudson Bay*. Toronto, ON: Champlain Society.

West, John. 1966. *The Substance of a Journal during a Residence at the Red River Colony*. New York, NY: S.R. Publishers, Johnson Reprint.

Wickwire, Wendy. 1992. *Nature Power: In the Spirit of an Okanagan Storyteller—Harry Robinson*. Vancouver, BC and Seattle, WA: Douglas and McIntyre and University of Washington Press.

Wiggins, Glenn B. 1977. *Larvae of the North American Caddisfly Genera (Trichoptera)*. Toronto, ON: University of Toronto Press.

———. 1998. *The Caddisfly Family Phryganeidae (Trichoptera)*. Toronto, ON: University of Toronto Press.

Williams, Glyndwyr (ed.) 1969. *Andrew Graham's Observations on Hudson's Bay, 1767–1791*. London: Hudson's Bay Record Society.

Young-Ing, Greg. 2001. "Talking Terminology: What's in a Word and What's Not." Special Issue: "First Voices, First Words." Ed. Thomas King. *Prairie Fire* 22.3 (2001): 130–40.

notes on contributors

LOUIS BIRD is a widely known storyteller and historian of his Omushkego (Swampy Cree) people. A member of Winisk First Nation, he resides in Peawanuck, Ontario, near the shore of Hudson Bay. He has devoted the last three decades to preserving Omushkego stories, language, and history on audio-tape and most recently on a website presenting over 80 of the stories he has gathered; see <http://www.ourvoices.ca>, produced by the Omushkego Oral History Project at the University of Winnipeg and funded by a grant from Canadian Heritage.

ROLAND BOIIR is a Ph.D. candidate in history at the University of Manitoba and has recently completed a dissertation on continuity and change in Native military and hunting technology on the Northern Great Plains and the Eastern Subarctic, 1670-1870. His studies draw upon the records of fur traders, travelers and military personnel, published Native biographies and oral history, cooperation with Native elders, examination of artifacts in museum collections, and the manufacture and testing of working replicas of bows, arrows and quivers. He teaches history at the University of Winnipeg.

JENNIFER S.H. BROWN is professor of history and director of the Centre for Rupert's Land Studies, University of Winnipeg, and holds a Canada Research Chair in Aboriginal Peoples in an Urban and Regional Context. She has authored, edited, and co-edited numerous volumes on Aboriginal and fur-trade history, and has published numerous articles and book chapters, often working collaboratively with colleagues and students of both anthropology and history.

PAUL W. DEPASQUALE is a member (Upper Mohawk) of the Six Nations of the Grand River Territory in Ontario. An associate professor of English, University of Winnipeg, he has published articles, essays, and book chapters on Early Modern colonial writings and on Aboriginal literature, including children's literature. He is the editor of a forthcoming book on treaties and land claims (University of Alberta Press) and co-editor of a forthcoming book on Aboriginal/Native American literary scholarship (Broadview Press).

M. ANNE LINDSAY is completing an Honours degree in history at the University of Winnipeg and was the Harington Fellow, 2003–04, at the Centre for Rupert's Land Studies, where she is now administrative assistant. Her chapter on the story of the Wailing Clouds grew out of her research while holding an Undergraduate Research Award in the Human Sciences in spring 2003.

MARK F. RUML is assistant professor of religious studies, University of Winnipeg, and teaches courses on Aboriginal spirituality, culture, and history. Recently he helped design and deliver an educational healing initiative "Walking the Red Road," for Aboriginal inmates at Stony Mountain Institute. The program, which received a national award, combines traditional teachings and ceremonies (delivered by Aboriginal elders) with academic perspectives.

DONNA G. SUTHERLAND is of Cree, Scottish, and Irish descent. She holds a B.A. from the University of Winnipeg in anthropology and psychology, and was the Harington Fellow at the Centre for Rupert's Land Studies in 2000–01. She is the author of *Peguis, A Noble Friend*, and is currently working on a new book entitled *Nahoway, A Distant Voice*. She played an active role in the Omushkego Oral History Project, organizing the collection, transcribing tapes, and contributing to its administration.

index